Manager's Portfolio of

Hard to Write Business Letters

Bernard Heller

PRENTICE HALL
Paramus, New Jersey 07652

Printed in the United States of America

10 9 8 7 6 5 4 3 2 1

ISBN 0-13-532441-6

ATTENTION: CORPORATIONS AND SCHOOLS

Prentice Hall books are available at quantity discounts with bulk purchase for educational, business, or sales promotional use. For information, please write to: Prentice Hall Career & Personal Development Special Sales, 240 Frisch Court, Paramus, NJ 07652. Please supply: title of book, ISBN, quantity, how the book will be used, date needed.

PRENTICE HALL
Career & Personal Development
Paramus, NJ 07652
A Simon & Schuster Company

On the World Wide Web at http://www.phdirect.com

Prentice Hall International (UK) Limited, *London*
Prentice Hall of Australia Pty. Limited, *Sydney*
Prentice Hall Canada, Inc., *Toronto*
Prentice Hall Hispanoamericana, S.A., *Mexico*
Prentice Hall of India Private Limited, *New Delhi*
Prentice Hall of Japan, Inc., *Tokyo*
Simon & Schuster Asia Pte. Ltd., *Singapore*
Editora Prentice Hall do Brasil, Ltda., *Rio de Janeiro*

ABOUT THE AUTHOR

Bernard Heller has four decades of experience as a creator of written communications and presentations. He has prepared reports, documents, letters, memos—any and all devices in which pen is put to paper or fingers stroke a keyboard.

These communications were written for companies of all sizes, ad agencies, marketing firms, and nonprofit organizations; various publics, boards, departments, bureaus, institutions, and executive task forces.

Mr. Heller has worked closely with scores of business managers at all levels—industrial titans, entrepreneurs, upper-level and mid-level executives, and rising stars. He has also taught university courses in persuasive writing.

Bernard Heller currently has his own private consulting practice. Among the clients he has worked with are Citibank, Colgate, and American Airlines.

PREFACE

Now you have the right letter or memo already written for you. The hundreds of letters in this book cover virtually all conceivable situations. The writing and rewriting, the fine-tuning, have been done for you. All you need do is personalize the message and make it relevant to your particular need.

Manager's Portfolio of Hard-to-Write Business Letters includes persuasive letters and memos you won't find in any other book. This is the source for a letter, memo, or presentation that grabs the reader's interest and expresses your thoughts clearly and convincingly.

Model letters are categorized so you can choose one that fits your needs and tailor it for your specific situation. Generally, these are actual letters pertaining to real incidents, with names, dates, and companies changed to assure privacy.

▌COMMUNICATING VIA E-MAIL AND THE INTERNET.

The new information highway is open now, and appears to be a major communications vehicle of the future. You must communicate more succinctly, sometimes without regard to the usual rules of grammar. Nevertheless, communication on the Internet and through e-mail must be clear and interesting. The principles of persuasion and motivation remain the same as in other correspondence media. The letters in this book can be easily converted to "e-mail speak."

▌STEP-BY-STEP INSTRUCTIONS TO HELP YOU.

So that you can see, through actual case studies, how to write a winning letter, about one-third of the letters are preceded by a scenario of the reasoning and strategy used, followed by the appropriate tactics and style.

You will learn how to make a dull, often unpleasant, and perhaps negative subject readable and interesting, and even how to earn a sympathetic response.

Good writing creates agreement; inspired writing induces admiration. This is the direction in which *Manager's Portfolio of Hard-to-Write Business Letters* is pointing you.

CONTENTS

2 INSPIRE YOUR TEAM TO PRODUCTIVE THINKING AND DOING. GET THE JOB DONE UNDER TOUGH CONDITIONS 49

5   COMBAT THREATS FROM WITHIN YOUR ORGANIZATION   117

6   PROTECT YOUR COMPANY FROM OUTSIDE DANGERS— CLIENTS, VENDORS, ETC.   146

12 THORNY JOB ISSUES 214

13   MONEY MATTERS   253

14 FIGHT BACK AFTER BUYING FAULTY, UNDER-PERFORMING, DEFECTIVE, OVERPRICED MERCHANDISE   287

15 CRITICIZE WITHOUT BEING OVERBEARING   301

16 CHEER UP SOMEONE WHO HAS HAD A BAD BREAK   311

YOUR IDEAS: ADVANCE, PROMOTE, AND PROTECT THEM

Ideas are the seeds of all endeavors. They must be planted before products are born, businesses thrive, technology is spawned, edifices rise, projects are mounted, books and publications come into being, art and literature are created, societies flourish. Good ideas are scarce, great ones are rare indeed, but they have no value unless they sprout and come into full bloom. Bad ones fail. Luckily some of the bad ones are discarded before they consume energy, time and money.

Charles Revson, an entrepreneurial legend who built ideas into a women's cosmetics empire, Revlon, said "Ideas mean nothing, they have no value, unless they are developed, made into real products and real sales campaigns that work. Give me someone who can do that."

If you conceive a winning idea you must let the world, or your company or your boss, know that you created it, are responsible for it, that without you nothing would have happened. Those who get the credit and the reward are sought after and prosper. That's why so many people seek out, steal, wangle, blatantly claim credit, for ideas they didn't, or couldn't, think up. There is much "ideanapping" going on in this world of competitive endeavor.

Many good ideas flounder because they are left hanging and are ignored. Inertia and laziness set in on those who are supposed to act on them. All too often you have to persuade, cajole and take a hard stance to have your idea emerge into a blossoming reality.

You must make certain you as the author reap whatever rewards or praise stem from your brainchild. On the other hand, take measures to evade blame if there is a chance the idea may be a dud. This has to be a classically delicate balance.

Following are letters to help you maneuver in these various situations.

▌GET FULL CREDIT AND REWARDS FOR YOUR IDEAS.

SITUATION: You are a marketing executive in a surgical supply company. The sales climate is changing rapidly. Your company is struggling to maintain its market share as new, agile competitors shoulder their way into the marketplace.

You are trying to adjust to recent structural changes in hospital and HMO purchasing procedures. It means you have to modify your data processing and billing framework, a daunting job. In addition, you have to realign your sales strategy to adequately service these important classes of trade.

How to cope and move ahead was the subject of a brainstorming meeting, moderated by the CEO. Thoughts were bandied about, hashed, rehashed and dashed. You had a few stunning ideas which you took the time to think through prior to the meeting.

Considering the tumultuous session that took place, your ideas stand a good chance of emerging much altered, if they survive at all. At the least, they will lose your stamp and be credited to the group, not to you personally.

You came up with some of the best solutions, but there will be no glory for your brilliance and toil.

STRATEGY: Send a memo to the moderator, copies to the rest of the group. Add a copy to the chairman who wasn't at the meeting.

Explain your ideas thoroughly and in detail as you voiced them originally, not what came out of the communal group. Now it will be on the record as coming from you. You rightfully give your assistant credit for the idea he had suggested. This gives evidence of your integrity, and stamps your name even more deeply on your ideas.

The format is a covering letter or memo outlining each of these ideas in brief, which will serve to claim credit for each one. Detailed descriptions of the ideas are attached to the letter.

February 13, 1996

To: Diana Horsman
        Karl DeEhmer
        Jeanie Felton
        Harold Scott
        Catherine Victor

From: Steve Chin

Re: 1/25/96 Brainstorming Meeting—Tackling the New Competition for
        Hospital and HMO Business.

Many things were bandied about at our meeting, and everyone, it seems,
came up with really good suggestions, including some ingenious ideas that
I believe should be taken off our note pads and put to practical use.
They are too good to be left dangling.

I've gotten some further insights on the ideas I had submitted, and I
think it's best to put these on paper since we may not meet in another
such session for some time.

This is the gist of the ideas I offered. A detailed explanation of each
one is on the pages that follow.

  1. An association with a major pharmaceutical manufacturer to jointly
     open up and service new hospital and HMO accounts in major markets.

  2. Self-study courses for doctors which will grant them continuing edu-
     cation credits. The courses deal, of course, with the diseases in
     which we are involved.

  3. Working hand-in-hand with inner-city groups and local governments
     on health and nutrition problems. This will give us a favored entree
     to public hospitals and Medicaid plans. We will be in a preferred
     position for huge volume potential.

  4. Product education seminars for personnel at major medical centers,
     HMOs and VA hospitals.

Number 4 came from my assistant, Bob McDonald, and he deserves credit
for a really bright idea.

Regards,

Steve

cc: Mr. C. Everett Fifer, Chairman

▐ GET YOUR BRILLIANT IDEA PAST THE GATEKEEPERS.

SITUATION: A sales representative for a data communications company,
              you were recently laid off because of a severe downsizing.
Now you are on your own as an independent sales promotion consultant.

You have a blockbuster idea for a long-distance phone company which will
substantially increase its business. It's an entirely new concept that entails

joint ventures with major travel companies to tap into their customers who travel for pleasure or business. It will benefit both the phone company and its joint-venture partners.

You had previously done promotional work for a long-distance provider, which gave you valuable insight into this business. You know its needs, and you know the competitive strengths and weaknesses of the leading players in this combative industry.

You have spoken to the marketing people at three travel companies. You didn't reveal the full concept, but gave them sufficient information so that you could gauge their attitudes. All were extremely positive—in fact, enthusiastic.

From this background, your idea materialized into a tangible, practical design for greatly expanding a phone company's customer base of frequent long-distance users.

You now have a wonderful idea that can make money for you by means of setting up the procedure with a phone company and helping to run it as a consultant. That is, if the company will go along.

STRATEGY: Now, how do you get a good hearing at a phone company that has the facilities, the resources, and the bankroll to make your idea blossom into a sustained, full-scale campaign? It has to be where you will be handsomely rewarded for your ingenuity and your ability to get this done.

How Do You Make the Approach?

Select your primary target—and targets two, three and four.

Where do you have a friend, or a friend of a friend, who can give you the corporate intelligence you need—the personalities, the decision makers, the doers, the formal and informal hierarchy, the sensors on what and who to avoid? This person should be a good starting point, someone who can ease you in, whether it be in company one, two or three—or perhaps number four as you go down the line.

If you have no such champion, you'll have to devise your own approach. Why not start with the company that can make the loudest noise, the one with the deep pockets? Is it likely to take a chance on something new and test-market the concept?

You may have to overcome the obstructionism, even enmity, against new and alien ideas originating beyond the company's sheltered confines.

After all, sales ideas are what they, or their various ad and sales promotion agencies, are paid to think up. A foreign idea, especially if it is good, becomes a personal threat. Very few feel secure enough to brook such intrusions from an outside source.

A subtle way of fending off interlopers, such as you, is to declare the idea, or any offshoot, as having already been considered and rejected at some time in the past. Of course, one idea breeds another, so don't be surprised if you see the intrinsic germ of your creation introduced at some later time, altered so that the company is able to disclaim any outside authorship.

How Do You Get Your Foot in the Door?

Several approaches can be considered.

1. Call and send a letter to the CEO, or the senior marketing executive.

   You may well be ignored completely. Then again, you may receive a short, respectful response from an underling, noting that the company doesn't consider ideas from outside sources. Or you may be instructed to get in touch with another (lower level) executive who is concerned with such things. Maybe your letter will be directed to a junior executive, who will get in touch with you.

   All of the above are the kiss of death.

   Then again, the executive who received your request for a hearing may call and have you explain your idea on the phone (this is bad for you), or ask that you come in for a meeting.

   The meeting, more than likely, will be with the marketing staff who will, with due respect, carefully lower your idea to the grave for the aforementioned "not invented here" reason.

   On the other hand, the meeting may be successful and your idea accepted for testing with agreed upon terms for compensating you. This is a long shot.

2. Another entry avenue is through the advertising, sales-promotion, or direct-marketing supplier—the people who are hired to come up with selling ideas.

   You'll have to share the glory, but half is better than none. And in this way, you will have a cheerleader fronting for you. Needless to say, the motive is to get credit for discovering a good idea and bringing it to the client. Nevertheless, you are still known as the author and will profit from your input and implementation.

3. Another way is to contact an outside member of the board of directors. Send a letter stating you have a well-conceived concept for increasing the company's business. Request it to be directed to the proper person at the company.

   The board member likely has no ax to grind and feels duty bound to see that anything that can help the company gets exposed to the people who are supposed to act on it.

   The board member may send your letter along to the CEO or a high executive and suggest contacting you. He/she may also send you the name of the person to see.

   You then send a letter to this person or persons saying that you were asked by Ms. Theresa Madalone, a member of the board of directors, to get in touch because you have a concept that Ms. Maladone thinks warrants serious consideration.

   If you don't get a decent review, write to the board member again, saying that the people you contacted don't appear to be interested in good ideas that can help raise the company's profits. At the least, they should give you a serious hearing. Isn't this their job?

   If you want to get more extreme, buy a few shares of the company's stock and pose as an irate shareholder.

   The board member may want to dispose of this matter and may, therefore, present your case to the CEO or chairperson. "Aren't you guys interested in seeing something that may be good for the company? It shouldn't be dismissed just because it's from someone on the outside."

   You may have to sign a waiver prior to a meeting at the company which will protect it from any claims you may make about usurping your idea if the company had thought of something like it before your presentation. You will have a hard time claiming authorship if the company appropriates the essence of your concept or alters it while retaining the core benefit.

   If the waiver is a condition of the meeting, you will have to sign it but add a clause giving you some protection.

These are some suggested methods of entry. There are others that may come up that will give you a lead to follow.

You must be persistent—and patience is essential regardless of your frustration. Above all, make sure your presentation is superlative. Preparation, preparation. Always be respectful of everyone from the top down. In turn, you must command respect yourself.

Good luck!

▌HOW TO PRESENT YOUR IDEA.

TO A SENIOR COMPANY MARKETING EXECUTIVE

February 18, 1996

Mr. Lester T. Middlebury
Group Product Manager
Northern Telephone, Inc.

_____

_____

Dear Mr. Middlebury:

> *"Four things come not back—the spoken word, the sped arrow,*
> *the past life, and the neglected opportunity."*
>
> (Arabian Proverb)

I have formulated and researched a marketing idea that will significantly benefit Northern Telephone, that I would be most happy to present to you.

No long-distance company, including Northern, has ever executed this kind of promotion. It is unique. And it has great promise of significantly increasing your long-distance sales and market share.

Briefly, it is designed to enlarge Northern's credit-card base among the most frequent long-distance users, with special emphasis on switching competitive phone customers. In fact, it will strengthen the competitive standing of any large long-distance provider.

I have been a marketing consultant for the past 10 years and have orig-inated a number of successful marketing programs for several giant com-panies. And I am experienced in long-distance marketing, so I know your industry quite well.

Northern Telephone is my first choice in making this presentation, pri-marily because of your creativity and keen marketing sense in recogniz-ing an original idea of exceptional merit and giving it the proper thrust to assure success. I'm aware of your reputation on this score, which is why I'm writing to you.

I suggest that we meet to go over this. If you wish, however, I will send you a written description prior to our meeting, with the understanding, of course, that the information is privileged.

Very truly yours,

TO THE AD AGENCY'S ACCOUNT SUPERVISOR

February 18, 1996

Ms. Elizabeth Bard Buckley
Vice President, Account Supervisor
Abbot, Hellman, O'Neill Advertising Co.

_____

_____

Dear Ms. Buckley:

> *"Each thought that is welcomed and recorded is a nest egg,*
> *by the side of which more will be laid."*

> (Thoreau)

I would like to share an idea with you that's in the interest of your client, Northern Telephone. It's a promotional system to increase Northern's credit-card customer base and encourage the use of the credit card for long-distance calls. It is specially designed to switch competitive long-distance customers. The idea can benefit any long-distance company, including Northern's closest competitors. But I prefer to bring it to you first.

In short, this concept is not merely a sudden flash of inspiration. Nor is it a simple germ of an idea. It's a carefully thought out and well-researched promotional plan, a stunning new concept for increasing Northern's share of the long-distance market. It can lead to a whole new advertising and promotional campaign. And it can be easily tested.

The concept involves partner relationships with certain major companies who have indicated a desire to seriously explore this kind of arrangement.

I have been a sales communications consultant for 10 years, and have originated a number of money-making concepts for several giant corporations.

There is, of course, the alternative of going directly to your client. But I prefer to present it to you first, since I'm aware of your reputation as having a very talented eye for exceptional selling ideas—and knowing how to make them work. And, in fact, you, personally, are quite famous for originating such sales concepts for Northern.

Let's get together and talk about it. I'm confident that you'll find it to be a great service to Northern and will want to get behind it. If you wish, I can describe it in writing prior to our meeting.

Regards,

T. Ross Tinker

TO AN OUTSIDE MEMBER OF THE BOARD OF DIRECTORS

February 18, 1996

Ms. Theresa Madalone
Member of the Board of Directors
Northern Telephone Co.
c/o Furlong Industries, Inc.

_____

_____

Dear Ms. Madalone:

> *"So long as new ideas are created, sales will continue*
> *to reach new highs."*
>
> (Charles F. Kettering)

May I ask your assistance in presenting a remarkable sales development concept—an eye-opening new opportunity for Northern Telephone.

I say this as an individual who has been in the marketing business for a long time, with a strong knowledge of the long-distance marketplace. I am willing to turn this over to Northern for its serious assessment. I am not representing a company or group.

The idea I am able to present has been carefully structured and researched, including a thorough examination of Northern's previous promotional campaigns. Northern has never done anything like this, nor has any other phone company.

In a nutshell, it is designed to significantly increase Northern's credit-card base among frequent long-distance users, with special emphasis on switching competitive phone customers. In fact, it could elevate the market share of any of the major long-distance companies.

I'm asking if you would be good enough to steer me to the proper person at Northern who is responsible for its marketing plans and is in a position to introduce this concept if. he or she finds it fitting.

If you wish, in advance of a meeting at Northern, I'll be pleased to describe the thrust of this idea to you in person or in a written document.

Very truly yours,

T. Ross Tinker

FOLLOW-UP TO BOARD MEMBER UPON COMPANY REFUSAL

March 3, 1996

Ms. Theresa Madalone
Member of the Board of Directors
Northern Telephone Co.
c/o Furlong Industries, Inc.

_____

_____

Dear Ms. Madalone:

You will recall that I requested the name of the right person at Northern Telephone who can evaluate and act on the sales enhancement concept that I developed.

It was good of you to give me the name of Mr. Wendell Josephs, Vice President of Marketing, to whom I've written. I sent a copy of the letter to Mr. Theodore McGracken, CEO.

However, regretfully—for me, and I should add for Northern as well—I received a rather curt negative response. Speaking as a stockholder, I'm sure you share my concern that the people at Northern feel so complacent about their business that they don't care to look at a marketing concept which may be of inestimable value. I say this as a professional marketing consultant with a background in the long-distance industry.

Northern, as everyone knows, is in a highly volatile and very competitive market. I don't believe its people are in a position to ignore what could be a powerful sales strategy that can strengthen its competitive position.

Thank you so much, Ms. Madalone, for the help you've given me to date. Perhaps you can guide me on pursuing this further with Northern. It seems that Northern should thank you as well.

Truly yours,

T. Ross Tinker

Prior to any presentation, the company may ask you to sign a waiver disclaiming original authorship if the company previously knew of the concept from another source.

In this case, a statement such as this should be appended.

I am signing this waiver with the understanding that other sales-building ideas that Northern Telephone may have conceived, and which are in their files, may possibly have certain similarities to the one I'm presenting. However, this is not a valid claim of proprietorship if such ideas do not have the same unique and original features.

The following "innovations" are hypothetical, for the purpose of demonstrating lucidity and style in presenting your position.

You are the owner of a small technical consulting company and you want to have a large advertising conglomerate adopt a system you developed, which will earn you considerable money. It's often best to bypass the bureaucracy and write directly to the person who runs the company or agency and sets policy.

(By Registered Mail)

Mr. Sheldon Bellinger
President

Dear Mr. Bellinger:

I have good news for you! . . . In the form of an exciting new ad medium that will increase your billings, be a powerful weapon in your new business efforts, and put you far out front as an industry innovator.

Here it is!

We have developed a greatly improved system for accessing the World Wide Web to promote products or services. This is a new way to exploit the information superhighway for commercial use. Our new system is perfectly suited for big budget advertisers or large agencies such as yours.

This exciting breakthrough has been eighteen months in development, under tight security so as to avoid a leak. We will invite media coverage when we license its use, and there is certain to be a tremendous amount of publicity.

If you agree to see our presentation we ask that you sign the enclosed nondisclosure agreement. This initial presentation will show how the system works, without all of the technical details. It will be about one hour.

You are the first person we have contacted.

Very truly yours,

You must regroup after a turndown by a mid-level executive. You presented your idea to a Senior V.P. of Product Marketing who, despite his title, turned out to have little decision-making responsibility. He sent you what seemed like a form letter: no interest at this time, keeping your product improvement idea on file, good luck in presenting it to someone else. It was an insulting response in view of your hard work and ingenuity in coming up with a wonderful idea.

Go over his head, write to the president. Enclose a copy of your letter to the misguided executive and his reply. Send it certified or registered, return receipt.

(By Registered Letter)
CONFIDENTIAL

Dear Mr. Morganstern—

> *"Our greatest weakness lies in giving up, the most*
> *certain way to succeed is to try just one more time."*
>
> (Thomas Edison)

I am trying one more time because I cannot believe your company is not interested in an exceptionally worthwhile product improvement, an innovation that will give you a big edge over your competition. I had presented this to your senior vice president of product development and he evidently showed no interest.

It is a recipe change that will significantly improve the taste, texture and feel of your low-calorie, fat-free salad dressing, without losing the fat-free benefit. It has resulted from considerable research and testing, using as a base your product that we bought from three different chains of supermarkets in my area.

This exclusive innovation was blind tested with twenty five men and women. The results were virtually unanimous. . . my new recipe is a decided improvement.

Considering that fat-free dressing is important to your product mix, and is fighting strong competitive brands for shelf space, the turn-down I got seems amazing if not ludicrous.

Mr. Morganstern, you are famous as a powerhouse marketer and peerless leader, with keen reverence for the bottom line. That's why I'm writing you rather than one of your competitors at this time.

Sometimes the chief has to take the ball!

Very truly yours,

Jose Mendoza

You must contact the same person who had previously turned you down. Your initial presentation letter to him was completely misinterpreted. He either hurriedly scanned it, or it was passed on to an assistant who missed the point. It's usually unrewarding to repeat your case with the same party, but try, it may work, and there's nothing to lose. Meanwhile you should also present your idea to the company's competitors.

As with your previous letter, send it registered, return receipt, with a sealed copy addressed to you to set the record that it was sent on a certain date.

(By Registered Letter)
CONFIDENTIAL

Dear Mr. Ackerman:

A second effort for me. . . A second chance for Leeward Corporation.

I'm making this second effort because I know my packaging improvement idea is exceptionally worthwhile. Without a doubt it will make money for your company—a great deal of money.

Mr. Ackerman, this is what your reputation tells me about you: You instinctively know when an idea clicks, and how to act on it. You are quick to dismiss irrelevancies and get to the core principles. You are also a very busy person and probably have little time to go through all your mail. That's the reason for this second effort.

In a nutshell, I am bringing you the following opportunity.

A diagrammed engineering design of a pouring spout for your syrup
containers. With a simple motion, it will automatically dispense
either a teaspoon or a tablespoon of product. No spoon or measurement device needed: it can dispense the required amount directly
from the bottle.

I am certain this will work in actual production quantities, which, of
course, you will test in mock-ups. If there is extra cost, which I
believe is unlikely, it will be minuscule, and will certainly be offset
through additional sales volume.

I'd be delighted to meet with you and your associates to display my
schematic diagram, which is patent pending. I will sign any legal documents that are reasonable.

Do you want to take a giant step ahead of your competition? You will by
being the first to try this packaging innovation with tremendous consumer appeal.

I will call you next week.

Very truly yours,

Jose Mendoza

P.S.   Thank you so much for your attention to this second effort.
        There's a saying: "Opportunities are never lost; if you won't
        grasp them, another will."

WHAT TO DO? YOUR PROPOSAL NEVER REACHED TOP MANAGEMENT. RESUBMIT IT.

TWO STRATEGIES:

Come Out Swinging
Walk Softly, Diplomatically

SITUATION 1:   A power utility had been getting a lot of flak from the com-
                munity it serves because of service problems and certain
overcharges. Local politicos had taken it up as a cause.

The chairman set up an ad hoc coordinating committee of four top-level
executives to solve the problem and turn around the public's hostility, which
was fueled by the media. As director of corporate communications, you were

assigned to create an effective plan of action—what to do, how to do it, and how to make sure it works. This was a tough mandate. The plan had to work; there was no second chance.

You gathered the forces in your department, with the help of other specialists in the company. You worked on it for weeks with little sleep. Here was a high-profile chance to show what you could do to be a hero. The day came for you to make an all-out presentation to the committee.

Your plan was creative, stunning, and forceful. Some operational factors didn't hang together neatly, but these were minuscule details that could be straightened out before the plan went into play.

What happened? The committee didn't focus on how the BIG IDEA could help the company. Instead, it seized on the small operational trivialities that needed fixing. It was like demolishing an exquisite building because the elevators were too slow.

You suspect that there was some underlying jealousy in all this. This innovative, daring stroke would have been a publicist's dream, would have undoubtedly singled you out as the originator, and would have made you the fairhaired boy, upstaging the executives on the committee.

No way can you let this die. The plan is too good, and the issue you are solving is vitally important to the utility and to the community—not to mention to your career.

STRATEGY I: You are sure you can safely go over the heads of the committee members and right to the chairman. The very top. Your plan is your best ally.

Write him a letter or memo. You have to be forceful to make your point and get a good second chance to score. You also have to be absolutely sure of yourself, which you are.

Go to it. Don't worry about ruffling egos. You are convinced your position is too good for you to lose. And there is so much to gain.

August 9, 1996

To: Mr. H. Peter Kennedy, Chairman
       Hampton Power & Light

From: Clarisa Gardineaux

"There has never been a statue set up in honor of a critic," so said Jean Sibelius, the Finnish composer.

The reason is that critics have a significant place, but they are not doers. Doers make the wheels spin. They innovate successful programs. They cause growth and profits, year after year.

My department managers and I worked day and night for a total of about 100 hours each on the community service plan I presented to the Can-Do Committee on Friday.

Hours spent are not a criterion of how good a piece of work is, of course. But this plan has tremendous merit. It will speed up our service to our consumers, greatly improve relations with our big customers, and focus our public-relations coverage.

The committee asked us for a concrete plan. We provided it. Certainly, there are details that have to be worked out, little knots that have to be untangled. This can be done with the help of the rest of the company staff. That is, if there is a willingness to put it on the company do-now schedule.

This plan is good. It will work. I exposed it to some of the people in other departments. They raved about its spunk and potential. We all agreed it needed some smoothing out here and there, but these are trivial details, which don't lessen the worth of the plan itself. The ingenuity of the idea as a means of solving our problem is valid. This is what counts.

It was not an open-minded committee that I made my presentation to. It was an adversarial session. The committee condemned it for these little, insignificant things rather than seeing what the big picture looks like.

We are asking that this be reviewed again. Give us a chance. Give this company a chance to fix a vexing problem and at the same time demonstrate its ingenuity and its committment to its civic responsibility.

Respectfully,

Clarisa Gardineaux

STRATEGY II: You follow the old adage—"You can sell anything if you don't mind sharing the credit." You know that the four committee members, all major executives, will get the glory, or most of it.

Write them a memo, with a copy to the chairman, saying that their help is necessary to get the plan operational. Only they can get it on track by smoothing out the rough spots. By doing this, the committee members will share the acclaim with the chairman. You know that esteem will come to you eventually. You will be recognized as the one who devised the idea and brought it to the committee. The chairman knows it, and your co-workers know it. It will surely be leaked to the press.

August 9, 1996

To: The Operation Can-Do Committee
        Lawrence Burnham
        Josephine Engelhart
        Harold Goodman
        Anita Rosenzweig

From: Clarisa Gardineaux

I'm grateful to the ad hoc committee and to each of you individually for pointing out certain operational problems with the plan I presented. I think we all agree that these are details—important ones to be sure—that can be easily fixed. When this is done the plan will be a roaring success.

The creative way you quickly realized what needs to be done sets us in a clear direction for successfully solving the company's problem. No other utility company in the country has done anything like this, which makes a fertile field for some really great publicity.

You indicated what the bugs are. Now we need your ingenuity in getting them out and getting the program onto the drawing board. This will be great for the company as well as for the community we serve.

It would also be good if you set the pace in getting media coverage. The company can get a lot of glory out of this. But I think it's appropriate that you, collectively and as individuals, be the spokespersons. Along with Mr. Kennedy, of course.

Thanks so much, and it's a remarkable experience working for you.

Regards,

Clarisa Gardineaux

cc: Mr. H. Peter Kennedy, Chairman

Make sure top management doesn't forget that you thought up the seminal idea that is now being put into play. Your contribution is becoming murky, and you are not involved in it. It is in the hands of the new products committee.

A MEMO TO THE PRESIDENT AND OTHER SENIOR MANAGERS

To: Mr. Stanley Bellinger, President
        Mr. David Schwartz
        Ms. Lindsey Somers
        Mr. Clark Sheldon

From: Gretchen Van Deusen

I sure got a euphoric lift from the enthusiasm you showed when you saw my concept on new-products planning. It inspired me to do more thinking, and I've come up with new ideas that will help make my original concept a practical reality.

I request that you allow me to participate in bringing my brainchild into fruition. You can be certain that I'll make a solid contribution.

Make I check with you tomorrow?

Sincerely,

Gretchen Van Deusen

Your proposal to a senior executive was stalled in its tracks.

LETTER TO MANAGER DELEGATED BY EXECUTIVE TO SCREEN PROPOSAL AND COMMENT

Example #1

Subject: Cloud Nine

Dear Mr. Halterman:

Ms. Buckley sure has a great deal of confidence in you. I've been told she passed my proposal on the Cloud Nine product over to you to look over, and then to forward it to her.

The user-friendly aspect of this system required complex engineering which we didn't deal with in this preliminary proposal. We felt the focus should be on the consumer benefits and the marketing at this time. The technology was to be presented later.

I'm available to answer questions, give you more information; in addition, I'm willing to make modifications that you may suggest.

Mr. Halterman, it would really be good if we met, even for a half-hour. I'm sure you'll find it to be an interesting and important half-hour. This is a product improvement of far-reaching benefits to your company— benefits that your company cannot afford to overlook !

I'll call you Thursday morning.

Sincerely,

Sheldon Brown

Example #2

Dear Craig,

Mr. Roger's executive assistant, Ms. Weinberger, told me that you are reviewing the material I sent him.

I'll be pleased to be of help in evaluating this product idea, since there is certain technical and background information that was not included in the preliminary proposal. This initial proposal is an overview of the major features and benefits, and I did not think it nec- essary to go into the production details at this time. You can be sure we can back up all the claims that are made.

One way to perceive its importance is to close your eyes and just imag- ine that your competitor is introducing this innovation. Wouldn't your associates and Mr. Rogers feel envious, remorseful and left behind? Now you are in the driver's seat. You are seeing it ahead of anyone else.

I'll call you in the next day or two to arrange a meeting.

Very truly,

Evans Larue

P.S. By the way, I've done focus-group consumer research which I can't wait to share with you. You will find it extremely enlightening. My associates said it was mind-boggling.

The following letter to the director of planning is to get you into the forefront of transforming your idea into a viable project. You happened to think of it during a sales meeting. Someone picked it up and added an extra flourish that gave it momentum.

Subject: The RO-4 Program

Dear Mr. Seabright:

I'm very grateful to Jerry Messenger and Jean Fritsch for picking up on my original idea, and turning it into a practical project. Without them nothing would have happened.

I'd like to be assigned to the RO-4 Development Committee. I've done a lot more thinking about this program and can be a big help in getting this innovation moving ahead and into the mainstream, on schedule and on budget. I'm sure my input will greatly help the Committee.

Truly yours,

Harry Cowan
Markham Cowan

Your idea was modified in order to make it more practical. You want to register that your idea was the seed germ that made the final product a reality. Without you it wouldn't have happened. It's sometimes good to be a bit boastful as long as you flatter someone else at the same time.

To: Sid Weintraub
       Marge Lin
       Rita Halpinberg
       John Warfield

I guess each of us should be congratulated on how we took a seminal idea and made it grow into a full-blown project that will be great for our company.

Trees grow, sprout leaves and flower. But a seed first had to be planted. I'm glad to have planted the seed. And I'm especially delighted that we are all nurturing it and bringing it to life.

It was your imagination and creativity that supplied the nourishment to make it grow. Without you my seed would have shriveled and died.

Thank you so much.

Best wishes,

Sonia Mizowski

Someone accused you of stealing his idea. You took the thought that had been ad-libbed, altered it and turned it into a practical concept. Your creative input took what was conjecture and made it into a full-fledged innovation.

He is now charging you with stealing his idea, and grumbled to the CEO that he deserves full credit for the innovation.

A LETTER TO YOUR ACCUSER, COPY TO THE CEO, IS NECESSARY.
THE MAIN POINT IS TO LET THE CEO UNDERSTAND THE ACCUSATION
IS NOT QUITE JUSTIFIED.

To: Perry Adolphus

Re: The new investment instrument we'll be launching in August.

I'm sorry, Perry, that you feel your idea was appropriated. Please understand that in practical terms it really wasn't. You surely deserve credit for coming up with the initial thought that led to a suggestion for this new investment product. No argument.

But please keep in mind that it was a long road, with more ideas and creative application, that took us to where we are today. Other people also deserve credit for the thinking that made it work.

Perry, I take your feelings seriously, and I know you appreciate what I'm saying. There is no reason for quibbling about who did what. Now is the time for all of us to pull the wagon.

None of us will enjoy any glory if this product doesn't fly. You, by all means, and the other people who contributed, will surely be congratulated when it is introduced. In the final analysis shouldn't we all put our minds and hearts and energies on what is best for the company?

This brings to mind the old adage. . . "Making an idea work is more difficult and more important than having the idea in the first place."

All the best,

Harriet

cc: Mr. Jackson Sweringen

KEEP YOUR WORK FROM BEING "CORRECTED" AND CENSORED.

SITUATION: You are a network TV producer working on a hot new program concept. The person responsible for standards and clearance is far more careful and conscientious than necessary. He cuts and slashes the script to the point where the audience interest will be stunted. You are convinced this timidity will make the program a bomb instead of a smash hit.

STRATEGY: Send him a strong but chummy memo with copies to the production chief and head of marketing saying that he's going too far. You note that the network can have ample protection without tearing the guts out of the script.

Example #1:

September 14, 1996

To: Jerry Turno
        Vice President, Internal Affairs and Program Clearance

From: Maggie Blackstone

Re: The "What Went Wrong?" Show . . . Slated for fall lineup.

Jerry, I well understand you have to be sure that we don't get pilloried by the people who are mentioned in the program, are not subject to any libel suits, avoid gratuitous sexual overtones, etc. As the guardian of this company's reputation and wealth, you have an acute responsibility, which I well understand.

However, it goes without saying that the company has to get out shows that attract audiences. As such, they must be timely, of blockbuster interest, and often provocative.

I understand your caution, but all I ask is that you reconsider some of the changes you called for in the scripts. Your omissions and disclaimers emasculate its interest, its excitement, the kind of talk-about we want, the publicity, and the reviews we hope for. In short, the ratings and the advertising sales.

Jerry, can't you pull in most of your changes and still have ample protection? You are excising the muscle and guts from the scripts.

It's like extracting all the teeth to prevent cavities.

Cordially,

Maggie

cc: Abbe Hill Curtin
        George Mopilos

Example #2:

To: Mary Beth Michaels

Mary Beth, have mercy!

The changes you made in my production forecasts were well taken, well thought out, and certainly well worth reviewing. In total, you made an excellent analysis, and thank you very much for it.

But I have to take issue with your suggested sales target of plus 8.5% in the first quarter and 15% for the year, which upped my projections by 25%. It puts us both on the spot.

You don't allow for contingencies—such as possible equipment stoppages, work slowdowns, supplier snags or whatever. Unfortunately, such "possibilities" can happen. These things happened before, as we are both unpleasantly aware.

Isn't it better to exceed our projection rather than fall short? Let's be as sure as possible of delivering good news, rather than taking the chance, and the brick bats, of not-so-good news.

Mary Beth, your cogent comments put solid muscle into what we're doing, and we'll both earn a round of applause when we go over forecast. Again, let's give ourselves a little room. To be sure, I'll keep you posted all the way.

Stephanie

P.S.   It brings to mind the sayings of two other smart people, like us—

> *"The world belongs to the enthusiast who keeps cool."*
>
> (William McFee)

> *"Boldness is ever blind, for it sees not danger or inconveniences."*
>
> (Francis Bacon)

YOUR CLIENT GIVES YOUR IDEA TO ITS OTHER AGENT TO IMPLEMENT.

SITUATION: You are a partner at a financial services company. Your function is to develop ideas for financial swaps and new equity placements. You have been doing this for one of your highly rated clients. You have discovered that this same client is now implementing an especially praiseworthy financial plan you had presented six months ago—but not with you. A rival financial house is making money and getting good publicity from your idea.

STRATEGY: Write a letter to your client pointing out your displeasure, but not so harshly as to cause ill feeling. You don't want to jeopardize the relationship, yet you must notify clearly that this must not go on.

December 3, 1996

James T. Reilly
Senior Vice President
Boomer Products, Inc.

_____

_____

Dear Jim:

This deals generally with the producing of IDEAS, one of the most impor-tant functions that we are privileged to provide for you. As such, it specifically discusses something that came up recently which is somewhat disturbing.

We value your account and we get much satisfaction out of the harmonious way we work together. One of the reasons is the way you encourage us to give vent to our ideas that help your business and ours too—indirectly, of course.

You appreciate a good idea when you see one. You know how to adapt an idea to your needs better than anyone I have ever known. That's why you inspire us. In short, you provide a lush environment for creativity.

Jim, you know, more than anyone, that good ideas are hard to come by. We strain. We research. We review. We argue, often into the night. We hope that when an idea is accepted we'll implement it for you. We want to make it into a valuable property so that you will make a lot of money and we'll make some, too.

So it was disturbing—and I must say, frustrating—when we saw one of the ideas we presented to you six months ago now being carried out by Boomer. Not with us, but with another shop.

Even though what we saw was practically what we presented, they might have thought of it independently. It happens sometimes. If so in this case, I apologize for mentioning it.

This is nothing very serious. I just wanted to let you know how we feel around here. We love handling your issues, and we're proud to have you as a client. You know we'll give you the best service and the best ideas in the business.

Cordially,

Lawrence O'Sullivan
Partner

YOUR IDEAS ARE BEING GIVEN TO A RIVAL COMPANY TO DEVELOP.

ADDITIONAL LETTERS:

You submitted an idea to an information network. It deals with an innovative way of assuring e-mail privacy. Its subsidiary corporation is following through on it. It was not patentable, not a strong lawsuit claim, but it's a steal nevertheless. Write the CEO. You may not get to work on it, or be compensated, but let him know he owes you a worthy future assignment.

Dear Mr. Zachary:

We feel happy . . . and we also feel sad! Sad and stung, that is!

Happy because you are adopting in principle the e-mail security idea we presented to you on November 18, four months ago, at a meeting which I had requested and you agreed to. My associates and I gave considerable thought and effort to this idea, and you were obviously impressed with our presentation.

Considering all that takes place between conception and birth, there was likely some mistake in not having us develop this concept further. We were probably lost in the shuffle after you turned it over to an associate.

We submitted this idea for the purpose of being given the assignment to develop it. If it is not possible to reassign it at this late stage, we look forward to being given another project of similar scope. I'm sure you have full confidence in us, now that you know what we can do.

Anyway, we're proud that you are acting on our idea. I'll keep in touch!

Cordially,

Melvin Pruitt
Senior Partner

An issue along similar lines, but a less friendly letter. You got wind that your client is about to give a building remodeling contract to another firm, using the plan and estimate you presented two months ago about an innovative computer-modeling idea that will be a sure money-saver. Don't take it lying down, but remain cordial. Express your rights but maintain good will, because you still want to get the contract turned over to you.

Re: Baltimore Construction Project

Dear Mr. Hawkins:

Someone in your office made an honest mistake, I'm sure. With all the proposals you must have received on the Baltimore project, there was an apparent mix-up by which our plan is being given to another firm to execute. I know this was not your intention because you greatly admired our presentation, and told us so.

The company that now has our plan may alter it somewhat, but the fact is that the key ideas, the basic principles, *were conceived by us.*

We are honored that you chose to use our innovation which will save your company considerable money, and we still stand ready to perform the construction job under your staff's direction. To be certain, we will get it done on time and within the budget, and you and your associates will be proud and pleased with the outcome.

I'll give you a call to go over the plan again. You will see a small modification we made since our last discussion; it is an improvement and will not affect costs.

Suffice it to say, our innovative plan was adopted and we deserve to be awarded the contract to continue on this project.

Sincerely,

Lauren French
Chief Operations Officer

You decide to take a determined, all-out stand against having your idea appropriated by the company you presented it to in good faith. That company gave it to a rival firm to reap the benefits in dollars and prestige.

```
Dear Mr. Mitchell:

We have been reliably informed that Leapold & Co. is fulfilling the
remodeling project on your Broadway property. It has further come to our
attention that that company will be utilizing, in large part, the plans
we submitted in good faith when we made our proposal.

Even if it had submitted a lower bid, which may have influenced your
decision, the use of our basic design in principle is a violation of our
rights, and we are prepared to protect our interests. On the other hand,
we stand ready to mediate this in an amicable manner which will satisfy
both our interests.

Please let us hear from you within the next two weeks.

Very truly yours,
```

Your idea was stolen. You, a production head of TV programming for a movie studio, have the responsibility for coming up with program ideas. You and your associates developed a novel plot for a series, including characterizations and casting suggestions. It had a new twist, different from anything that had ever been aired. It was submitted to an ad agency for its client, a talent agency and a few other people in the industry in order to be sold.

Five months later—a lot of interest but no specific offers. You then read in the trade press that another studio had sold the same idea to a TV network. The description, as reported, had some wording identical to your proposal. A leak, no doubt, and your program idea was appropriated. You don't want to take it lying down.

A MEMO TO THE STAFF

```
To:    All the people who worked on Heavenly Bodies, or knew about
       this original programming concept.

You all saw it in the trade press—the idea was stolen right out from
under us. It was leaked to the wrong people. I'm certain it was not from
inside here. (At least I hope not.) Most likely it was stolen by one of
the outside people who were exposed to our proposal.

This is war. And I'm going to attack it in accordance with the Army Field
Manual's three levels of warfare: strategy, operational art, tactics.
```

Translated into our idiom this means—work the trade press, then the people who received our proposal, then the culpable studio.

There will be a meeting this afternoon, 3 o'clock to discuss it. All of you attend.

Tony

NEXT, A LETTER TO THE EDITOR OF THE PUBLICATION THAT REPORTED IT. COPY TO THE PUBLICATION'S CEO, AND COPIES TO THE OTHER LEADING MAGAZINES IN THIS FIELD

Dear Mr. Berger:

You were unintentionally erroneous in reporting that Diamond Star Productions had come up with a new and interesting twist to a program series and the Antelope TV Syndicate picked it up. It is not true. We created this program and submitted the idea to the Regis Cable network, the Trueblue Talent Providers and several other well-known people in the industry. Nothing came of it for us. But this same program idea which originated with us was apparently filched by Diamond Star. This is unmistakenly proven by the fact that parts of the description reported in your publication were word-for-word the same as we used in our proposal.

As a responsible and well-respected publisher, we know you will want to publish the fact that our idea was stolen, and that your previous report that it was a Diamond Star creation was an error. You are invited to confirm this by reading our proposal.

Very truly,

Abigail Rector
President

FOLLOWED UP BY A LETTER TO THE HEAD OF THE STUDIO WHICH WAS REPORTED TO BE PRODUCING THE PROGRAM SERIES IN QUESTION

Dear Mr. Oglethorpe:

I know it may come as a shock when I tell you the facts behind the series you just contracted to produce for the Design Network.

Whomever submitted it to you had stolen the idea from us. There will be no question when you see our proposal on the identical series idea that was pitched to several production studios and talent agents during a three-month period ending November of last year. Part of the press release you submitted had virtually the same wording as we had written in our proposal.

I'm sure you agree, it is clear we must get together.

Truly,

Ben Terranova

▌YOUR HIGHLY ACCLAIMED MARKETING PROJECT IS ▌FLOUNDERING ON YOUR CLIENT'S BACK BURNER.

SITUATION: You are a principal at an ad agency supervising a world-class health-care account. You have presented an innovative sales-building plan that was applauded by all as a startling concept. All signals called for moving ahead with gusto. That was six months ago, and nothing has happened.

All the people involved have been busy with ongoing projects, while this marketing gem has been relegated to the back burner. For the good of the company, the starting switch has to be turned on.

STRATEGY: Send a letter to the company's marketing chief in charge of this project. Prod him to start the action without seeming too critical of his past stalling.

October 3, 1996

Conrad D. Van Devander
Executive Vice President, Marketing
Denoyer Health Care, Ltd.

———————————————
———————————————

        Roger Baldwin
        Dorothy Su
        Lindsey Schreiber

Dear Conrad:

What a great idea! Just what we need! It will demolish our competition!

This is what was said six months ago, when the agency presented our business-building plan for Nemenosa 3. You'll recall we had it all buttoned up, ready to go. We said it would take three months to get this operational, and we were virtually told to get ready for a test in four states. But the go-button wasn't pressed.

Since then, we have done as much as we could to keep it moving: letters, meetings, reminders. But everyone—and it goes for your people and ours—has been so bogged down on immediate projects that they couldn't spend time on this, as important as it is.

As you have often said, Conrad, the business depends on forward think-ing. We presented an exciting, forward-thinking plan that was accepted without question. Six months have passed, and there is still no forward involvement. We can't afford to allow this to languish.

Imagine how we would all feel if a competitor came out with a similar marketing program. Think of how foolish we'd all look. It would be trag-ic. We must be absolutely sure this doesn't happen.

Conrad, your people do a wonderful job, and ours do, too. We work well together. Let's get the Nemenosa 3 business-builder off the back-burner now. Now's the time to put your finger on the go button.

Best wishes to Clara and the kids,

Phil Cleary

PREVENT A PROSPECTIVE CLIENT FROM STEALING AN IDEA YOU ARE PRESENTING.

SITUATION: Your company, Sales Promotion, Inc. is going to present an innovative sales-boosting idea to Ideal Vacations, Inc. It will be a good piece of business for you if they buy it. The relationship is such that it would not be wise to put a legalistic protection agreement in front of them to sign because they probably would call off the meeting. At best, they would consult their lawyer, which would hold up the presentation. It would then become a legal maneuvering game.

You are anxious to get going with them, but you want it clear that you own the idea. You must tactfully state that they would have a problem if it's used without your involvement.

STRATEGY: Have a letter to show preceding your presentation. It should be the front page of the bound write-up you leave with them. It must say that the idea is your property and that you are the one to implement it, which, incidentally, is to their benefit as well as yours.

The letter should point up the business-building value of your idea. You did this in the presentation, but reiterate because you must give it the hype it deserves.

Indicate that you are exposing this idea to them as your first choice. But, understandably, it will be presented to a competitor if they turn it down.

Keep in mind that this may not necessarily give you iron-clad legal protection. But it establishes you as the innovator and could strengthen your case if they steal the idea from you and you choose to take legal action.

September 15, 1996

Ideal Vacations, Inc.

_____

_____

Attn: Gordon Sessions, Senior Vice President
        Tomaso Estrada, Vice President
        Virginia Hooper, Vice President

Here's our presentation for the business-building plan we had discussed with you. It is being made to Ideal exclusively at this time.

Based on our projections, which are backed up by our research data, we're confident you will add 10 to 15 percent in sales above your normal volume in the first year following the introduction of this promotion.

In effect, you will build a bigger sales base and increase your market share.

The basic marketing ideas and operational procedures in the presentation are confidential and proprietary to Sales Promotion, Inc. If you elect to implement this program, the promotional campaign and data processing are to be supervised by our company under Ideal's direction.

As you can imagine, we put months of time and a great deal of out-of-pocket expense plus a good amount of creative thinking into the task of developing this marketing idea and its implementation. Sales Promotion, Inc., is undoubtedly in the best position to launch the program and keep it running successfully.

Now to an important point, which I'm sure you agree with. This startling new vacation concept will create tremendous noise in the travel market and give you a big leg up on your competition. There will likely be copy-cats, but you'll have the clear benefit that goes with being first. You'll be out front with the strongest promotion concept in many years.

Very truly,

Stephen Mandel
President

FIGHT BACK AT AN IDEA THIEF. YOUR IDEA WAS APPROPRIATED BY THE COMPANY YOU PRESENTED IT TO.

SITUATION: You are the owner of a direct-marketing company. You devised a new concept for switching customers from one brand of a packaged-goods product to another. Better yet, the acquired customers are encouraged to stay with the product they switched to and not go back to their former brand. In other words, it is a long-range business building campaign for a packaged-goods company. It's done by means of a multimedia program using telemarketing, direct mail, and advertising.

You whetted the interest of marketing executives at a big liquor company. You knew this approach would be a superb marketing tool for a whiskey brand. That's why you contacted them. They agreed to see what you had, and you made a formal presentation.

They went for it, or so it seemed to you. It was right, they said, for their vodka product, which, although still a big seller, was gradually losing market share. You left two bound presentations behind. They said they'd get back.

There was no signed confidentiality agreement. You trusted them. Frankly, if you had insisted on such an agreement, you likely would not have had the meeting.

During the next four months or so, calls were made for questions, but not for commitments. Eight months after your presentation, you saw something that gave you a fifty-point blood-pressure surge. The company had introduced your concept—or its clone—to the marketplace, supported by a big ad campaign through its regular ad agency. Everything you have seen tells you it's an out-and-out theft of your idea.

STRATEGY: You don't want to run to high-priced lawyers right away.

You send a certified or registered letter, return receipt, to the president, stating your case. Enclose a copy of the document you had given the marketing people. Your letter should be dispassionate and businesslike, chief executive to chief executive. This is a matter of protecting your rights: consummately firm, with a hint of more to come if need be.

You don't say it outright, but you imply subtly that you will be willing to settle for a very decent fee rather than bring it to litigation. You, a small entrepreneur, are hardly in a position to engage in a drawn-out, costly, time consuming, high-powered legal proceeding versus an industrial giant.

You check your letter with a lawyer friend to make sure it won't jeopardize a legal case if it comes to that.

By Certified Mail

September 23, 1996

Mr. C. Stevens McLaury
President
Bryant Distillers International, Ltd.

_____
_____

Dear Mr. McLaury:

I saw something in the newspaper yesterday that left me very much disturbed. It should disturb you too. It touches at the heart of how we make a living here at our company.

Let me explain:

On December 12, 1995, eight months ago, we made a presentation of a new concept—unique, never done before—to get a market share lift of your top-selling vodka brand. In other words, this was a plan to switch consumers

of a competitive brand of vodka to your brand and to maintain the loyalty of a significant percentage of these new customers. Of particular
significance was that this idea encouraged the continued perceptible rise
of the market share long range.

We had an eighty-page document for implementing this project which
included trade and consumer advertising plus direct mail and telemarketing. Two copies were left at the meeting with your executives who told
us without reservations that they liked and admired our idea very much.

I saw our concept in a magazine ad yesterday, in full bloom. Or something so close to our basic idea and its implementation that you'll be
hard put to distinguish between the two. It's being run by your regular
agency, not by us.

As I noted before, marketing ideas are our business. We get paid for
them. That's how we make a living. We've been doing fine because we are
creative as well as good businesspeople who know how to hit the jugular
of consumer persuasion.

I'm sure you will be fair. We will be too.

We're looking forward to hearing from you shortly.

Very truly yours,

Bob Stevens, President

AN ASSOCIATE IS HACKING AT YOUR PROPOSAL

SITUATION: Your big idea on which you made a written presentation
                   was virtually demolished by the critical memo of an asso-
ciate at your company. It really centered on details rather than substance. His
caustic comments are putting it to rest even though you believe the idea has
excellent merit.

You know he is engaging his highly developed political infighting skills to put
you down, which is a good clue that your proposal is exceptional. You have
to undo the damage, get your proposal on line, and repair your reputation.

STRATEGY: Tell the criticizer in a memo, with copies to the other execs,
                  that his concern lies with operational details, not the idea
itself, which has eminent merit.

You have created an innovative business-enhancement concept. No need for
operational purity at this juncture; that comes later. Emphasize that he
shouldn't nitpick a good idea to death.

Play on the criticizer's ego—his amazing gift of recognizing a good concept and the ability to make it work.

Enlist the cooperation of your colleagues, including the criticizer, to work out the operation and get it going.

Putting this idea to work will bring the company industrywide acclaim, which will rub off on everyone involved in it; therefore, it warrants everyone pitching in.

This is the way to get your plan on the front burner. When the operational procedures are ironed out, you will write up the program in its final form, under your name, and take charge. Let's face it. You originated the idea and deserve the glory.

March 15, 1996

To: Bob Travis

From: Peggy Wallenberg

IN EXTREMIS—In the last extreme, next to death.

I'm sure this is not what you intended. But in effect, this is what your comments could conceivably cause to happen to the real-estate investment plan my group put together.

This was a preliminary proposal. Its intent was to lay out the big picture; there was no time to button down all the details. I'm sure you didn't mean to kill it; indeed, you have a unique gift to build on an essentially good idea, not discard it.

Others who have read the proposal think the idea is intriguing and has great merit. We all realize, of course, that there are some rough edges to be smoothed out. Indeed, your comments confirmed this, and at the same time were helpful in indicating how this can be made into a very vital program.

Let's all meet on Thursday to discuss the implementation of this plan that will enable us to enhance our company's net worth. We now have the head and body in place; all we need is the bloodstream to give it life. It all boils down to our determination to make a good thing work.

My group will then prepare a final plan based on everyone's input, which will include the operational methodology and a timing schedule for the introduction. We'll then be ready for an early spring start.

This will be a big coup for all of us, for which we all deserve credit
and the praise when it's introduced.

Regards,

Peggy

cc: Zoe Callaway
       Mel Hirsch
       Elena Munoz

▌COMPANY POLITICS OBLIGE YOU TO ENDORSE AN IDEA
▌TO YOUR CLIENT THAT WILL UNDERMINE YOU.

SITUATION: You are an account executive at a company that acts as a
                    sales broker for various record labels. An important
account you handle is number two in pop music records. A senior executive in your company has an idea for promoting your clients' new releases
in a novel way: using the loudspeakers at race tracks and betting parlors.

First of all, it's not good to have ideas for your client coming from anyone but
you. It dilutes your importance on the account.

Second, you particularly don't like it coming from this guy, who is trying to
wheedle his way into supervising you on this piece of business. Initiating an
innovative idea is a good way for him to start.

Third, the idea doesn't fit your client's customer profile. Indeed, his idea is
lousy, and you would look bad if you approved it.

STRATEGY: Ask the senior executive to give his recommendation to
                   you in a memo. Send a copy to your client, with a covering
letter. Your letter can't appear negative because the senior guy expects you to
support him, and you are obliged to do so. But you also do not want to show
your unabashed agreement.

Bottom line: You don't want your client to accept this idea, but you have to
appear gung-ho loyal within your company.

You will meet with your client later and give him a more pointed oral opinion.

October 27, 1996

Mr. Sheldon Kaplan
Vice President
Dynamo Records Corporation

_____

_____

Dear Shelly:

One of our senior people here, Dick Rogers, has an idea for hyping some of your new releases that he thinks you should consider. A good idea can come from any source, which is why I don't hold back on putting it in front of you. Dick explained his idea in a memo to me, which I'm attaching.

Please don't brush it off strictly because it may not be consistent with the marketing plan we formulated. The audience he suggests we promote may be out of kilter with your target consumers, which we pointed out to Dick. So think of this, if you will, from the viewpoint of broadening your customer base, which is a noteworthy point.

Please hold off on any negative opinions you may have until I talk to you about it when we meet this coming Thursday.

Regards,

Conner

▌PREVENT YOUR IDEA FROM BEING NEUTERED BY
▌CORPORATE INERTIA.

SITUATION: You were recently hired for a top spot, exec VP, director of planning, at a giant retailer. Its image and sales have been slipping the past couple of years, gradually outdistanced by smart, hungry competitors.

The chairman and CEO saw you several times before you got this coveted brass ring. You obviously impressed him, and he put his blessing on you, pushing your name to the top of the list. Apparently he wanted a quarterback who could turn the game around. Your reputation is that of a catalyst who gets things done in a hurry. After looking at all the plays and players, you are convinced you can come up with the game plan that gets the company out of its slump to start winning.

Your first presentation to go about building the business is scheduled for review by a new Project Growth Committee. You clearly sense opposition and resistance because your groundbreaking concepts are antithetical to the corporate psyche of the committee members.

STRATEGY: Send a pre-presentation letter to the chairman, who will
                   not be at the committee session, preparing him for the
anticipated negativism. Serve notice that the ingrained attitude of fear-of-the-new retards progress and prevents ground-gaining offensives.

You assume you were hired to turn things around, but it can't happen with the stodgy attitude that you fear will choke the life out of the plans you will be presenting.

November 15, 1996

To: Ms. Loretta Springfield
       Chairman and CEO
       Sherwood & Company, Inc.

From: Steven Danouski

This letter will only take you two minutes. It's an important two minutes.

I'm scheduled to deliver my new-horizons presentation to the Project Growth Committee next Friday. It's my first real performance here since I came on the scene. I just want to make a few private pre-presentation comments to you.

I notice a resistance here to new thinking that does not conform to the way things have been done, to ideas that seem to upset tradition. I know you agree that we should not stay within a well-worn, narrow decision-making path.

"We can't do it here" is unfortunately what I've heard so often in the short time I've been around. We both know this stifles progress in building income and net worth, which is what I was hired to do.

Some of the ideas I'm going to present are new marketing concepts that will give us a competitive advantage and increase our sales volume. One is structured to improve our image and our customer franchises rather than see our image continue to decline. Another will recommend that we abandon properties and projects that are losers.

My presentation should be given serious consideration on its creativity and its merits rather than its adherence to corporate folklore. How soon each of the ideas can be made operative is the key issue—the sooner the better. We have to dispense with the "it's not right for us" syndrome. I know you agree, and will have an open mind on my proposals.

I'll finish up my two minutes with this Oscar Wilde quote which I know reflects your own thinking—"Conformity is the refuge of the unimaginative."

Best wishes,

Steve

YOUR SEMINAL IDEA WAS APPROVED BY A CLIENT BUT NOTHING WAS DONE ABOUT IT.

TWO SITUATIONS:

The ideas are presented to a company on a freelance basis. There is no formal client relationship.

The ideas are presented to a valuable client under a client-agency contract.

SITUATION I: Your company, a marketing communications enterprise, came up with a powerful idea to substantially increase subscriptions to a magazine that's been around for a long time and is still popular, but inching downward. You developed a unique concept to reverse this baleful trend and breathe new life into the publication. Acting as a freelance consultant, you presented it to the publishing and editorial staffs. It was unanimously acknowledged as a bright new concept that is just the ticket for reviving the publication. The implied message was "go," and the staff personnel were to meet internally on timing and details.

Six weeks have passed and you haven't heard anything of substance. Where is the former enthusiasm? A great deal of time and money was spent on this proposal. You must know if it will fly.

STRATEGY I: You urge them to formally tell you whether they will make your concept operational, and, if so, when. You advise them of your option to take it elsewhere if it is turned down or remains in a nether world much longer.

September 27, 1996

Mr. Henry Wisniak
President and Publisher
Merriwether Publications

Re: Follow up to meeting of 8/9—Ideas for X12 Project

Dear Hank:

The meeting was a great success. Everyone thought our idea for renewals and new subscriptions was marvelous. Jerry Tramiel used the word "incredible." It wasn't my word, but I happen to agree with Jerry.

You were also very gung-ho, noting it as an innovative coordination of telemarketing, direct mail and integrative TV, with a creative copy concept—all designed to give birth to a super-powerful campaign.

That was six weeks ago, and we haven't heard anything from you or your people. Our phone calls didn't get any substantive response. You know as well as anyone, Hank, that ideas don't come easily. Good ideas are valuable. Great money-making ideas are precious.

We really have to know how it stands. If you still want to make your target launch date, we have to clear our decks now because there's a tremendous amount of up-front work to be done.

If you are still serious about the program but are holding it up for a later date, let us know, so we can rearrange our in-house work schedules. Or, perhaps if it is far down the line, we may consider taking this idea elsewhere, after discussing this option with you.

On the other hand, we need to know if you have abandoned the program or if it is in an indefinite hiatus. In this event, we will be free to present it to another publisher as soon as feasible. It goes without saying that we will not divulge any confidential information you gave us.

I realize you and your staff are swamped right now. But can you please give us an answer soon, say by October 15?

Thanks, Hank, I'm looking forward to hearing from you, and most of all, working with you on this stunning breakthrough project.

Regards,

Felix Casablanco
Executive Vice-President

SITUATION II: Your direct-marketing agency is under contract to a leading magazine publisher to create and implement circulation-enhancement programs. The title you service has a circulation over a million, which has been slowly eroding.

Your company was given the assignment of turning the situation around; you came up with an ingenious method to stop the skid and move circulation in the right direction. It was presented to the publishing and editorial staffs and was given its rightful accolades. There was every indication of getting this project into high gear promptly. "This is what we're looking for" was the clear message—or so you thought.

It's now six weeks later, and there has been no definite word despite your specific, yet deferential, prodding. This is a valuable client, and there must be no risk of alienation.

STRATEGY II: Write a normal company-client letter, respectful but to the point. Ask about the status of your recommendation, noting that it got an exuberant go-ahead reception.

You need to know because you require about a month's notice to tool up, and it is getting close to the most opportune launch date.

```
Mr. Henry Wisniak
President and Publisher
Merriwether Publications
```

```
Re:  Follow-up to 8/9 Meeting—Recommended Plan for X12 Project
```

Dear Hank:

I am bringing this up because there has been no decision as yet about this project, and we may miss out on the most advantageous launching date. We had agreed, I believe, that it should be in the early fall. We need at least four weeks to tool up.

It's hard to keep an innovative idea like this under wraps for long, especially with the possibility of leaks. So the sooner we go to work, the better off we'll all be.

Imagine how we'd feel if we saw another publisher start a campaign like this, or even one that's pretty close. We would be chastising ourselves for not moving ahead when we had the chance. Let's make sure we keep this jewel for ourselves and get a good step ahead of competition.

I recently came across this quote from Thomas Kennedy, the author: "Ideas lose themselves as quickly as quail, and one must wing them the minute they rise out of the grass—or they are gone."

I'll call you to find out the status. With the hope, please, that we will decide on a starting date.

Best regards,

Felix

Your client accepted your idea and asked you to develop it. The staff people assigned to work with you have been lackadaisical. Send them a memo, with a copy to the president.

Special to: Jack, Mary, Heather—
               The Elite Task Force Assigned to the Beta Project

The client was fired up about the Beta Project, and so were we. But little has been done about it these past four weeks because everyone got involved with our regular business activity.

Nevertheless, we all—this means *all*—have to get going right away on Beta. Our client hasn't said anything so far, because of involvement with other day-to-day problems, but something is sure to pop soon. Mr. Leonard approved a meeting on this tomorrow, 2 o'clock, for responsibilities to (again) be assigned. It will mean extra work, but this must be done, and please, there's no more time to waste.

Each of us will surely enjoy kudos when Beta becomes a successful reality. Who knows. . . maybe a bonus? Are you listening, Mr. Leonard?

Dan Gross

cc: Mr. Joseph Leonard, President

MEMO TO YOUR COMPANY PRESIDENT WHO HAD APPROVED GOING AHEAD WITH YOUR IDEA

Mr. Joseph Leonard, President

Subject: The Beta Project is Languishing. It bodes bad news.

It's been four weeks since the client enthusiastically asked us to proceed on Beta, but I'm afraid little has been done so far. You'll recall it mentioned that Beta will accelerate its growth, *and will increase our business with it.* Our progress is too slow—much too slow!

The people assigned to help me—the task force—have been very busy on other things and weren't able to take on this extra responsibility. Let's say it's no one's fault. Not now.

I need your help. The task force personnel should be relieved of some of their day-to-day duties in order to devote the bulk of their time to this assignment until it's completed.

With a big push and priority effort we'll have a plan ready in four weeks, which I know will make the client very happy. And we can then start making money on Beta—and a good chance at other business from this client, who will be very grateful to us.

Tim Wilshaw

ANOTHER LETTER TO SHAKE UP PEOPLE AND SPUR ACTIVITY BUT WITHOUT MISTAKES DUE TO HASTE

Dear Rochelle,

Time is of the essence. If ever this well-worn maxim is true, it's now.

Rochelle, can you please put more people on the Internet Information Development Program? Otherwise, we won't have it ready when we told the media it was to be announced. For sure, we'll both look foolish. In spades!

A word of caution. In speeding this up, mistakes can happen. They must be avoided. I'll cite another wise observation (Shakespeare). . . "Too swift arrives as tardy as too slow."

Call on me for any help I can give.

Regards,

Bud

ANOTHER LETTER IN THIS PROBLEM CATEGORY

Your client approved your wonderful idea, and asked you to get a team together to make it workable. The team members haven't done much so far. Push them. Motivate them.

To: Jackie DeMarco
        Joseph Gimbel
        Brian Sullivan

About the Aureole II Effort

A sensation within our grasp. . . Within but not *in*, yet.

The client approved our idea and thought it sensational. And we were asked to resubmit it in a "doable" form. That was two months ago, there were several starts, but the effort seems to have petered out.

This new service will be on the money, when it's released to the public and the press. We have the means to do it. But not the end, yet. We also have the right team—the four of us. Getting the means to the end will take another four weeks—IF !

IF we work hard at it—with personal sacrifice. I don't have to tell you that the sacrifice entails long days, but please have your spouses understand. Tell them their indulgence will pay off. *It will!*

Regards to you fellow heros,

Your client is faltering in helping to carry out your idea which is to be a joint effort. Fire up its marketing director to complete work before competition goes one-up on you and gets there first.

Dear Rita:

Project Alpha. . . Is it floundering? If so, we have problems.

We're all geared up here, and surging forward on this important program. You have been doing some excellent work too, but I understand a few snags are now holding your people up. It is unhappily putting us at a standstill.

It would be good, Rita, if you could estimate when these glitches will be taken care of so that we can plan the next phase of our assignment. If it's resolved in the next two weeks it will be possible to launch Alpha before a competitor comes on the scene with a similar idea.

I got word, and I'm sure you did too, that practically everyone in the industry is feverishly searching for product innovations, and neither of us wants an interloper to shove us aside and come out ahead. Especially when we are within striking distance of launching. What a disaster that would be!

How about getting together at lunch? Are you clear next Thursday?

Cheers,

Jeffrey

OTHER LETTERS TO PREVENT YOUR PROJECT
FROM BEING BOGGED DOWN

You are the client, and your vendor who is enrolled in your effort is not delivering on time.

Subject: New Analytical Tool

Dear Alphonse:

Let's pull together to get this to market. It's languishing—we're behind schedule and getting further behind every day. We have to catch up!

You are an important part of this revolutionary breakthrough that will shake up the whole industry. It takes hard work—and serious dedication—but you and I know it will pay off for both our companies.

I will send you a new schedule in the next couple of days. It's tight—it has to be adhered to. I assume you won't have any questions.

Let's pull together and win. We can't drop the ball, Alphonse. The rewards are too big.

Joe Mooney

Dear Lindsay:

We've lost momentum on bringing TRIUMPH to market. I'm sure you realize it will cause both our companies to lose money. What started as a great idea will end up as a dream—a nightmare—if we don't step up the effort.

It's essential to get this project back on track and on schedule. The introduction is already in the rumor stage, which means it has practically been announced. I made drastic moves to pull out all stops here; please let me know tomorrow what's being done at your shop.

By the way, are you free for lunch either next Tuesday or Wednesday?

Warm regards,

Hortense Bradley

OTHER LETTERS ON THE SAME POINT

To: Ginny Epstein

Re: The Plan for Product X

Hey guys. . . Victory is in sight. We can see the light at the end of the tunnel. But we're kind of stuck in the tunnel.

You get the picture. We have to have the plan ready by February 8—that's three weeks. Three short weeks. Will we have it?

It's hard to fully appreciate the results at this time because we're so close to it. However, clearly and without doubt, the introduction *will be a sensation.* Think of the recognition you will get. . . not to mention the pride of accomplishment.

If anyone cannot put the necessary time in, please let me know *now,* and I'll have to get someone else to fill in. It's only three more weeks. After all your magnificent efforts so far, why let someone else get the glory?

I'll be in touch,

Mike Hansen

cc: Vin Esposito
       Sara Musikant
       John Warfield

ANOTHER LETTER

To: Arthur Simmons, Team Leader of Program Skylark
       David Kahn
       Laura Simon

Dear Arthur,

The two pages that are attached tell precisely what needs to be done, with a four-week schedule. It's important to get back to me fast if any-one on your team suggests any modification *that will be an improvement.* Improvements are the only changes to be considered. The weary, faint-hearted or naysayers need not get back.

Please bear with me; this job has to get done on time, and much time has been wasted so far. Let's pick up the ball and run.

We'll have a big party when this is finished. Promise!

Regards,

Steve Brill

Inspire your people to step up work on your project, by letting them know they are an elite group. They are, and must work harder and faster, on a vital development that must be kept absolutely secret right up to the time of its announcement.

```
CONFIDENTIAL
Subject:  X5 Task Force

Dear Ronald:

It's vital that everyone on this select team makes sure there are no leaks.
It's hush, hush on any news getting out. That would be a calamity!!

We also have to keep a lid on any rumors, hints or innuendos, within the
company as well as outside. Be deadpan if there are any inquiries—lie if
necessary. Even a wink could spill the beans. All notes, scribbling etc.
are to be shredded at the end of each day.

Unfortunately, progress is too slow. We all have to pull harder. Anyone
who drops the ball will pull us all down. Please don't let it happen!

There will be plenty of chances to relax and bask in the limelight when
this job is successfully completed. I'm proud to be part of this team.

All the best,

Ben
```

Be willing to share the credit for your great idea, if that's what it takes to get it to fly. There has to be a working relationship between your company, the manufacturer, and the agency you hired to do your advertising and promotion. If the agency hasn't delivered, shake it up.

A LETTER TO THE AGENCY PRESIDENT

```
Dear Frank,

Status Report: Operation RT901—A marriage gone awry?

The close working relationship between your folks and ours seems to be
breaking down. The software structure that we are engineering is moving
along O.K. But your company's job, the promotional campaign, is way
behind. How come?
```

Your people made two formal presentations, and showed work at several impromptu meetings, but so far we don't have the blockbuster that's needed. I know your guys are talented, creative and great, so I know you can do a sensational job.

Perhaps we, here, have not given them good enough guidance, for which I'm willing to take a smidgeon of blame. It won't continue.

The bottom line is that we have to get RT 901 introduced famously and on time. It will make us both look like the geniuses we are.

Cordially,

Jim Strasburg

INSPIRE YOUR TEAM TO PRODUCTIVE THINKING AND DOING. GET THE JOB DONE UNDER TOUGH CONDITIONS

As a supervisor, do you often see your reports at cross-purposes? People differ on how a project is to be done. Disparate goals and attitudes, conflicting opinions, not to mention individual jealousies, ambitions, strivings to shine. No pulling together, no real teamwork to get a job done well, so you can be proud of the results and look good to your superiors.

An able, results-driven administrator at times has to declare what has to be done, how it should be done, and who should do it.

You are ultimately responsible. Cajole, praise, motivate, or do whatever will work to accomplish your objective—and shine.

CUT THROUGH VOLUMINOUS DATA, AND CHANGE DEBATE INTO DOING.

SITUATION: You are the top guy responsible for marketing policy at a durable goods manufacturer, a worldwide behemoth. You commissioned a market-research company to conduct a consumer survey in order to get helpful information for marketing and advertising planning. The research report is a detailed 258-page document with tables, charts, and graphs—a voluminous compilation of data tabulated by groups, subgroups, with regressions and digressions.

You asked your marketing personnel to analyze the study to determine what to do about it. You got numerous recommendations, some exceptional, some good, some abstruse, some impractical, some narrowly focused, as well as a host of conflicting viewpoints.

STRATEGY: You have to get this planning to move forward. Send a
                    memo to all your marketing division heads. Zero in on the
nitty-gritty findings without going into nonessential detail.

This means reducing 258 pages of complex data to a practical few. It's the
starting point for getting the salient research findings out of binders and into
the real world.

You want to arrive at a total marketing strategy that is effective and makes
sense. You note that further cogent comments are welcome, but positive
action has to start in one month.

IN-HOUSE MEMO TO YOUR ENTIRE STAFF

February 11, 1996

To: All Marketing Supervisors and Advertising Managers

From: Betty Freeman

Re: Consumer Research Survey—On the Opinions of Consolidated
        Electronics Corp., Its Products, and Its Advertising

We've all had a chance to digest this expensive 258-page survey. By the
way, it's a very good study. It could be incredibly good if used properly.

I made an aggressive assault on this document, piercing through every
finding. I also studied everyone's comments, written and oral. There were
many opinions and many conflicting interpretations. If we followed everybody's recommendations, it would take many years and an inestimable
amount of money.

Unlike the federal government, we cannot sustain a policy of "Try it,
see if it works. If not, try something else." Also, unlike the federal
government, we cannot operate at a deficit for long.

After sifting through all that I mentioned, I've zeroed in on a number
of bedrock findings from which we can build a plan of action.

- Everybody we care about knows of our company.

- Most have a good opinion of us. A fairly significant minority
  have a less-than-good or poor opinion. Enough so that we should
  do something about it. The study tells the reasons—for example,
  what these people are thinking. We should keep these negatives
  in mind in all our consumer-communications venues.

- Our products are liked by almost everyone who is familiar with them. High numbers rate them "superior." This should be the case, considering all the measures we take to assure high quality and the links we set up with customers for the fast redressing of grievances. We must keep up what we're doing in this regard.
- Our pricing is considered fair.
- Our advertising is remembered by more than half of consumers but few remember our slogan. Not too bad, but not great, either.

What I got out of all this is that we do a good job producing products, pricing them well, and giving good customer service. We could do a better job of reinforcing these facts and building on this positive image with the public. And, by the way, with the trade.

Let anyone who has anything cogent to add please do so. Study the research report again. We have to arrive at a common agreement on what to do: what to tell our ad and PR agencies, our employees, service sector, and so on.

Let's have agreement on all this in four weeks, which is March 11. On this date, we'll have our first action meeting—the most important one, because it will initiate action on our new strategy.

I know we'll go into this in a spirit of cooperation to do what's best; to ensure this, I suggest these rules:

No gridlock

No defensive postures

No adversarial overtones

No contentious expressions or thoughts

No self-serving statements

No focusing on a problem without a contravening solution

No eulogizing of previous strategies

No gratuitous praise or criticism

No wasted motion

No wishful thinking

When our whole program is in place, it will be enshrined on stone tablets and all will bow in reverence.

Have a great weekend,

Betty

▌CUT THROUGH ABSTRACTIONS AND FOCUS ON THE
▌SALIENT POINT.

SITUATION: You are the head of a well-recognized architectural firm. Profits took a dive, meaning trouble. You must get your employees on track in order to change minus earnings to plus.

STRATEGY: Your staff has to understand one basic premise: you are in business to make money to pay bills and have some left over. They have to set their thinking straight on getting the business back on track. You asked your staff architects to write you a memo with the answer to the bedrock question—"What are we in business for?" See what they have to say, and then get back to them.

February 11, 1996

To: Jake Davidoff
       Lindsey Anderson
       Diane Quester
       Lars Stenveld

From: Seth Herman

I asked you to specify what this architectural company is in business for. What is our cardinal purpose?

I don't have to tell you this is to address the basic thing we are supposed to do. It is a first step in overcoming the big slide in profits during the last three quarters and get us on to a growth curve.

The answers I've seen are. . .

   Design outstanding structures we can be proud of.

   Get new standards of construction integrity.

   Lead our clients to innovative and greater architectural achievements.

These are all nice, but no one gave the right answer, which is our hard-core objective, our unalterable responsibility that's ahead of anything else.

We are in business to make money. The other words of wisdom are relevant, no doubt, but they are not the bedrock reason for our being here. It's profits that make for these nice offices and the perks we enjoy, as well as pay our salaries. Their absence will cause cessation of same.

Let's keep this in mind as number 1.

Have a great day,

▌RESTORE WORKER MORALE AFTER A FIRING BLOODBATH.

SITUATION: Your company had a severe downsizing, caused by two years of plummeting earnings. Twenty-five percent of the employees have been pink-slipped. You have to keep a charge-ahead attitude in the sales department, which you head up. You cannot afford a downcast demeanor. Your salespeople have to be upbeat and optimistic in explaining the new company structure to their customers.

STRATEGY: Send a memo to your division managers for distribution.
          Tell them that things are fine and that business will be moving ahead at a much better pace because of greater efficiencies now in force. Everyone now here is secure, with a chance to make more money and to move up the ladder faster.

October 18, 1996

To: Joe Durso
        Felice D'Amico
        Bernie Bronsweig
        Carol Bloom
        John Farley

From: Harry Medina

Re: Reorganization of the Sales Department—The Facts.

Q. Why did we make this move?

A. We at times bumped into each other, causing problems with our accounts. There were instances when two of our salespeople contacted the same customer. It was necessary to have a more orderly sales structure.

Q. Why were so many people laid off?

A. We had a lot more people than necessary for the volume of our business; moreover, the new technology we installed in the last couple of years in itself entailed a work-force reduction. This streamlining allows for more individual opportunity. And, insofar as the sales department is concerned, there will be more commissions for those who are here now.

Q. Will there be any more layoffs?

A. I can't forecast the future, but the answer at this time is no. The reorganization is complete. No more layoffs are contemplated. Everyone here is important. There is a new opportunity now, to stay and thrive, which we want all of you to take advantage of.

Q. How is business right now?

A. Very good. There are fewer sales now, but they are more profitable because of the efficiencies we put into place. Business looks like it's growing. We're happy. You should be, too.

Q. What changes are going on in our information processing?

A. Our computer programming was falling behind the new technology. We are now getting data faster and more in tune with the marketplace.

Q. Will more people be hired later on?

A. Yes, as the business grows and it gets too much to handle for you guys. We'll let you know what goes on. The people on board now will get the first crack at the best positions and promotions.

This should dispel the rumors and put us on track. And every one of you, please let me know if there is anything else on your mind that you want answered.

My thanks to you all; I'm convinced we have the best sales force in the business. So is our chairman and president.

Best wishes,

Harry

P.S.   Please distribute copies of this to all the people in your divisions. I want them to know as much as you do.

▌GET PRACTICAL—GET "DOING"!

Indecisiveness, disparate decisions and conflicting agendas run wild. Why? Because a corporate dictum calling for consensus and collegiality, in line with a new wave theory on decision making. A corporate department is supposed to deliver a recommendation. Progress is plodding. Send a letter to the head of the department to get practical, and get the work out.

Dear Alexis:

A decision has to be made on what to do about the Norwalk assignment. We are patiently waiting for a plan of action.

The culture here says that a policy plan needs a consensus. Everyone should have a hearing—all have the right and the duty to express their opinions. In this way decisions will result from the organization genius, not from one strong individual or group. It's like a democracy. It sounds laudable.

In this case, however, you have to put the finish on the endless bandying, philosophical skirmishes, and senseless debating. As the linchpin you must accelerate the process to a pragmatic conclusion.

Please, no more wasted time. We're tired of reading status reports. We need a final determination. Can we have your department's report by May 16? If not, call me and tell me why not.

Regards,

Adelaide

You are the one in charge of getting out a budget plan for the coming years' production schedule. The people reporting to you on this project are in perpetual disagreement. It's mostly the starry-eyed vs. the somber-eyed.

Dear Team-Mates—

About the production plan and budget for the next fiscal year:

Time is running out. We have to come to a decision on how much material and personnel we will need for the next fiscal year. Can we be decisive—and at the same time correct? If not, we are not doing our jobs.

There have been forecasts of forecasts, and this is not meant to criticize the fine analyses that were made. They have been thoughtful and worthwhile, even though they have come to differing conclusions as earnings go, from high, to low, to in-between.

I'm afraid that philosophical differences and nitpicking have taken over. Why? Pride, each one's desire to shine, the urge to debate, and the big bogey, a fear of being wrong!

To be sure, we *must* exercise caution—but not overcaution. Right now we're in lethargy, gridlock, and at this rate we'll be sinking.

Let's not make the fatal mistake of abandoning native intelligence—that is, GOOD SENSE! And keep in mind, we must come to the best decision for now, not for eternity. We are living in the present. Posterity will be addressed later.

Have a good day,

Bernie

ANOTHER LETTER

Mr. Thomas Eckhart
Vice-President
Financial Descriptions, Ltd.

Dear Tom,

About our strategic investment plan. . . Next Monday, the 11th, is the deadline.

This document will not be engraved on stone tablets. Nor will it be submitted for the Pulitzer Prize. But it has to be smart and beautiful, and be right, and be able to withstand scrutiny. You are a superb professional leading other superb professionals. You know how.

Remember, there don't have to be any necks sticking out. We will put in alarm signals, with the option of monthly adjustments, if necessary, as we progress. Get it? The word is progress!!

Your friend,

cc: Blair Jones
       Carol Kingsley
       Loretta Siegel

ANOTHER LETTER

An important policy recommendation and plan of action is bogged down waiting for economic forecasts by the god-like predictors of the future.

You are a senior officer who has to put your stamp on the recommendation; this is a memo to the executives and grunts who are working on it.

Good morning, members of the Planning Committee:

We're in the midst of our annual plan, as well as our awesome epic, the 3-year and 5-year blueprint. I see us being enslaved by prophets, the celebrated economic forecasters who earn huge sums through our insecurities and guru reverence.

In deciding what should happen, and what is going to happen with our company, we obviously have to keep in mind the prospects for the industry and the national and world economies. A slavish dependence on the forecasts of the economic intelligentsia makes the job easy. Like a day at the beach.

But it is not the intelligent way!

Everyone knows that economic forecasting is not a science. Shrewd and learned as the economic Olympiads are, they hardly ever agree on what's going to happen. The further into the future—2,3,5 years—the less reliable are their prognostications.

If four seers all forecast one way and a fifth has a contradictory view, who is to say the fifth is wrong? And keep in mind the old saw: If you ask ten economists a question, you are liable to get eleven answers. In other words, economic forecasting at best is imprecise and often wrong. It is one of the tools for planning our business, to be taken seriously but not rigidly, not unthinkingly.

The economists, psychologists, statisticians, sociologists, pollsters and so on, from whom we draw knowledge, are very important, but they don't run our business. You do. They have an out, and can detach themselves, when things go wrong. You don't, and you can't.

Get your brilliant minds lit up and stop the gridlock. You know the business better than anyone on the outside. Let's meet on what facts, data, surmises we're to go on and then get the plans done. This meeting is on Wednesday, September 4th at 10 o'clock, and it should last one hour.

Regards,

Pat

▌ PRAISE A WINNING ACCOMPLISHMENT BY YOUR ▌ COLLEAGUES.

SITUATION: You are an ad agency VP account supervisor on the shop's biggest account, a world-renowned toiletries company. Your creative people have been in a strenuous and stressful exercise on a new TV commercial for your client's shampoo brand.

The advertising theme is a new creative idea. The commercial, in pre-production format, has gone through extensive testing among consumer panels along with commercials from two other agencies that are trying to get this business.

Hooray! Yours came out on top.

STRATEGY: Get the good news out to the creative team quickly in an interoffice memo, heaping praise on the people directly responsible. Copies go to all the key people, including the agency's chairman and president.

Without taking the edge off their pride of accomplishment, you have to point out that the job is far from over and that there's much more to do to get this commercial on the air. You don't want them to wallow in a euphoric glow when there is so much work ahead. Give the memo a smile to take the edge off your pushing them back to the workbench.

You will have solidified their loyalty and inspired a continued effort by demonstrating that this is the kind of wide recognition everyone in the agency can expect when they do a good job.

October 1, 1996

To: Candy Steinman
      Norm Sanchez
      Penelope Durgin
      Steffi Smith
      and others who had a hand in Commercial TF103

From: Ethan Warfield

You produced a winner. It sure makes everyone here look good.

The client just gave me the results of the three commercials tested. Yours came out on top. I always knew it was great advertising, but it's so nice to have it confirmed. Best of all, the client is delighted with it, supremely so. So are we.

Before you decide to take the rest of the day off or go into a euphoric glaze, think of what has to be done.

1. First, walk around a bit, greet your friends; praise each other. Then sit down and look out the window for 5 minutes or so.

2. Take a long lunch. (1-1/2 hours.)

3. Later this afternoon, start getting ready for production. Casting, sets, studio, location, etc., and figure out the final budget.

4. All of this has to be client approved by October 22. Sooner is better, because it must be on the air in March.

5. Other assignments will be coming up, starting a few days from now. I'm sure you'll take these new creative challenges in your usual masterful strides.

6. Have a nice weekend.

Be especially proud in that we beat out two other top agencies. Congratulations to everyone!

Admiringly,

Ethan

cc: Sigmund Brandberg, Chairman
        Theodora Ramos, President
        The Staff

ADMONISH THE NEW-BUSINESS PITCH TEAM AFTER A COSTLY DEFEAT. IT SHOULD HAVE BEEN A VICTORY.

SITUATION: The new-business team at the marketing communications agency which you preside over is generally composed of five or six of the star performers. It is an ad hoc group that is selected for each presentation. They pull together and deliver the presentation, drawing on other staff members for specialized input.

One such team made a costly endeavor for a foremost account plum that had two other agencies also running after it. Your group wasn't successful, even though you consider them more talented than the winning agency's team.

They didn't prepare as well. They were also overconfident. They knew they were good, and they knew they had superlative ideas to show off. But their ideas weren't spelled out convincingly. All of this added up to losing instead of winning.

STRATEGY: Send them a group memo. Bring them to reality as to what makes a successful new business team. Point out their foibles, what they did wrong, and what they didn't do right.

Tear them apart and then brace them up for the next new business encounter.

April 8, 1993

To: The Performers Who Made the Presentation for the
          Sugarland Account
       Rowena Balterman
       Mary Beth Innis
       Casper Winters
       Gene Koenig

From: Barbara Thomas

One Step Back. . . Let's Make It Two Steps Forward Next Time.

I don't have to tell you that Will, Ruby & Partners aren't as good as
we are. So how come they beat us out on the Sugarland business?

We had wonderful ideas to show Sugarland. We were confident. We had a
good attitude. We were the best team in the tournament. We didn't score
the winning run. Why?

We would have won. . . IF. . .

> *IF* we had spent more time at Sugarland in order to learn more
> about their business. We thought we knew it. But we didn't know
> it well enough. We were badly out of sync on one of our sug-
> gestions. It hurt our image.
>
> *IF* we had consulted with the trade press to find out what the
> competition was doing. One of our gold-plated ideas had recent-
> ly been done by a competitor. That was a major embarrassment.
>
> *IF* we had given ourselves more time to thoroughly check our
> write-up. Some of the typos made us look small-time.
>
> *IF* we weren't so damn cocky. Some of our shoot-from-the-hip
> answers were evasive, one was double talk and one was plain
> wrong.

Every championship team and every superstar must train constantly to be
in top condition, to be thoroughly prepared for every single game, men-
tally and physically.

Repeat: thoroughly prepared.

Talent alone does not win. A lot of behind-the-scenes hard work is an
absolute necessity. That's what makes a winning team. That's what brings
in big salaries.

We learned a lesson. A costly one. Did you add up the cost of this presentation? You'll be shocked!

Let's make sure we're ready when the next one comes up.

B.T.

▌GET YOUR STAFF—AND YOUR VENDOR—FIRMLY INTO LINE.

TWO LETTERS:

"Correct" Your Vendor
"Correct" Your Staff

SITUATION: You are the Director of Marketing Communications of a top packaged-goods toiletries manufacturer. The executive level supervisors are youthful cream of the crop from top MBA schools. They are clever, eager, and often oblivious to rules and procedures that may slow their drive for recognition and riches.

Each one wants to be the first to get data from your consumer research supplier, sometimes even before it is assembled, so that they can present it to upper management with their intelligent comments. Being the first with inside information brings attention and kudos.

This helter-skelter drive to be the bearer of tidings causes confusion, mistakes, and misguided analyses. It makes you look bad. It causes your department to be perceived as disorganized and leaderless.

STRATEGY: Send a letter to the head of the research company saying that all information it gathers—every little piece of it—is to come to you first. It must not comply with individual requests from your staff. Point out the reason and that the former confusion was not the fault of the research people. They were taking orders from a client, yes, but from the wrong staff member. Only you represent the client.

Then send a memo to your staff, with a copy of the letter you sent to the market-research company. Specify the new dictum. Enlist their support and praise them for their intelligence, their striving to excel, and the wonderful job they are doing.

```
Mr. Anthony DiLoresta, President
Target Marketing Research
_____
_____

Subject:  The Transmitting of Information

Dear Tony:

I very much appreciate the consumer data you are bringing to light.
```

But there is a problem with how you transmit the information to us. It affects our judgment on what to do with it, which in turn affects our decision-making process, which, in turn affects the value of the information itself.

Here's the chain of command on your dealings with this company:

1. All your data—reports, top-line, bottom-line, objective, subjective, interpretive, inferential, or whatever, phoned or written—come to me first. No other copies are to go to anybody.

2. This office will look it over, discuss it with you or with whomever you may designate. I will then review it with the appropriate people here. We'll then come to a judgment as to how to handle it.

3. I, or one of my staff, may then ask you to send along multiple copies of one or more of your reports. That is, your own data and analysis, which is not to include any interpretation by anyone outside your office.

We are pretty much a free-wheeling organization peopled by smart young "turks" who work hard and accomplish a lot. It's great for this company.

They have often called you for top-line data or early results—even before they are fully compiled. They have asked to see reports, or your interpretations, before they have been formally prepared. Several have received reports before anyone else here. You have complied with their requests but it's not your company's fault. You answered a client's requests.

It has, however, gotten out of hand. It is bad business procedure, and it's going to stop. From this time on!

If anyone at your place gets such a request from anyone here without my approval, that person is to refer to the statements in this letter and then inform me.

I'm sure, Tony, that you are in accord with what I'm saying. I'm also certain you are happy to see it changed. Keep up the good work.

Best regards,

Betty Jo

P.S.   My staff has seen a copy of this letter.

```
To:    Shelley Bogart
       Oscar Fogarty
       Nancy Hanna
       Bud Kingman
       Linda Miranda
From:  Betty Jo Anderson
```

Attached is a letter I sent yesterday to Tony DiLoresta of Target Research. Read it before starting on the rest of this memo.

Now that you've read the attached, here are my comments to all of you.

First of all, I'm proud of the superb job you are doing. You handle it with intelligence, verve, and an insatiable eagerness to excel. It's good for this company. In fact, it's great.

Now for the sticky rules that you see in my letter to Tony. It may confine your exuberance, but it increases your effectiveness and your value to this department and the company.

We have to be a team. Let's each have the advantage of the others' judgments. This is not to say everything has to be dictated by consensus. But we must have collegiality. There is a huge advantage to having the combined wisdom of several brilliant minds in reviewing a problem.

At the same time we should take into account what a very clever guy, Henry L. Doherty, once said ... "Some of our problems can no more be solved by majority opinion than a problem in arithmetic."

The bottom line on marketing research—

> All reports, comments, results, judgments, opinions, and surmises must come from my office. The positive input of each of you will be fed into what is distributed to the other people here, with full credit given.

> You will have better recognition of your good thinking than before. What's more, you won't be caught giving premature or partial results, which can be, and often are, misleading. Be happy.

I'm glad you are here,

Susan

You are a consultant and your client wants you to provide a sound sales forecast and the reasoning behind it. To avoid wrangling when your client sees the outcome, you want to get agreement on the principal factors that will guide you to a conclusion.

Dear Carla,

Thank you for giving us the Alliance sales plan assignment. With all humility, we are experts at this kind of work, and have an exceptionally good track record.

Before proceeding, we should agree on a few basic guidelines:

A. We want to consider all the facts. We need this from your people, and we'll dig through it and sift out all the decision-influencing data. Facts not conjectures, no wishful thinking, no undue bleakness.

B. Opinions, yes. Hunches, yes. Caveats, yes. But they must be based on realities of hard knowledge and experience. Industry experience, your company experience, your personal experience and your staff's personal experience. And our experience.

C. In the mix of data we will review are macro changes and shifts taking place in the industry, and microanalyses of your company and your customers.

D. From all this we will analyze known factors and probabilities that will affect your sales.

E. We will insert flexibility into the plan, so you can pull back, retrench, surge forward as the actual situation unfolds month-to-month, week-to-week, even day-by-day. The point is to avoid surprises. Most of all, to avoid getting into a hole and being late in getting out.

Planning discipline like this diminishes aimless debates, time-wasting discussions, unworthy recriminations.

The umbrella guideline is: . . . Aim carefully and keep your powder dry!

Warm regards,

Casper Simpson

ANOTHER LETTER

Dear Team-mates:

Time is running out. Two weeks from today, we have to come to a decision on material, personnel and technological needs.

There have been forecasts ad infinitum, arguments, philosophical differences, nitpicking, and self-serving urges. Added to this is the deaden-
ing fear of taking an absolute stand. Mostly from not knowing what outside forces will take hold—i.e. shortages, currency fluctuations, wars,
you name it.

Only God knows what is going to happen! We mortals can't portend the
future so, of course, we must exercise caution—but not paralyzing caution. Right now we're in atrophy and we have to get out of it.

Let's put into the decision-making mix all of the publicly known facts,
the behind-the-scenes information, the history that bears on the problem, the opinions of experts, a good dose of intelligent analysis, and
a fall-back safety factor. And do the best job we possibly can.

Best regards,

Marie Munoz

Your company does business with the government. You're subject to the
winds of change in legislative agendas, regulations, policies, public attitudes,
voters' moods and on and on. But you have to plan ahead regardless. There
is gridlock, mostly due to a dependence on political forecasts of voter ten-
dencies, election trends, and the psyches of politicians.

YOU ARE IN CHARGE—CITE YOUR DECISION-MAKING PRINCIPLES.

Re: The two-year capital projection

Dear Mr. Ross:

We're in pretty much of a dilemma in arriving at a clear-cut agenda on
specific steps to take over the next two years. We have been looking at
opinion polls and the forecasts of the famous political pundits. The pundits, however, don't have to take any flak if we guess wrong. We do, from
top to bottom.

At the very best the pollsters may give us clues. Clues are not necessarily facts, not hard data that will lead to success or failure. I know
you agree that we simply can't have political polltakers and forecasters run our business. It could well drive us to distraction, and destruc-
tion.

Let's look on these people as helpmates. That is, helpers, not doers. We are the doers. We have to use this help PLUS common sense. Now, let's get it done.

Best regards,

Danny Dexter

To: John Warfield, Ann Stein, et al.

Re: Suggested factors in developing our next fiscal year profit projection, taking into account R &D costs.

I'd like to put these guiding principles on the table.

1. Top priority is to service what we have right now—what is taking place now. In other words, the government contracts and concrete assignments now in hand, as well as the private sector contracts to which we are committed.

2. Concentrate on the likely upgrading of these contracts—due to technical improvements, re-engineering, safety considerations and other influences that will make them providers of additional work and income.

3. Remember also contracts now being considered which we are confident of getting. Prices have been approved, but they are held up by details.

4. We should have a financial cushion to service contracts which are in the competitive bidding stage—in which, say, there is at least a 50-50 chance.

5. Of utmost importance, we must set aside money for realistic research and development. That is, R&D with agreed upon objectives based on present and near-future science and technology that have practical and profitable commercial applications. And we must keep an eagle eye on research being done by the government, our suppliers, and our competitors. We must try as best we can, within legal constraints, to avoid having a competitor do one-upmanship on us.

Some of what we do here may be speculative, but it's worthwhile if we don't go overboard or get recklessly embroiled in future science.

From all that you have said, I know you concur that this makes good business sense, and I assume we have your approval to move ahead on these precepts.

Jerry Rosen

▌GET DISSENSION UNDER CONTROL.

There's dissension at your local union hall. Meetings are chaotic. Voting is overly contentious; the domineering voices win out. An open letter to the president of the local—addressed to him personally and a copy posted on the bulletin board for all to see.

Dear Bob:

Please take the time to read this letter—it is respectfully intended for our rank and file and for the good of our union.

Our last two meetings were disasters. Very important issues were brought to us by national headquarters, and we weren't able to discuss them rationally. The shouting, name calling and cursing were disgraceful. Worse, we couldn't come to any real conclusions—and some members didn't vote at all out of protest. Some weren't even sure what the vote was about.

May I make these suggestions. . .

    A. Before we are to vote on anything important, let's say a week or two before, the specific issue and the pros and cons should be in a letter or printed in a circular and mailed to each member's home.

    B. People at a meeting must ask for recognition to speak. No loud talk without getting permission from the platform. Clearance to speak must be impartial, all sides heard.

    C. If a number of members find they have a common opinion, one person should talk for the group, mentioning who and how many he or she represents.

    D. No more than three minutes for any speaker from the floor. An intelligent point of view can be voiced in that time. No foul words, no insults, and respect for all members, including those in opposition.

    E. Those who wish to make a longer talk must ask permission and come front and center.

    F. No loud voices from the floor to be tolerated. People who persist in shouting are to be told to leave the hall.

It comes down to democracy in action, and also common courtesy. That's how we'll make this union strong, as well as each and every member.

Your loyal brother in combat,

Terry Hammond

A craft union's membership disagrees about voting on a new industrial contract, particularly as it applies to a specific large company. You want the fighting to stop.

```
To Our Local Rank and File:

I've written this poem to all of my brothers and sisters. It is not great,
but I believe it says everything. Say it to yourself, to each other. Keep
it in mind.

                    Stay always together in friendship
                      and we'll keep on flying high.

                    But grudges, sneers, hostility
                      will make us crash and die.

                    Everyone who wears our badge
                      is your true and loyal friend.

                    See the badge and you will know
                      they are with you to the end.

                    When all of us will fight as one
                      we can go to any length.

                    Let's not forget, one and all,
                      in Union there is strength!!

Let's stop wrangling and meet as friends. There is much at stake.
```

Gridlock at the local school-board meetings. As a member, you send a letter to the rest of the board to stop endless conflicts and inflexibility which thwart getting things accomplished.

```
Dear Fellow Members—

We all agree that we are up against issues of utmost importance, a sit-
uation which gives each one of us a scary responsibility. Sorrowfully,
our deep responsibility is the only thing we can all agree on. I mean
agree without reservations, points of difference, a need for more debate,
and on and on with endless talk.

May I raise my small voice to say we are not getting things done right.
I don't mean right for me or right for you, but right for the children
and parents of our community.

May I respectfully request that the Board president get tough about
insisting on orderly meetings, judiciously tied to an agenda. We should
not conduct any business until proper procedure is strictly adhered to.
```

We must see to it that we treat the problem, not the symptom. And let everyone keep uppermost our true purpose. A quote from a past statesman, Robert Schuller, is appropriate—"Problems are not stop signs, they are guidelines."

Samantha Brandman

ANOTHER LETTER TO BRING A SPIRIT OF CORDIAL DIALOGUE TO A CONTENTIOUS ISSUE

Dear Fellow Members—

Free speech is noble, but endless jockeying is not. Can't you see the stultifying inflexibility and mulishness in many of our deliberations? Why don't we adopt the attitude of coming to a conclusion that's right for the community at large, not necessarily perfect for every single individual? It means yielding, and compromise. . . Yes, and respect for each one on our board.

Otherwise we'll be of disservice to our community members who depend on us.

Respectfully,

ANOTHER LETTER TO SPECIFY RULES OF CONDUCT

To: All members of the Seaview School Board
From: Board Chairman

Here are the simple rules for conducting meetings: All viewpoints are to be heard and discussed in order, quickly, with limited debating, and issues intelligently discussed. No rancor, no one out of order. The majority wins.

Isn't that the way democracy should be run? Sometimes it runs the way we like it, sometimes not, but it runs. Otherwise, there will be chaos and anarchy in the governance of our school system, which must be avoided at all costs. . . It is bad for all of us, for each individual and family.

O.K., let's make what I said here a unanimous decision. I don't think *this* has to be debated.

Your fellow member,

Sanford Roberts

ANOTHER LETTER

A local taxpayer committee meeting. A disgusted committee leader delivers a letter to the members deploring chaotic, ego-thumping meetings of the past which throttled any real accomplishments—and aimed at establishing rules of conduct.

Dear Fellow Members:

The last two meetings were hardly worth attending—and I was embarrassed at having been elected your leader.

With that said, I'm setting down these hard-and-fast rules—

- The labyrinthine maze of disparate opinions, theories and bombast, adds up to chaos. Well, maybe not as far as chaos, but it sure isn't getting our job done. This must cease. Right now!

- The culture here is to bring out the best in each of us. To evoke a communal genius in facing what must be accomplished. We cannot and will not make this a battle of conflicting and stubborn wills.

- There is no room for shovers, self-servers, macho wavemakers—nor the timid and scared for that matter. I'll see to it that the glib, the garrulous and the chest thumpers do not dominate the agenda.

- We're going to have sessions here which harness our common wisdom to common goals.

All of these points are now to be agreed upon—in total. It must be a unanimous vote. There are to be no dissenters, no abstentions.

Your thankful leader,

Augusta Shine

▌RECOMMEND HOLD-OFF ON NEW BUSINESS.

Send a report to the company president, with the objective of walking away from what appears to be a lucrative contract. Your company is not equipped to handle it. Chaos would erupt if it were attempted. But you don't want to appear negative or unwilling. (Before sending the report, you had a meeting to agree on this conclusion. Thus the recommendation to hold off is a group decision.) Present your position so that it appears positive, but almost impossible, for the president to want to take on this new business.

To: Bennett Schacten
From: Harold V.
Re: The A & D Contract Proposal

I met with Eloise, Sidney, Bryan, Arlene. This is our collective wisdom as to the various choices that can be made regarding this new business assignment.

  1. We have neither the production capacity nor the expertise for all that's involved. To accomplish what is required will entail an investment in technical equipment and personnel of uncertain cost at this time.

  2. Handle what we are able to do well and farm out the rest under our supervision. This will need extra supervisory people and sufficient time to find the right suppliers. It means asking the client to extend its desired time frame for developing a plan of operation. We cannot now assess how much extra time is needed.

  3. Say we will do what we can—and offer our assistance to the client in getting vendors for the rest.

If you like option 3, which seems the most practical for us, we will make a presentation on this theme. However, I believe it wouldn't be acceptable because this client wants everything done under one roof.

You might want to give it a try. If so, we should get started right away, and hold up other projects that don't have a tight deadline.

There's more on your plate than you can do well and it has become overwhelming. Get the human resources manager's permission to have others help you, under your supervision.

Mr. Jackson Derona
Vice President, Human Resources

Good morning, Jackson:

There are three important projects I'm working on, all with tight deadlines—two due at the same time. However, I am able to reschedule so that we'll manage, but we'll need extra effort, overtime work--and more help.

I can break these projects down into performance modules so that people can be assigned individual units of production. This will, with my supervision, work out well, and we can save some overtime expenses.

I'd like to have Doug, Rita and Mario assigned to head up these units, and I will give them instructions and pull together all of their input.

If any one of them is absolutely unavailable, I'll need his/her equiva-
lent, but it would have to be someone of equal ability.

Thanks, Jackson, your okay will make it possible to get all of this work
very capably completed—on time and within budget. I'll call you today.

Jerry Spero

▌REQUEST ADDITIONAL HELP TO GET WORK DONE.

A letter to your boss, saying you are delegating certain tasks to help you get
your assignments done. In this case you are making the decision as to who
will be assigned to help you. Praising these people will likely get their cooperation.

To: Mr. G.K. Summers

From: Tony Coleman

Subject: The Code Name T38 Presentation

In order to get all the pieces together for the best presentation we
can do—or that any company can do for that matter—I'm asking Doug, Carl
and Rebecca to pitch in to write the sections they are preeminently
qualified for. Who, anywhere, can do their specialties as well as they?

I will pull together the sections they complete so as to have a cohesive
and persuasive presentation. Needless to say, this will be an important
piece of business for us, and I'm sure you want to be certain it gets
our best effort.

A letter to the VP and manager of the company division asking permission to hire consultants to take up the slack on a project you are responsible
for.

Mr. Sean O'Rourke
Vice President, Administration

Good morning, Sean—

I need your help on the P.D.R. project I'm working on.

There are several areas in which we need some outside help to evaluate
some of the options I'm including in the report, and for writing up a

few sections. I will edit what they write and put the total report into final form.

Utilizing our own people would not be wise at this time since they could be more productive on other assignments.

This is why I strongly recommend hiring consultants to fill in the gap. I've already met with two who I think are very well qualified. (The cost involved is shown on the next page.) Undoubtedly, we will be saving money in the long run and at the same time get the job done on time.

All the best,

Bennett LeBow

Delegate an assistant to supervise and turn around a project that is slowly going downhill and into a state of chaos. Confirm this in a memo to her, copying the COO. It must be done diplomatically, and without a negative reflection on you.

To: Debbie Robinson
        Neary Processing, Inc. Division
        Headquarter Building, 11th Floor

We need capable hands, mind and skills to organize the Delta Project which is in a state of confusion, close to chaos. There is a deplorable lack of direction, which we spoke about yesterday.

Starting tomorrow you will be running this project. Please let me know if you get any flack from the people who will be assigned to work under you.

Debbie, you will report to me, and I expect a report every Thursday AM giving all pertinent details as to progress, problems and so on. I have complete confidence you will get this under control and running smoothly. I'm sure you realize that this project, if run effectively, will be an important contribution to corporate profits.

John Waldorf

cc: Mr. H.P. Warren

▌RECONCILE DISPARATE VIEWPOINTS.

Pull together disparate viewpoints and dispel confusions.

```
To:    Jack Thomas
       Yoni Farsa
       Mary Goldberg
       Juan Romera

From:  Len Plattner
```

You are the people responsible for getting the Customer Service Department in line and on line so that it effectively promotes and implements our mission. Namely, total, unequivocal customer service. Nothing less than 100%.

We've been operating at 50% effectiveness. Do you know why? I'll put my finger on it.

It's because we have disparate views of our objectives and confusion as to methods—mainly fueled by individual egos, self-serving goals, and working at loggerheads. Get rid of it all! I'm in charge and this is my statement!

We're having a meeting on Tuesday, February 9th, at 9 A.M., on how we are to reorganize and conduct customer service—and how you are to lead the people who report to you. Bring to the meeting a spirit of cooperation, of amity, and of working together for the good of our whole endeavor.

Remember, our whole group, working in harmony, can accomplish much more than any single individual. This is how our company will grow.

I expect a lot from you on Tuesday, 9 A.M.

Form an ad hoc committee to organize and run an event for your civic association.

LETTER TO THE ELECTED CHAIRMAN AND THE MEMBERSHIP AT LARGE

```
Ms. Audrey Blattner, Chairman
Trustees:   Sheila Rosenberg
            Jack Lewis
            Stu Hopkins
            and All Members
```

Having been honored to head up the arrangements for our annual ball—and having considered the many suggestions by all of you as well as by other members—I am now forming a committee of four to take care of the numerous arrangements. . . As follows—

> *Date and place:* Sheila Rosenberg
>
> *Music and entertainment:* Harry Wells
>
> *Printed material,* i.e.
> invitations, schedules,
> mailing pieces etc: Ginny Leonard
>
> *Financial*—the budget
> and its maintenance: Mort Kevin

All others—Please don't be dismayed if you are not included. We will probably have other duties to be assigned.

All the above named are to submit firm suggestions to me, and I will report the final decisions to the chairman and trustees. This will then be sent to all members and there will be a special meeting to review any constructive comments members may have.

If any of you who have been appointed cannot, for a good reason, carry out your assignment, I will assign your duties to another member.

Harold Vogel,
Member-in-charge

You are the organizer of a Political Action Committee that is getting out of control, and falling apart. You want to revive it and make it effective.

To: All Members

Never Say Die!
Yes, we can come to a programmed effort we all agree with.
Yes, we can recruit new members to give us more strength.
Yes, we can raise more money.
Yes, we can be effective in accomplishing our goals.

Money and members will give us the strength to reach the right legislators, the right committees, the right administrators—and get them to pay attention to what we want—and to act accordingly.

I am putting forward Adelaide Johnson to be the Operations Officer of this P.A.C. She has agreed to tackle this difficult, time-consuming job. If there is any dissent or disagreement, let me know about it in writing. Quickly. I'm confident, however, that everyone has confidence in Adelaide, and will give her full support.

Adelaide will select five members to help her, and assign them specific duties. All volunteers are to contact Adelaide.

Let's all work for our common good, and contribute money and time. Otherwise, we'll be overwhelmed by events and our legislative goals will fall by the wayside.

Your friend and fellow believer,

Richard Finnegan

Reconcile and direct your church's ad hoc building committee. Too much oratory, too little action.

Trustees of the Building Committee:

"Democracy means government by discussion but it is only effective if you can stop people from talking too much" (Clement Attlee, a former British Prime Minister).

I am directing this message to my seven fellow trustees with whom I share the honor and responsibility of managing this congregation and making it an influential force in our community.

Sadly, our Building Committee of 12 members is not functioning as it should. Some may think it is, but it is not.

Reason: Too much talking. Our meetings have become oratorical encounters. People are talking at cross purposes, and too often for the sake of voicing opinions with an air of authority.

I therefore suggest that this committee be given one more chance to meet. We are to put four resolutions (i.e. action choices) on the table that make sense. We should then *not* formally meet for a month. In the meantime we will have informal discussions on these choices in social or ad hoc sessions in order to arrive at some conclusion as to their wisdom and feasibility.

If progress is not made, and our next meeting continues as before, I believe this committee should be dissolved, and another one formed with different people.

I call upon your Reverence, the President and the Board of Trustees to concur.

Jerome Smith

cc: The Most Reverent Peter Smith

The large governing body of a charitable foundation must make some crossroads decisions on future activities. A committee was formed to resolve various details and come up with final determinations. You, the foundation's Chief Executive Officer, sees stultifying conflicts and disparate opinions bogging down decisive results. Send a letter to the committee chairperson—copies to the foundation's officers.

Dear Ms. Robinson:

May I please ask for serious attention to my following suggestion regarding the discussions taking place. As you know, what we decide is quite monumental, with repercussions far into the future.

I think we are going too far, too fast and perhaps at cross-purposes.

On this note, I quote a statement reportedly spoken by Napoleon Bonaparte. . . "Order marches with weighty and measured steps; disorder is always in a hurry."

I respectfully suggest that you divide equally your sixteen-person committee into four bodies. Divide the issues that need to be resolved among these bodies. Next, review the results with the officers of this organization and make appropriate conclusions.

Thanks so much for your attention and I'm anxious to hear what you think of this suggestion.

Special thanks for your efforts; I admire what you are doing.

Timothy Gordon

P.S.   I recently read a wise and witty quote in an article by Eileen Shanahan in the *New York Times Magazine* . . . "The length of a meeting rises with the square of the number of people present."

A corporate division head has to install another bureaucratic entity to settle disputes between the research-and-development committee and the marketing committee.

To: Cynthia Morgan
      Leonard Schwartz

You are both doing exceptional jobs running your committees, and coming up with some very thoughtful conclusions. It goes without saying, however, that due to different skills, training and responsibilities, you

are working on different agendas. And at times, understandably, at conflicting purposes.

I am therefore forming a steering committee, composed of myself, a representative of the financial department, someone from human resources and
a headquarters staff officer, to resolve any disputes.

This is not to dictate what you are to do. It is to smooth things along
and arbitrate any conflicting determinations. Naturally, you can question this outside committee's resolutions.

ANOTHER LETTER—TO LESSEN CONFLICTING DECLARATIONS

> *"Good order is the foundation of all things"*
>
> (Edmund Burke)

That's what we need, good order, and we are not getting it. This department is regressing into disorder.

I'll tell you why!

You are not discussing things in a collegial fashion. Many do not listen to what is being said. Listen! listen! Another's opinion may be just
as smart as yours, perhaps more so. Don't take a disagreement as a
threat.

Each one should keep this in mind: bargaining, compromising, not dick-
ering, is what brings the best results. It is best for this department
and best for each one in it.

Another wise saying—

> *"Do not condemn the judgment of another because it differs
> from your own. You may both be wrong."*
>
> (Dandemis)

MEMO FROM THE MODERATOR OF A STEERING COMMITTEE

Dear hard-working steering committee, with a thankless job:

I'll use seamanship metaphors to describe the way we have to operate in
coming up with a definitive financial allocation plan.

We have to have in mind a rudder so that we do not veer off our course.
We must negotiate and compromise, and I'll stop anyone who does not

navigate our assigned route or stalls the engine that keeps us moving forward.

So let's set our course and move full speed ahead—straight on course.

With friendship,

Gene Atkins

PACIFY ANGRY DISSENTERS TO A GOVERNMENT REGULATION

To fellow dissenters of State Regulation 2.43:

I know some are protesting it, some want to ignore it, a few want to fight it. And all find it needlessly involved and time consuming to fill out all the forms and answer all the questions.

But this is a rule from on high. It's the law. We're not going to protest because it won't do any good, and if we don't satisfactorily comply there will be trouble.

To be sure, we're not going to tilt at windmills. By all means, we're certainly not going to contest this needlessly complex regulation in court. Some of our peers have compared it to a Communist-style doctrine. We will combat it within the rules, legally, forthrightly.

Stiff upper lip, comrades.

Genevieve Sothern

CONFRONT DISSENTERS TO A CORPORATE REGULATION THAT MANDATES A SPECIFIC FORMAT FOR ALL REPORTS AND PRESENTATIONS

To the staff—

A few words about the management's requirements for plans, proposals and reports.

Regardless of what you may think, and to those who advanced their criticisms—we are all part of Excelsior Corp. and must put our best efforts toward getting the work done as management wants it done. Capably, enthusiastically and with dispatch. And, needless to say, we must act like the professionals we are.

Remember, we may not be privy to all the knowledge that resulted in the mandate of what is required. Further, management welcomes any sensible suggestion for improvement that is sent via proper channels.

So let's do it the right way—management's way—until we are told differ-
ently.

Dirk Sylvester
General Manager

ANOTHER LETTER OR MEMO BUT WITH A BACK-SLAPPING TONE. DOWN TO EARTH, FRIEND-TO-FRIEND

To all associates in the Marketing Dept:

Hey, let's stop griping and get to work, and get the job done with the
excellence we're all capable of. Whining, criticizing, grumbling takes
up time that should be better spent in meeting the deadline—and it does-
n't do the least bit of good.

Further, moping and grumbling is small-time and makes us look bad. We're
all proud of being looked upon as professionals. Let's act that way!!

Rob Calvert

∎ ENFORCE EFFICIENCY PROCEDURES.

Since bureaucracy has gotten out of hand, cut the timetable of committee or
council meetings drastically. If it is not reduced to a minimum, other projects
will bog down.

To: Members of our Management Committee

I think it's best to reduce the schedule of our Management Committee
meetings since it infringes on the important projects being done by the
attendees. I've gotten comments about this, which is why I'm writing to
you.

I'm sure you agree that meeting at three or four month intervals will be
just as effective as doing it monthly. Perhaps more so, since we'll have
more experience with any changes that come from each of these meetings.

This will put more of your thinking and energies into the many important
day-to-day and week-to-week issues you are responsible for.

Many thanks for your cooperation on this decision.

Pia Wendos

A service company has grown, but the sales department is still operating casually and informally in putting orders through the various departments. You have to enforce tight procedures or expenses will go out of sight.

To: Nick Kernlitis
        Arne Norquist
        Ralph Griffin
        Debbie Stone

Re: Procedures on orders and department instructions

Cost Estimates

Starting immediately we must institute tight procedures on all estimates you give customers both for their various requests and for the time the operating departments require to service these requests (time schedules). A cost will be applied to each department's work so that you can then provide the customer with a much more accurate price than just a "feel-good" price.

Time Schedules and Cost Estimates

You must give each customer a realistic time schedule. And similarly, a realistic schedule from department heads together with the hourly rates they will get from accounting. Overtime for rush jobs, etc. will be assigned the appropriate—and again, realistic—overtime rates.

Please pick up the necessary forms from Jim Seaver in accounting and he will answer any questions. No job will be processed without a filled-out form approved by accounting.

Lee Roberts

A SIMILAR LETTER, LESS FORMAL

For all sales and operations personnel, and all others involved—

The sales and operating departments have been going by seat-of-the-pants cost estimates and time schedules on the work we've been doing for customers.

It's got to stop!

Fortunately, we're a big league company now, thanks to the growth we've enjoyed the past couple of years—for which you all deserve credit.

So blame yourselves if we have to establish bureaucratic procedures and forms. From now on, as of this minute, Tuesday, January 12, 11:15 A.M., you will have to fill out the forms that are attached for each job request, so that a realistic time schedule, and a realistic cost, can be assigned to every single job we do.

I know this is less pleasant than the way we did things before, not as easygoing, but please cooperate. In fact, you must cooperate, for everyone's good.

Thanks for the great work you're done to make us grow.

Manny Rose

ANOTHER LETTER:
ADMONISH PEOPLE FOR NOT FOLLOWING PROCEDURES

To All Sales Reps—

Operating departments have complained that some of you—you know who—are requesting that work for customers be done without getting the proper time estimate forms *signed* by the respective department manager. They are being urged to start, in the interest of saving time, before the form is filled out and properly acknowledged.

From now on, cost estimates to customers are invalid without the procedure mentioned above.

This is another way of saying that procedures have to change because of company growth.

> Someone, I forget who, made a wise comment—"Growth is inherently embarrassing."

> Someone else made another pertinent comment. "A company can lose money by growing."

There has to be (and I as well as you hate this next word) *discipline* in following the proper procedures to get work assigned and started around here. Sorry, we've gotten too big to go by happy-go-lucky methods.

It's no more "you're my buddy, I'm your buddy." So let's get it done by the book. Otherwise costs get out of control and we can wind up losing money—and jobs.

Seriously, we have to be more businesslike. Some of you call it stuffed-shirt bureaucracy. Too bad—everyone has to follow company policy. It won't be annoying when you all get used to it.

John Sorentino

These letters apply to many industries, many companies, groups, associations etc.

To: Jerry Lassiter
                Emily Brown
                Lisa Fong
                Lew Ben-Stein

Subject: Concentration of research efforts.

We must get our heads pointing in a common direction. It has to do with market knowledge, our corporate resources, skills and experience; and of utmost importance, the risk/reward ratio of what we recommend.

As to risk/reward, forget what you learned that the greater the risk the higher the reward. This is gambling, playing the odds—we don't do that.

Think in terms of this formula: reduce risk to the minimum, increase reward to the maximum. Keep the other things I mentioned in focus too—resources, skills, experience. We must concentrate on what we do best, not venture into uncharted territory which can be dangerous.

Now let's move ahead. We'll have a meeting next Thursday, June 12, for a positive, sensible discussion. Feel free to offer creative suggestions in accordance with what was said here. I know we'll get some great ideas.

Len

ANOTHER LETTER

It sounds like a cliché, but it is important to say: "Answering problems goes a long way toward preventing crises."

We have to be honest and objective in our approach, not timid about stepping on toes, negating someone's favorite brainchild, and so on. Otherwise we'll make wrong decisions, move in wrong directions, and waste a lot of time.

Let's approach our next weekly meeting in terms of what's good for all of us collectively. We can do this and still be respectful of each one's opinions.

ANOTHER LETTER

I noticed that in the planning sessions we've had there are biased comments, a lack of forthrightness, and too strong a desire to please top management. Too much currying favor, keeping friends happy, rather than saying it as it is, telling what you really think.

Naturally, you tend to acquiesce to what your manager says, whether you agree or not. But it leads to bad decisions.

A certain cultural climate may support a business theory because it jibes with the story people close by want to hear at the moment. It's a frequent reason for wrong decisions and unfortunate acts.

Noting this, let's strive to come up with right decisions—and no one should be thin-skinned about having any pet theories shot down.

A BULLETIN TO A DEPARTMENT HEAD

Change "try" to "do."

Your staff is trying. They're trying hard. Good. Give them a little shove to talk in terms of "do."

A MEMO ON THE SAME NOTE

To: The techno intelligentsia that is developing a breakthrough shopping mall concept for the internet—Doug, Fleur, Hortense, Naken.

I'm not tossing a gratuitous morale-booster in saying that we're all grateful for the effort you are putting into this project. As you said, you are trying very hard. I'm sure you don't really mean "try"—in this business there is no such word. The only thing that counts is "do," which is different from trying.

Do, do well, get things done, do right, do to succeed, etc. Unquestionably you agree, and you sometimes use words incorrectly. However, you are not linguists, you arc computer engineers of the highest order.

If we didn't think you able to do this, you wouldn't be doing what you are doing.

Keep up the great work, we all know you will succeed.

Kerri

Brainstorming on top of brainstorming at company headquarters. Plans are discussed for (1) future survival and (2) growth. They haven't been explored in terms of profits. You want to stir things up and get people on the right track.

MEMO TO THE HEADS OF THE KEY DEPARTMENTS— R & D, MARKETING AND FINANCE

```
To:         Lucretia Kaudos—Director, R & D
            John Liebowitz—CFO
            Larry Malone—Marketing

From:       Bob Winston

Subject:    The 2-Year Game Plan
```

I attended several of the meetings and read the interim reports. It seems that we have some good ideas in the cooking stage. I'd like to interject one guiding principle in all of this that we should keep uppermost in our thinking.

What I see so far is that there seems to be an active hostility to making money. Real money, that is, not ephemeral, annual report money. Money that goes into the cash register, actual income, not assets that we can't spend.

Your recommendations must contain a well-thought-out cost estimate year by year, and a return-on-investment (ROI) analysis—carefully and realistically arrived at. Without this there is no recommendation.

Competitive assaults, share of market boosts and such are interesting, but ROI is meat and bones.

Get to sensible decisions—there are too many arguments. Develop solutions. No more chaos.

A memo to the staff people charged with coming up with a new computer platform to correct a certain system defect.

A message to: Melinda, Li, Brady, Irv.

The last few meetings uncovered some thoughtful hypotheses—which mostly developed into controversies.

Controversy is good in a way, since it breeds progress. But it has gone on too long! The big satisfactions seem to be in winning arguments. Let's not try to win any arguments—look to win a point that spells forward movement.

Please, let's get this done—and it's a tough task—by complementing each other's talents and ideas.

There's a big consumer market out there waiting for our solutions.

There's a meeting on this tomorrow at 8:30 A.M.

Syl

Some young "turks" are aggressively pushing ahead with new ideas on marketing via the Internet, and disdaining—even disparaging—all that had been done before. A brash outburst of creative energy.

You are the client who will be investing in it. Keep them in line without discouraging bold, innovative thinking.

LETTER TO THE RESEARCH GROUP HEAD

Dear Laurel,

What I've seen so far looks real good, and I encourage you to move ahead with your bold, new creative ideas.

May I make a suggestion?

Please have your young "turks"—I should say industry pacesetters—temper their ideas with industry experience. Not everything that happened before is necessarily bad. Everybody wants to invent something new, but don't summarily toss aside what's been done before even though it was successful, or partly successful. Build on it if it shows promise.

I like to peer ahead through the windshield. But I must also look through the rear-view mirror.

Laurel, this is not a criticism by any means. I love what you are doing. This is just a suggestion to make me more comfortable.

Best wishes,

Mark

SETTING A HIGH STANDARD OF PERFORMANCE FOR YOUR STAFF TO FOLLOW.

The project you and your staff are working on has a few minor production problems. There is a willingness to settle for a fix-up that will make it good. It should be better than good.

To: The Demon II production team

We're about to come out with a "good" product. That's not good *enough*. We built our reputation by building superior products. Let's not give up on this one by settling for "good." We have to keep trying to make it superior.

We must make a judgment—is it good or better or much superior to what the consumer expects? We should aim at much superior.

The following is a list of distinctions in evaluating the results of our product development efforts. It goes from "terrible" to "excellent" in descending order.

1	Disaster
2	Bad
3	Not too bad
4	Mediocre
5	Okay—average
6	Pretty Good
7	Good
8	Very Good
9	Exceptional
10	Excellent—Congratulations, Clap hands

Let's not accept anything less than 9 but preferably 10. We must have a result that will make us proud. I know you are with me on this.

Lee

Your company is embarking on an aggressive sales campaign—Personal calls, phone, letters, presentations. Set a high goal and fire up your sales force to make an extreme effort.

To: The Sales Team

As you know, we're starting a very aggressive sales campaign targeted to achieve a *25% increase* in dollar-volume business—and the acquisition of *ten* new customers—in the next *12 weeks.*

This is ambitious, but it must be accomplished, and it can be, if we all work extra hard at it. It means you will be doing double duty: (1) taking care of your present clients on their routine requirements and increasing the amount of business from them, and (2) acquiring new clients.

Did I say "double duty?" Actually, it is what I believe you normally do as a matter of course. But the next 12 weeks is an extra big push.

This is what to stress. . .

THE COMPETITIVE EDGE

We will give them a competitive edge by the products and the service we provide them with. *We* are their competitive edge.

The market has changed drastically—it's a marketing revolution. Companies in our industry need a competitive edge to survive, let alone forge ahead. We will provide it.

You must think hard about new ideas for the people you talk to. New thrusts, new techniques—and present it to them as *our* innovations. I say again, this company is their competitive edge in this hectic and ravenous market.

Everyone here is ready to support you. You will get the input and assistance of all department heads—and I am ready, willing and eager to pitch in.

We *have* to accomplish this. I *know* we can. There will be a big party in 12 weeks when we break the news of our success, and the three highest performers will get valuable gifts which will be announced later.

Remember—THE COMPETITIVE EDGE! That's what we provide our customers. That's what we're in business for.

Charles Tobias

RECOVER FROM A MISHAP THAT IS NOT NECESSARILY OF YOUR DOING

You tried to resolve a tough situation, and it turned sour. Now you have to get things back on an even keel.

A resident community organization set up various committees to push through a number of "improvements." Each committee had different missions to accomplish. All were vigorously pursued, without any recognition of priorities. Result: out-of-hand turf conflicts and explosive budgets.

Try to rescue the situation and make intelligent progress. Send a letter to all concerned.

To: Members of the three "Progress Committees"

May I humbly make a recommendation as to how to proceed from our present stand-still position. I say "humbly" because I am as guilty as anyone, perhaps more so.

It's a nonsequitur to say that we are getting nowhere, except going way over budget because of turf conflicts. Each committee wants to pursue its own agenda to the bitter end and crowd out all other initiatives.

This is supposed to be each one's right. But it's wrong. . . obviously. I see this is happening and I'm sure you do too.

Yes, we do have problems. Some are important and should be fixed in a hurry, others not so bad and could wait, and others would be nice to fix but could be abandoned until there are more utopian times.

Here's my suggestion. I'm sure you are thinking along this line too, but I just happen to be the first to write it down.

1. Each committee separate its tasks into three categories, labeled as follows . . ."Go" "Slow" "No."

2. Be ruthless in defining each task. First put it in "No," and think a lot about raising it to "Slow." And think again about saying "Go." The idea is to have as few "Go" tasks as possible. In other words, only the absolute necessities are "Go."

Obviously, we have to work on getting the very important things done right away, but it can only happen if we cut the "Go's" to a minimum.

Humbly submitted,

Samantha Barnes

LETTERS INVOLVING RECOVERY FROM BLUNDERS, NEGLECT, THOUGHTLESSNESS, INDIFFERENCE, LAZINESS, ARBITRARINESS

Dear Llewellyn,

I looked at the figures and projections for our real-estate variance procedures, and how much money the town will make—or lose. The plan shows a fairly good plus income and at the same time it looks like it will "prettify" our habitat and increase our real-estate values.

What could be better? Too good to be true? Unfortunately, I believe so after taking time to put all the data, projections, surmises, etc., through a microscope. It turns out to be wishful thinking, that's why it couldn't be true.

The math was done with smoke and mirrors. Which is why we have to go to the drawing board and start over again, now before everyone starts to believe the present report, rationalizes it, and it becomes an official (yet unrealizable) agenda.

Regards,

Eve Martin

ANOTHER LETTER

Dear Kao,

Re: The end of the line . . . we're running out of money.

All dreams must end. Eventually, we all wake up from our peaceful slumbers.

We've been making blue-sky prognoses of the results of our research efforts on our new software. But they may not stand up to empirical testing.

Let's modify our projected results and our hype, so that we can claim a winner when we report the results. In other words, let's be practical and be heroes, instead of dreamers and be losers.

We'll get together tomorrow to map this out and decide what to tell our staffs.

Good wishes,

Ben

ANOTHER LETTER

Good morning, Mr. Friedman:

The day of reckoning has come! The direct-marketing test for Legion Beverages does not show good enough results to justify a roll-out. This is not as bad as it sounds because we can still cut our losses and recoup. Yes—we will come up with a solution on constructing a successful direct-marketing campaign for Legion.

As I see it, we blundered into our present predicament. We should have stopped when it was opportune instead of plunging ahead and trying to solve the unsolvable. Chalk it up to human nature. You can also chalk it up to dogged determination to charge against cannon fire when it's wiser to retreat and live to fight another day.

Let's redeploy our forces, assign battle stations, put out patrols, gather intelligence, and move ahead to a triumph.

Pardon the war analogy. What is war? It has been called focused violence (in our case focused effort) toward an achievable end. This is exactly what we'll be doing.

Yours in victory,

Mary Ellen Stewart

cc: Gina Lopez
       Michael Scott
       Jennifer Leary

ENHANCE YOUR POWER AND PRESTIGE

Competition at the workplace. It's healthy, it causes a company to progress, it stimulates ingenuity, problem solving, it energizes an individual's effort to exceed, and succeed.

However, dog-eat-dog competition among peers, endemic in almost every work habitat, can also be corrosive. It may lead to political maneuvering, backbiting, deviousness. It can defeat progress, damage your reputation, stunt your upward movement. It can cause you to lose customer loyalty or management esteem.

Here are such common situations, and how to act, react, overcome and win.

ELIMINATE AN UNWANTED HEIR TO YOUR JOB WHO IS SLATED TO DISPOSSESS YOU.

SITUATION: A leading White House staffer once said, "Politics is a contact sport." This is true as well in the executive suite of TGF Broadcasting Network, where you are the major-domo of sales. You've been there for 18 years, credited with billions in sales, an often quoted leader in the industry. Just the same, your slip is showing. Sales slip, that is. Down 14%.

TGF's chief of chiefs thinks you've had it, and rumors are he wants you eased out. He has picked a young doberman with sharp teeth, a loud-mouth sales ace from a rival network, to come in and work under you. Of course, you met with the newcomer in advance of hiring and "approved."

Was there a choice? "After all, Jerry, you should be very happy to get this kind of help. Why should you be working day and night? We had a hard time getting this guy, and had to pay a lot to move him. We did it just for you."

It doesn't make sense for a hot shot at this newcomer's level to be your assistant. You see the chief's grand plan starting to go into action. Doberman will be an undercover agent, there to learn what is needed to have you become redundant, and then you will be delicately eased out to well-deserved pastureland.

STRATEGY: You are not ready for it. You will not be jostled up and out this way. You whole-heartedly welcome your heir-to-be and start training.

First, he must get a grounding on the station affiliate setup because he must acquire expertise on the network before he can sell it. As an assignment, you tell him to write a report on how to improve whatever needs improving.

He must also gather intelligence on the future plans of the rival networks and report his analysis of their prospective ratings, prices, audiences, and so forth.

Give Doberman this schedule, so essential to his career at the network, in a letter to his home a few days before he steps into the office.

These assignments will take months and require lots of on-the-road travel, making him almost invisible on the executive floor. Further, the reports are bound to be disasters. You, of course, will give him all the help possible. If he is discredited, you are blameless. After all, this network demands the most talented and brilliant.

April 18, 1994

Mr. Harvey Duran
38 Heather Drive
_____
_____

Dear Harvey:

Great news! For both of us. I'll have the widest open arms to welcome you here at TGF Broadcasting.

As Chuck told you, you'll be reporting to me, and I sure need your help. Indeed, I'll be looking to you to take over a big part of my duties, so that I'll be able to move on to other things that I can't talk about now.

I know, Harvey, that you want to get a close hold on sales as soon as possible. However, I'd first like you to take hold of a couple of other very important operations which need doing. In addition to helping us out tremendously at this time, it will give you a good handle of knowledge that will be extremely essential when you get into the thick of sales.

1. Get to know our major affiliate stations. Find out their gripes, their hopes, what they like about us and how they think we can improve. I've covered this with Jim Erhart, in charge of affiliate relations, and he's all for it. By the same token, sit with the managers of our owned-and-operated stations.

   Then write a complete report of what you found out, your analysis, and conclusions. This will be extremely valuable, as I'm sure you clearly see. This is a wonderful opportunity for you to learn our station lineup and become an expert on the network. Frankly, the people here can't wait to see your report.

2. When the above report is finished, carry out surveillance of what our competition will be doing this fall, particularly daytime programming. Try to get a fix on the ratings they anticipate and how likely they are to make it happen. Cable, of course, has to be part of the picture.

   Naturally, this will have to be a product of your expert reasoning and intuition based on the intelligence you gather. I don't have to tell you how important this will be when we get into the major selling season.

These are tall missions, Harvey, and so important in getting our sales pitch in excellent shape. We're all depending on you. Don't forget, I'll be the first one to lend a hand if you need any help. Just give me a holler.

I have a whole orientation and greeting procedure lined up for you right from the starting whistle. Lunches, cocktail meetings and so on. See me as soon as you step in the door.

I won't say the best of luck, because I know you'll make your luck. We all know you'll do great.

Jerry Sullivan

▌ A HIGH-VISIBILITY PROJECT THAT YOU DEVISED TURNED ▌ OUT TO BE A BUST. AVOID THE BLAME. MAINTAIN YOUR ▌ HIGH STANDING.

SITUATION: You are the dynamo head of marketing at a long distance phone company. You engineered a joint promotional venture with a famous packaged baked-goods marketer, Happy Bakers, for their popular cake and cookie brands.

Getting in bed with this huge consumer franchise looked like a marvelous coup. You proudly pulled it off. Your company's brass was excited.

You assigned the program's operation to one of your managers, Jason Miller, who was conscientious in carrying out his assignments.

The promotion flopped. The latest hot-line data from the field confirmed the bad news. The consumer offer was not good, and Happy Bakers' consumer characteristics do not coincide with your customer profile. Jason had pointed this out right away, but when he was quickly overruled, he bowed to your wishes and took charge of the promotion.

He is willing to take the blame for this fiasco in order to protect you. He figures you will then owe him a favor to be bestowed at some future time.

STRATEGY: Send a memo on the baleful news of the promotion to the Chief Executive Officer and the Chief Operating Officer.

Downplay the downside. Emphasize an upside. Avoid any indebtedness to Jason Miller while subtly indicating that he is blameworthy.

```
September 10, 1993

Mr. Roger Sears, President & CEO
Speedvoice, Inc.

_____

_____

Carlos Podesta, COO

Re:   The Happy Bakers Tie-In

Dear Mr. Sears:

I just got our new hot-line report from the field on our Happy Bakers
joint promotion.
```

Surprisingly, it doesn't demonstrate any renewed life to the point where it can be profitable for us to continue. The two market tests showed good promise, so it's hard to account for this. It's too soon to determine why it didn't work on the roll-out. We all thought it would be great, including everyone at headquarters.

I recommend aborting it now. We will then analyze the figures, find out how the promotion was carried out and whether the problem is conceptual, systemic, or whatever.

Fortunately, I decided to move this ahead gradually and also to put it into an intensive-care posture and monitor it every step of the way. So far, we only went to 30% of the country, so we caught the negatives early. And because we watched our expenses carefully, there is no big loss. This caution certainly paid off.

The good news is that our excellent rapport with Happy Bakers is undiminished. They will still do joint promotions with us, which could involve any one or more of their popular brand franchises.

In addition, we will be working on joint ventures with other class A companies.

As mentioned before, we'll look into why this one didn't measure up to what we all expected. Thus, it will turn out to be a wonderful test for future promotions, which is what we need.

Jason Miller, in my department, spearheaded the program. I selected him because he had always been very reliable on other projects. He put the market test data together which gave us the green light. However, I held him back from making a fast national roll-out. I can't really fault Jason since I obviously have to shoulder the responsibility.

It's pretty difficult to bat 1,000. Our batting average is still very good, and there are some great promotions in the pipeline. You'll be thrilled when you hear about them.

Regards,

A COLLEAGUE'S PROPOSAL UNDERMINED YOU. KILL IT WITH HIGH PRAISE.

SITUATION: You are a group product manager with a large manufacturer of health-care equipment. A colleague wrote a product introduction plan for two products soon to be ready for launching. One is a product she is responsible for; the other is your product. She recommends that the same procedure is right for both and that doing them in tandem will save the company a load of money. She is willing to handle the duo introduction.

It makes sense, but, with this highly visible, bold move, isn't she trespassing on your turf? You have been outmaneuvered.

The plan is competently documented and well written. It focuses on your colleague's brand, with adroit references to your product as a logical companion entry in the introductory launch.

STRATEGY: You can't condemn the plan. You have to join other management people in a common show of admiration, particularly since your brand is directly involved. But this must not be allowed to continue.

You decide to play a bureaucratic game by urging a series of meetings, reviews, assessments, profit analyses, more meetings, and so forth—supposedly to get the plan into play, but effectively making it inoperative.

Meanwhile, you will write your own plan for your product, holding it in abeyance but be ready to spring when the time is right.

November 16, 1993

To: Heidi Sherwood
       Colin Burke
       Luisa Alvarez
       Kathy Marshall

From: Sheridan Johnson

Your market penetration plan is a great piece of work—and very well documented, especially in terms of ethnic and seasonal variables. And certainly well presented. Congratulations, Heidi, you must have worked on this a long time.

My unqualified vote is to put this on mainstream for further review and on the way to implementation. The initial aim, of course, is to get it to a market test as soon as possible.

Since my brand is involved, I suggest we all write down the factors to address in the next stage of decision making, including any inherent problems that must be addressed. As a start, here are my recommendations on what needs to be reviewed:

What kind of market testing should we do before we roll out? How many cities, what information should we look for, etc.? Should we follow the procedure in the plan as written or try to get additional data before making a final decision?

Does the profit projection for each product warrant the amount of investment that is recommended? How much do we actually save with a dual introduction when the extra sales department costs are considered?

Will the detail people be confused? Will our trade accounts be confused as well?

Will the impact of either or both products be diluted by launching them together?

What effect will this have on doctors' prescriptions? Will they be confused?

I believe these questions have logical answers, but it's important they be addressed, since this is an introduction of two important products.

I would like to see this plan go. Let's all get behind it and make it work.

cc: Gerald Rosen, CEO
       The New Product Planning Committee

GIVE SUPPORT TO YOUR COLLEAGUE'S PLAN, WHILE MAKING SURE *YOUR* PLAN REPLACES IT.

SITUATION: A fellow executive came up with an innovative plan for a new business-acquisition process. It sounds great—on paper—and it could work. That is, if certain details are straightened out, if the operational procedure is put into place, and if it gets staff support.

You want to make an end run around it with your own plan, formulated in your mind but not yet on paper. Why shouldn't you be the big player in an important business-development program?

You need time to develop your idea, which is why you have to stall your friend's plan. It has to be consigned to the "good but never will be" pile.

You can't be negative. You want to seem supportive, a loyal team member. By all means you want to maintain his comradeship.

STRATEGY: Send a memo to your colleagues, with copies to the other executives involved and the COO, stating your enthusiastic endorsement. Say it's a function of perfecting the operational details in order to make it a winner. It will require thinking, meetings, and the delegation of responsibilities. You are gung-ho, and you say the others should give their active support too.

Actually, your colleague's plan could be trouble-free if sufficient time is spent in setting up the procedure. However, you have created a bureaucratic quagmire. In effect, your so-called enthusiastic endorsement has put this plan into a corporate dung heap.

December 7, 1993

```
To:    Tim Spiegel
       Ambrose Adams
       Laura Cohen
From:  Allen Schroeder
```

Great work! Your proposal for realigning our new business-development committee into an action-oriented department is innovative, and then some. It's a well-conceived, expertly prepared document, and it looks like it could be very effective. You have created a fine blueprint.

It would be good if we all hopped on board to iron out the procedures and make it work, keeping in mind the oft-quoted caveat, "there's a devil in the details." I'm confident the details can be worked out if we all pitch in. This is too good to be allowed to sit by the wayside.

Tim, please get a task force together to get this moving. I believe this group should start by defining the purpose and the goals. I suggest they then set up a procedure for each facet of the operation, with the specific people designated for handling each step, even if more personnel have to be hired.

To show my enthusiasm in concrete terms, I'm volunteering my services to develop an outline of the steps that have to be taken. I want to do this even though it looks like I'll be extremely busy for the next few weeks.

Congratulations,

cc: Mr. James E. Johnson, President

❙ MAKE AN ALLY OUT OF A RIVAL.

TWO STRATEGIES, TWO LETTERS

SITUATION: You are a group product manager at a packaged foods
                  titan—bright, resourceful, glib, and ambitious. A few doors
down the hall sits another group product manager—about your age, also
bright, resourceful, glib, and ambitious. The nature of the work environment,
your personalities, and the air that permeates the halls create an unspoken
rivalry between you. You each try to outshine the other, albeit with an outward display of camaraderie, and you are both stressing out.

You decide that a blending of talents and intelligence will make you each go
farther, faster. There's plenty of room for two near the top. Once you both
get there, of course, the rivalry can commence once again.

STRATEGY I: An opportunity comes up. You are both engaged in devel-
                  oping your product plans for the coming year. Each must
follow the same outline guide, which includes a forecast of the total corporate growth pattern over the next five years.

It makes sense to have both plans show the same forecast figures. Having different data would reflect badly on both plans. There will be questions. Which
one is correct? Why the difference? Why not get together to work on the corporate forecast? This is the conception of a powerful alliance.

STRATEGY II: You happen to be at a lull. Your rival is in a hectic overtime
                  mode. Make an altruistic offer to help. Say you would be
willing to work under him, as an assistant if need be, in order to get him over
the hump.

This is a way to get a partnership started. It is a comradely do-what's-best-for-
the-company gesture. You know the assistant role won't be taken seriously once
you become involved. Again, this is the conception of a powerful alliance.

(STRATEGY I MEMO)

September 16, 1993

To: Jerry Hoppindale
From: JoAnn Raab

It doesn't make sense. What doesn't make sense, you might ask?

It doesn't make sense for me to work on a project in which I have to analyze and make forecasts on a set of data when you are working on another project that requires the same kind of forecasts on the same data. 2 + 2 = 8—why not forecast together?

It's likely that our concerted effort will produce a more intelligent prognostication of the future growth of the company than each doing it solo. More importantly, two different forecasts will confuse management which won't believe either one. It will be a lot less work for each of us. Finally, it is efficient and more effective.

As so well stated by Samuel Goldwyn, the movie tycoon—"Forecasts are dangerous, especially about the future."

Regards,

(STRATEGY II MEMO)

September 16, 1993

To: Jerry Hoppindale

From: JoAnn Raab

I see you are snowed under right now with much to do and virtually impossible deadlines. I'll be in a relative lull for another couple of weeks because I have to wait for more product test results before I can start to develop my plans.

Why not let me help you get over the hump? It won't solve your entire problem, but another body working for you should ease it up a bit.

I'm not familiar with your products, but I'll take orders from you, just as if I'm one of your assistants. Jerry, I hate to say this, but this is not entirely unselfish. Your help would be more than welcome if I were in a similar spot and you could find the time to pitch in.

Regards,

▌YOUR NEW OFFICE IS NOT SATISFACTORY.

SITUATION: You've been appointed as a senior executive at a bank holding company. You appeared at your new office and got a startling shock. You wonder, is this the right place? The right address? Did they forget about your job title? Did you really get this job? Have I been had?

Your office is certainly not what your title calls for. It's small. An inside location. Further, it's rather unkempt. Obviously, there's been a mistake.

STRATEGY: Inform the office manager in writing, right away. There has to be an immediate change of location. However, you don't want to start off by throwing your weight around and demanding the proper trappings of your authority. You want your image to be nice guy, an officer with a feeling for the enlisted folks. You are aware of the current management principle that the best way to win loyalty and obedience is through love and admiration, not fear.

Your message to the office manager must be firm, but not overbearing. It must be insistent, yet with a light approach. Putting it in the form of a poem is a good touch. Make it whimsical, marking you from the beginning as a smart, creative, easy-to-get-along-with executive who knows what he wants—and knows he must get it.

(TO BE WRITTEN TO THE OFFICE MANAGER IN LONGHAND.)

November 17, 1993

To: Todd Franklin, may I record a complaint.
Proper and businesslike, with calm restraint.

An appeal to you, Todd, I ask for your pity.
No intent to amuse, or to seem smart or witty.

I'm bereft, bewildered, befuddled, bemused.
Feeling so weary, so wanting, so woefully abused.

Why hasn't it happened, what I should expect?
No window, no couch, nor even respect.

Should I leave quietly, go home for a week?
And when I return find in place what I seek?

Pardon the longhand, Todd, I have no secretary.
Please call me on 941, I'm not in the directory.

Seth Hamilton
Senior Vice President
Consumer Banking

▌ YOU ARE ON YOUR COMPANY'S BOARD OF DIRECTORS BY ▌ SPECIAL MANDATE. TELL THEM WHY YOU ARE A FIRST- ▌ RATE CHOICE.

SITUATION: You are a senior pilot at Global Airlines and were appointed a member of the Board of Directors. It came about because, after a hard fight with the pilots' union, it was agreed, among other things, that the union could have one seat on the Board. You were the one chosen.

The other Board members perceive you as an incongruity that was forced on them.

STRATEGY: Send a formal message to the Board members explaining why you are just as qualified as of any of them to be seated in the Board room. In fact, you bring a meaningful perspective to the board that was previously lacking. You have a vital interest in the future of the airline, a deep knowledge of the company at all levels, and a good business sense as well, particularly as it pertains to flight operations. Be deferential but firm in stating this rationale.

May 18, 1994

A Message to the Board of Directors of Global Airlines, Inc.
From Your Newest Member, Leon Harrison

_____   _____
_____   _____
_____   _____

I am honored to serve with you on the Board of this company. I'm a senior pilot at Global, as you all know, and have worked here for 25 years.

I suppose you may consider me an incongruity, since my appointment is due to an agreement the pilots union made with the company to include one member on the Board. I'm the one that was selected.

As well as being an employee in a senior position, I'm also a stockholder, with a good part of my savings invested here. My interest, as is yours, is in having this company prosper. If it doesn't I'm out of a job,

as will be the case with the many thousands of other people who work
here. So you see, my future, my retirement, the happiness of my family,
and my kids' college education, all depend on this company's success.
All my thinking and all my efforts are for the whole company, not just
for the pilots, the maintenance people, the clerks, the executives, or
any other group.

My training has been very specialized. All I do is fly passengers around
the world. (Let's face it, isn't this the raison d'etre of this company?) But I also read a lot about the business functions—finance, marketing, legal, customer service, and so on. I know the character and culture of Global intimately.

What I also bring to the Board are common sense, integrity, loyalty, and
a deep-seated conviction to make this company vital and prosperous in
this dog-eat-dog industry.

I am gratified to be joining you in helping to shape the destiny of Global
Airlines.

Leon Harrison,
Member of the Board of Directors

cc: Spencer Rosencrans, Chairman

▌MAKE YOUR DEMOTION LOOK LIKE A PROMOTION.

SITUATION: You've been an employee of a food-processing company
                   for 26 years, the past 12 as the National Sales Manager.
You've been transferred, actually demoted, to special-markets sales. It's kind
of a backwater slot. A youthful executive was brought in to take your place.
A matter of young blood replacing an old-timer.

The company wants to keep you on because of the friendships you built up
with customers. Everybody likes you. It would be bad customer relations to
put you on the street. The company would seem grubby and heartless.

STRATEGY: Send a letter to the customer-friends you have been con-
                  tacting for so many years. Describe your new position as
an upward move. Management wants you to help in planning for the
future. Your know-how and creativity will be indispensable for this assignment.

Management must be satisfied with the way your letter is phrased. Check it out with them. Also, show the letter to your replacement with the notation that it has management approval.

LETTER TO ALL YOUR EXCUSTOMERS

September 22, 1993

Mr. George T. Mitolokis
Vice President
Selective Food Wholesalers, Inc.

_____

Dear George:

I want you to know this good news before you hear about it officially. My job here has been changed to a front-office position. I'm moving from Sales Manager-National to Sales Manager-Special Markets Planning.

Management and I agree that it will give me a chance to take a step back, take my mind off day-to-day pressures, and help in long-range planning. It's a way of taking advantage of my knowledge and creative talents to help the company grow.

It's a big responsibility, and I'm delighted management saw fit to put me in this spot. I'm not happy that I won't see you regularly, but I'll certainly stay in touch. You can be sure I'll drop by when I'm in your area.

Steve Callahan is taking over as National Sales Manager, and I'll be working with him so that there will be a clean transfer of customer responsibilities. Steve is a great guy and knowledgeable in the business. I know you'll like him.

Thanks, George, for all you've done for me. It was wonderful doing business with you. Having you as a friend puts delicious icing on the cake.

Best wishes,

▌TURN DOWN A JOB OFFER BEFORE YOU ARE REJECTED.

TWO STRATEGIES:

I. You Are Presently Employed
II. You Are Out of Work

SITUATION: A high-level marketing position is open at a big-name hotel
               chain. The search is well publicized with various con-
tenders identified in the press. You made the final round but you found out
through leaks that you will not get the offer. It's going to someone else.

STRATEGY I: You are working for a hotel chain, and you wanted to
               switch to this new post, which would be a nice step up.
Your company knows you are in the competition and wishes you well since
it's a good upward move it can't match.

You want to avoid the stigma of losing out to someone else. It signifies, in a
way, a failure to measure up, which deals a sharp blow to your image inside
and outside your present workplace.

Write a letter requesting that you not be considered, giving a plausible rationale. The letter should be suitable for distribution to your colleagues and the
press, if need be.

STRATEGY II: You are out of work. You don't want the world to know you
               were an also-ran for this position. Send a letter withdraw-
ing your name so that you don't bear the stigma of rejection.

Make it appear that you are very busy with consulting assignments that must
be completed, which precludes your taking on this responsibility at the present time. Leave yourself open for the possibility of a future opportunity with
the company.

(STRATEGY I)

March 14, 1994

Mr. John Mashida
President
Sigma Hotels, Inc.

_____

_____

Dear John:

This may come as a surprise to you in view of the close discussions we've
had over the past several weeks relative to the position of Senior VP,

Marketing Director. I understand from rumors that it's coming down to the wire and my name is on the front-runner list.

It is, therefore, important that I get this message to you quickly. I thought about it for the last few days, talked it over with my family and associates, and finally came to the difficult decision of asking you to withdraw my name.

There is much to do in my present position, including certain important projects that I started which I am obligated to see through to completion. I thought more and more about this as we got into final discussions. In good conscience, I cannot now abandon my present responsibilities.

I am honored by your consideration of me. And I'm most pleased that we got to know each other, which I hope will be the start of a lasting friendship.

Sincerely yours,

(STRATEGY II)

March 14, 1994

Mr. John Mashida
President
Sigma Hotels, Inc.

_____

_____

Dear John:

As I had mentioned in our discussions, I have been in the midst of an important consulting assignment which I hoped would be winding down by this time. However, it is still going strong. In addition, I was recently called on by a major hospitality franchiser which could lead to another assignment.

I, therefore, ask that my name be withdrawn from consideration for the position we had been reviewing, since I am presently unable to assume this responsibility in good conscience.

I am honored by your consideration and am most pleased to have met with you and your colleagues. Let's stay in touch. I hope the future will open up another opportunity to work together.

Most sincerely,

▌PUT AN END TO SNIPING, BOTH INTERNAL AND ▌EXTERNAL.

You are in charge of getting a project completed requiring the work of an outside vendor. Another executive introduced a particular vendor into the company and he has done good work. For convenience sake you also use him. However, you have become aware that he is talking critically to this other executive about what you are doing. When you speak to the executive about it, he says that since he introduced this vendor to the company, he is his prime contact.

To: Jerry Haggerty

Re: Production Concepts, Inc.

We have to make certain things very clear, or there will be unnecessary confusion and discord which will be counterproductive.

Al is performing for *me* on *my job* that *I'm* responsible for. If he has any complaints, criticisms, thoughts or whatever, he must talk it over with *me*.

I don't want him gossiping to anyone else. You introduced him to this company, but that's where it ends. Again, Al works for me on the job I'm now doing with him. I have control over what, how and why he performs. If Al thinks otherwise I cannot use him. I'm sure you understand.

I suggest you tell Al, as I will.

A follow-up memo, two days later. Or it can be the first and only memo. Remain friends. Why have discord? It could characterize you as a hothead and unsure of yourself.

To: Jerry Haggerty

Re: Production Concepts, Inc.

It seems ridiculous to bring up the matter of Al making stupid comments to others about the work he's doing for me.

My gripe is with Al, not you, of course. You've been helpful in bringing Al into the company since he's good at what he does, However, he is not indispensable.

Jerry, it's all very silly. We shouldn't have any differences just because Al is unbusinesslike. He'll be replaced if he doesn't perform well.

Sherwood Michaels

A colleague is sniping at a statement in your report in which you recommended a software system for the company's research projects. The kind of response shown here could also apply to an ad you recommend, or a machine tool, a website or whatever.

Dear Jason:

I appreciate your comment as to my recommendation of the EJS software because it leads me to believe that I may not have made my recommendation rationale absolutely clear.

The suggestion to use EJS was very carefully evaluated. We used Allard Computer Consultants—well recognized in the industry—to help us come to a decision. You can be sure they gave the EJS system the most thorough and extensive testing imaginable before filing their report. I also spoke with other companies who are using it.

Jason, this does not unequivocally guarantee perfect satisfaction in our environment. But it suggests a good choice to be made at this time. Naturally we will monitor it carefully for possible bugs, and make necessary adjustments.

Thanks again for taking the trouble to bring this up.

All the best,

Sidney

INVITE A WELL-KNOWN PERSON TO PARTICIPATE IN COMPANY ACTIVITY.

You want to invite a well-known executive from a large noncompetitive company to speak at your company's business seminar so that you can display your high connections in the business world.

Dear Mr. Gentry:

May we call on you for your celebrated expertise on American corporate standards?

We operate at a high level of customer service and management effectiveness as indicated by various studies we have conducted of companies in our industry. But we don't want to stand on whatever laurels we enjoy.

We look to further improve customer loyalty and the efficiency of our management structure—and what we believe is our state-of-the-art communications technology.

We plan to conduct a private seminar, to be attended by our chairman, president, and top management executives, to discuss these issues. It would certainly be illuminating and interesting to hear your views of the current state of American commerce and business. Some of this has been published, but it would be exciting to have you discuss your comments in person. Further, we all look forward to meeting you.

I will call you shortly to provide more information, and, I hope you will agree to attend.

Most respectfully,

You want to make a connection with a well-known person in your industry, or celebrity, government official, author, etc. An association with the elite gives you cachet.

Invite such a celebrity to be present at your company or organization.

Dear Senator Gardiner:

On behalf of the Granite City Education Association, I am inviting you to appear at our special parent-teacher seminar. There will be approximately 200 members present who would enjoy hearing some of your insights on the coming education legislation.

I know your agenda is full, but, again, we would appreciate it if you could spare some time to meet with us. We all admire the wisdom you've shown in regard to the subject of education funding.

Respectfully,

Jeannette Rosenwal
Committee Chairperson
Granite City Education Assoc.

▌HANDLE COMMUNICATION SNAFUS.

You goofed by failing to put an employee overtime notice in the payroll records. The employee complained. Management asked you to explain in a memo. Give the facts without saying you personally made a mistake.

```
To:    Harvey Gould
From:  Michael Doran
```

A mistake was made. Mr. Torentino's overtime notification wasn't in the overtime slot in the Payroll Dept. I corrected it and explained the matter to Mr. Torentino.

ANOTHER LETTER, ON A SIMILAR SITUATION

Due to your mistake, there was a mixup in communications procedure.

Dear Mr. Thorndike:

Our forwarding system works 99%—which is great considering the best of procedures governed by technology is often at an 85% success rate. That's not to say a "normal" snafu is an excuse. The one in question was rectified—everybody's happy.

ANOTHER LETTER

There was a glitch in the forwarding of information from my department to the controller's office. Rather than get into the matter of what-and-why I'll just say it's been fixed, and we're now on track.

Best regards,

Blair Stone

ANOTHER LETTER

Dear Mr. Cohen:

I remember the saying from schooldays, "There's often a slip twixt the cup and the lip." I think it came from Shakespeare.

Anyway, the slip, which caused wrong information to get into the report you received, has been corrected. Thanks for bringing it to my attention and I've told the person involved who will be nameless.

Regards,

Dori Hoffman

▌ENHANCE YOUR IMAGE.

There is a fine line between noting your good deeds and boasting. While you have to enhance your image, self-praise must be stated inferentially, without seeming to brag or gloat.

Good morning, Laurel. And it is a *good* morning!

The results are starting to come in. Advance sales figures show we are starting to turn around.

The promotion that was recommended looks like it's working—thanks to your help. Although I suggested this promotion, it couldn't have happened without your input, and the others who pitched in. That is what helped it to succeed.

Thanks so much for your part in making it work.

Your proposal to generate favorable publicity about your company was put into effect, and now some good results are starting to come in. Emphasize your "success." Remind management it was your proposal that started it all.

Remember the advice I gave on a program to enhance our image and get good media coverage? It was written up as part of my proposal this past June 14.

Well, two months later, now there is cold, hard, black-and-white proof that it's working. (See the attached press clippings and other documentation.) We had gotten some black eyes from the press about having lagging technology—which wasn't true. . . but such things, even if untrue, have a negative effect with the public.

I said in my proposal that we shouldn't let the bad notices go by, and a number of countermoves were suggested. We should all be pleased we agreed to get this started.

OTHER MEMOS

"It's not too late to turn things around!"

This is what I said last July, when I presented my proposal. You all believed it, bought it, got behind it, and now it's come to pass.

No one can operate as a lone voice. We all had the imagination and the perception to latch onto a good campaign—good only because everybody added their skills and pitched in.

My thanks to you all.

ANOTHER LETTER

There's a fine shade of difference between acceptance and enthusiasm. Oh, but the distinction is so important!

It makes the difference between success and failure.

I want to thank all of you for supporting my research initiative with enthusiasm. It is now paying off, and we are all basking in its accomplishment.

I'm very grateful for your support.

ANOTHER LETTER

"Productivity needs cooperation."

This cliché is universally acknowledged.

It certainly was the case in bringing my software initiative into fruition. There were occasions, as we all know, when it could have gotten nowhere, but your combined skills and creativity helped overcome the mishaps.

Now we have a really competitive product. Thanks so much for all your help.

ANOTHER LETTER

The results are in. Our market share has taken an uptick. Small, but it's a turnaround. Our downtrend has apparently stopped.

It didn't happen by itself—or without us all working like demons.

Thanks are due to the marketing plan described in my presentation of June 13. But more thanks are due to the way Debbie, Charles, Genevieve and Harry all worked so hard to make it happen. I should add, worked with such wonderful professional skill that it makes us all proud.

▌ASSERT YOUR NEW AUTHORITY OVER FORMER PEERS.

You have been promoted to manager of a department. You now have a management title, added responsibility and three people reporting to you who were formerly at your level. The need is to show you are the boss of this unit and should be taken seriously by your staff, who have been your buddies. You have to show your authority while maintaining a comradely spirit.

A series of meetings to revamp department policy is a good start.

```
To:    Hilda, Jack, Kristel
```

I hope that my being in charge of this department is not too much of a shock to you. It is to me, even though I was told of this move by the president two months ago and was sworn to secrecy. Things will have to change, but there's no reason for any of you to have the least concern about your job, or your status.

I'm going to meet with each of you individually to review your work and reporting procedure. Most importantly, I want to listen to your concerns, if any, and address them.

My first meeting is with Kristel—Friday, June 11, 9:30.

Best of luck,

Gene Rossman

ANOTHER KIND OF MEMO ON THE SAME SITUATION

```
To:    Hilda, Jack, Kristel
```

This is to tell you of immediate steps in regard to our new setup.

The first thing to do: settle down and continue the good work that you've done in the past. As before, carry on all the routine things and any new requests that come up.

Obviously, some things have to change, which is why this department was restructured and I was put in charge. Let's have a meeting tomorrow, 9 A.M. promptly, and we'll go over it. Your constructive comments will be welcome.

Gene Rossman

▌ SHOW POSITIVE FACE WHEN THINGS LOOK BAD.

The work you did is not turning out as well as you and others expected. This lack of success puts you on the spot, but you have to show a positive face and look good.

To: Gordon

We got a lot out of the development work I've been doing on the new Windows Software design even though it wasn't positive as we had hoped. We must keep in mind, negative results in research are important too.

I've shown that we cannot succeed if we use the logic that we had thought of so highly, and we should try another path. It was good that we did this work. It proved we should abandon this procedure and thus avoid digging dry wells. It will save a lot of money and grief.

Regards,

Naomi

cc: Shiela
        Aubrey

ANOTHER LETTER

Dear James,

Sometimes bad news is good. And this is one of those times.

It's a good thing I checked out the feasibility of what was hoped would be a software solution for diagnostic medical screening. The alley I went down doesn't work. We have to try a new logic if we want to pursue this solution.

If we had introduced this product it would have been a debacle. This research caused us to avoid a lot of trouble—ill-will, bad publicity, law suits, shall I go on?

I believe the experience I gained makes me the logical candidate to continue in an attempt to develop a successful product. The potential reward is by all means well worth this effort.

Naomi Landau

ANOTHER LETTER, MAKING THE BAD LOOK NOT SO BAD

Dear Winthrop:

Here's a case of taking one step back so we can go two steps forward.

My development work on formula 3Z is not working out well, and I don't see how it can be turned around. Recommendation: abandon it and let's go on to another approach.

We all know it takes a number of trials—sometimes a great many—before you hit pay dirt. This latest exploration was very worthwhile because we learned a lot from it that paves the way to a final success.

On with the search for the solution.

Rita Lorenzo

COMBAT THREATS FROM WITHIN YOUR ORGANIZATION

YOUR PLAN WAS TURNED DOWN FOR ANOTHER'S. MAKE A COMEBACK—WITH STYLE.

SITUATION: You are a computer engineer at a software company. For the past three months you have been working to develop a software program for medical diagnosis. It will greatly reduce the time for amassing and analyzing huge amounts of data from a large number of medical tests and present them in a gestalt image—an important advance with a sizeable market potential.

Another engineer in your company produced a plan for the same purpose. Ipso facto, the two of you were competing.

Your rival got a thumbs up. You know his plan is not as good as what you were developing. His report to management was more spectacular—literate, colorful, replete with blue-sky analyses, full of bells and whistles. You can see that the staginess covers up snags and faults, but management went for it. You can't fight it. Not now.

The winner is a marvelous politician, a supreme infighter. He's glib with the answers, fast on his feet, rattles off intricate data with aplomb. A master at inducing smiles and affirmative head shaking.

Sidle off with your tail between your legs? No. Your plan is better. It's not yet history.

STRATEGY: You now enlist in your competitor's camp. Pitch in with
                   enthusiasm. Offer to spearhead his project, under him. You
will do the spade work—developing, testing, perfecting—and relieve the creator of the day-to-day pressures. You'll keep him apprised of everything, of
course, but he can now lean back and keep his mind on the big picture—on
the meetings, the marketing, and the hype.

Your offer will sound very good, since your rival really doesn't want to get
involved in the humdrum details. You've given him an excellent alternative.
He's sure to take it.

You know his plan will not work without certain critical adjustments. There
will be problems of complaints and recalls, if and when it is introduced to
consumers as is. At this point your compatriot will be in over his head in rem-
edying these glitches.

This will be done in the development and testing stages, which you will be in
charge of. Inch by inch, the plan's virtues will be chiseled away. One small
error at a time will be uncovered by the careful, tedious testing you will be
putting it through.

Finally, it will have to be abandoned. Your friend's bluster will then look silly,
his jokes no longer funny.

Then, your plan will go into operation. You will be working on the side, hon-
ing it, improving it, perfecting it. It will be ready on time as a replacement.

A smoke-screen maneuver? Yes, for a good purpose. You will have performed
an exceptionally valuable service for your company.


```
April 28, 1994

To:     Lawrence Aldrich
From:   Sam Berger
Re:     Pitching in to Help on Your Trilateral Project

Let's get started now. This is too good to hold up even for a day.

Here's my suggestion on getting your project to completion in the least
amount of time—

I will take it upon myself to be the point man, reporting to you. We can
have Meg handle the beta, and Nimmo the gamma components, and start pro-
ducing them.
```

After there is enough to work with, even if it's not in finished form, we can start the testing of components. This should be done concurrently with the production which will save a good three months in coming up with a marketable product.

There will be a final testing stage when production is completed, to make sure there are no bugs before bringing this new software to market.

We have to give it a sexy name. It's up to you because you have such a good feel for what will grab the public.

This will give you the time you need for evaluating the reports and planning each step. You can handle the big picture without being diverted by day-to-day details. You will, of course, know everything that goes on every step of the way.

Best ever,

Sam

cc: Dick Devoe
      Meg Quinn
      Nimmo Kanaga

▋ YOU LOST OUT ON A PITCH FOR A MAJOR ACCOUNT.

FOUR LETTERS AND MEMOS

SITUATION: You are the new-business impresario at an advertising agency. You just got word that you came a close second in a six-agency scuffle for a much-coveted electronics account. Very little comfort there: close second might as well have been 22nd.

STRATEGY SCENARIO:

Memo to You from Your CEO:

He asks how come we didn't win, since we are a big-league agency which put so much time and money into this proposal.

Your Memo to the CEO of Your Company and the Troops:

You want to express whatever positives can be squeezed out and help alleviate the pain of your position. There's hope for the future—not all is lost.

Your presentation was very impressive and admired, even though you didn't win.

Your pitch to this prospect hasn't stopped. There's still hope for winning some business from them.

The President Sends a Letter to the Head of the Winning Agency:

Congratulations. The Best Man Won. (That is, the best presentation.)

The CEO Sends a Letter to the COO of the Company It Pitched:

He wants to say that the COO made a good choice in the agency selected. It is good; so are we, but apparently not good enough in this encounter. He admires the way the COO is running his company and is impressed with his executives. Now that they got to know each other, he doesn't want to let the relationship lapse.

It took a lot of money and hard work to establish this contact. It would be very foolish not to build on it. You never know; it might pay off later.

MEMO TO YOU FROM YOUR CEO

March 10, 1994

To: Brian MacDunn (Senior VP, Fuller Advertising, Inc.)

From: Jim Domaster (CEO, Fuller Advertising)

Well, we didn't get the DPI account, and I have to say we were all taken aback by the news. I'm disappointed, because your team put so much time and personnel into this presentation, not to say expense.

It's especially hard to take because we're better than Harris & Beeman, the winner over all the six agencies competing.

Was it the quality of the presentation? The way it was pitched? Our demeanor? Personalities? Inside politics? A bias towards the winning agency? What was it?

Let's analyze it for the future to make sure we get the maximum strength and advantage on the next new-business presentation.

You have to keep pitching on DPI. It still has potential for business. And don't forget, we're the best ad agency in the business. And you are one of the folks here who makes us this way.

You mentioned that you and your people did your best.

We're not paid to do our best. . . We're paid to win!

YOUR MEMO TO THE CEO OF YOUR COMPANY AND THE TROOPS

March 11, 1994

To: Jim Domaster, CEO

From: Brian Goldsmith

We're now rising from the ashes after the DPI shoot-out. We came out second among the six agencies competing—actually, a very close second. I got this from the people I spoke with at DPI.

But second doesn't mean anything. It's like an election; either you win, or you lose. Winner takes all.

That's for now. Let's look to the future on this account. We made a good solid presentation with innovative ideas. It was eminently professional. Some of DPI's people said it was admirable. We earned a lot of respect for Fuller Advertising.

We also made some friends at DPI. We'll keep up these contacts. We have a big size-12 foot in the door. DPI has other business it could give us. And who knows what will happen in six months or a year on this business that we lost out on?

We'll take advantage of this valuable "in." It will pay off.

cc: Sandi Solomon
        Bob Milkowski
        Serena Nukarab

THE CEO'S LETTER TO THE HEAD OF THE WINNING AGENCY

March 11, 1994

Mr. Emmon Beeman
President & CEO
Harris & Beeman

_____

_____

Dear Emmon:

It is with personal sadness and envy that I congratulate you on winning the DPI account.

Your shop made a stunning presentation. We were great, but you were superb.

I know you'll do a marvelous job on this business, and I wish you the best of luck.

How about getting together for a drink? I'd like to toast your well-deserved good fortune in person.

Best ever,

Jim Domaster
Chief Executive Officer
Fuller Advertising, Inc.

THE CEO'S LETTER TO THE COO OF THE COMPANY IT PITCHED

March 11, 1994

Mr. Milton D. Loquester
President & Chief Operating Officer
Data Processing International, Inc.

_____

_____

Dear Mr. Loquester:

You picked an excellent agency. We wish it were us, because we're excellent too, but obviously our presentation wasn't quite up to their level in this case.

In making this presentation, we got to know your people very well. We greatly admire them and their cooperation in giving us a fair shot.

I should also say that in our business we have contacts with a great many companies, and we're so impressed with the way you run yours. It is par excellence in every way. Naturally, everything we learned about DPI will remain confidential.

Now that we've gotten to know each other, let's not have our acquaintanceship lapse. I trust I can call you for advice from time to time. Likewise, I'm at your disposal.

Best regards,

Jim Domaster
Chief Executive Officer
Fuller Advertising, Inc.

▌YOU MUST JUSTIFY YOUR DEPARTMENT'S EXISTENCE TO NEW MANAGEMENT.

SITUATION: Your company was taken over by a financial consortium. You now have new bosses, eager to quickly increase profits. They walked in with the attitude that efficiency must now rule, or they won't get their investment back. They seized on the perception that there are too many bodies around. So there was cut, cut—and likely more to come.

They ask you, the manager of procurement, to tell them what your department does, your personal duties, what each of your staff does, and what efficiencies can be made. Your staff has already been reduced from eight to six because of the cutting frenzy.

STRATEGY: You decide to send them a narrative piece specifying the theory of procurement, your department's place in the company, and the extraordinary importance of what it does. You must emphasize procurement's crucial involvement in the whole business. Without you, everything ceases.

You note that you and your people are overworked to the limit of endurance, but you perform gladly with pride. Essentially, you want to avoid losing any more of your people and to get the new overseers off your back.

October 6, 1993

To: The Management Committee on Resource Usage
            J. Edgar Sawman, Chairman

From: Richard C. Donovan
            Director of Procurement

Subject: The Procurement Department—Our Mission and Structure

What We Do

Ordering supplies, equipment and materials, and distributing them to the people at our plants is a simple, straightforward way of describing our task.

However, it doesn't seem simple when you consider that our responsibility is enormous. We obtain the goods that make this whole company run. If we don't do it economically—and with expert precision—everything will stop dead in the water.

Who Does It

The staff personnel reporting to me have been downsized to five buyers and one information technician. We are now three-fourths of our former staff. We've been reduced, restructured, programmed and deprogrammed, and we came out of it with undiminished dedication to doing the best possible job. It hasn't been easy, but we have a strong spirit of achievement, because we want to help make this company prosper.

The Parts of Our Mission

Our personnel responsibilities consist of three basic functions. Each is MOST IMPORTANT.

1. KEEP THE ROUTINE ORDERING AND TRAFFICKING FLOWING WITHOUT A HITCH. Getting everything our plants and offices need, no matter how near or far. Getting it on time, in good condition, with the best quality for the purpose at the lowest price. Whew!

   Every executive, each and everyone in the whole company, sees this going on every single day, like clockwork.

   The next two functions are behind the scenes. You don't see them taking place.

2. SUPPLIER RELATIONS. We must make sure we have the best vendors. Their production capabilities, their shipping facilities, their financial strength, and much more all have to be checked and rechecked. This is to assure an efficient, on time, and reliable supply stream.

3. Now for the glamour part—NEW VISTAS. It's crucial that we keep up with new technology, new ways to improve quality, increase efficiency, save money, and get ahead of the trend and the competition. All of this is little noticed until a new system gets put in the works for all to see.

As mentioned before, people and space have been cut here. We're lean, to the point of skinny, but not malnourished. Very often we work without any thought of hours or weekends. We do it with enthusiasm and pride.

Think about it. What we do impacts on everything that takes place here. We deliver the goods that make this company run.

Respectfully submitted,

Richard C. Donovan

▌SURVIVE A CORPORATE DOWNSIZING.

SITUATION: You are a mid-level customer-service manager at a field office of a world-renowned computer company. It is undergoing a severe downsizing. Rumors are running wild throughout the company about who is marked for termination and who will survive. Everyone from the bottom up is scared. The underground company semaphore is signaling that your job is destined for the discard heap.

STRATEGY: You decide you can't just sit there defenseless with your neck on the guillotine block. You need your job, and you will do anything to avoid the upcoming carnage.

The first act of preservation is to send a seemingly routine letter to the head-quarters executive in charge of the downsizing, with a copy to the human-resources chief, to inform them of your work activities. You emphasize that on your own you go far beyond your job description, which enhances your value many times over.

You have excellent rapport with major customers in your area. In addition to keeping them happy, you advise them on peripherals, software, and equipment upgrading, all of which leads to extra sales.

In fact, considering your effectiveness in generating new business, you request that part of your workweek be officially allocated to the sales department. Make yourself seem as indispensable as possible.

You've done the best you can to avoid being an unemployment statistic.

September 21, 1993

Mr. Clemson G. Acheson
Executive Vice President
Majestic Computers, Inc.

_____

_____

Ms. Gwendolyn Hartnett Ritchie
Vice President, Human Resources

Re: My Current Job Duties as Assistant
       Customer Service Manager—Houston Office

For management review, this will update you about my present work activity in the Houston office. As you will see, what I'm doing goes far beyond my prescribed duties.

Naturally, I fulfill all my responsibilities in handling service requests and complaints. However, I also anticipate customer problems and head them off; I also advise customers about upgrades, peripherals, and software.

In so doing, I have developed a personal relationship with several of our more important customers. They often call me for guidance on utilizing their hardware more effectively and for equipment they may need.

When there is a lull, I visit customers to chat with them eye-to-eye. This is the best way to find out the technical details of our customers' programs and to advise them on using our equipment more efficiently.

This has led to a large number of sales we would not have otherwise obtained.

I'm convinced that my contribution to the company would be even further enhanced if part of my time were officially registered to the sales department. I could carry out this assignment concurrently with my customer-service duties.

I believe this brings you up-to-date on my activities. Thank you for the opportunity to review this with you.

Very truly yours,

Otto G. Rickhoffer
Assistant Customer-Service Manager
Houston Office

CORRECT PROBLEMS THAT CAME UP AFTER YOU MERGED YOUR FIRM INTO A LARGER OPERATION.

SITUATION: You are a respected attorney and the owner of a moderate-size law firm. After thirty-six years of building and nurturing it to its present highly reputable and profitable state, you decide to take it easy. The wisest course is to merge into a larger firm with plenty of personnel and facilities to handle your needs.

You will continue to take care of your clients but be relieved of most of the details and management travails.

Your personal income is in relation to the income you generate. This was the plan when you spoke at length with the owners of the firm who succeeded in luring you.

Your business was much in demand. You had been courted by many medium and large law firms. The final winner pushed all the right buttons to get you to agree.

Two months have gone by, and you are worse off than before. There is lip service to your needs, nothing else. You are working harder and longer, with mounting pressure. And you are falling further and further behind.

Bottom line: You are disheartened. It's not working out. The owner-partners are sincere, but fail to make it work for you.

They know they made a great deal in acquiring you. Since they have already spent several hundreds of thousands of dollars on this deal, they don't want to rock the boat. Having you undo what's been done would be very sorry news for them—unthinkable, in fact.

STRATEGY: You have leverage. You know the partners don't want to lose you. If you hint at dissolution, they will get panicky.

It won't take a lot to please you, but they have to roll up their sleeves, take charge, and give the necessary orders to their staff. They have to sign the requisitions for the needed personnel and equipment.

You are meeting with them tomorrow to go over the matter of "How is it going?" You send them a memo today—a day in advance of your meeting—to specify your grievances and throw the problem in their laps. They have advance notice and can start thinking about what has to be done.

Give them a week to rectify your situation.

April 7, 1997

To: Podesta, Saul, Weiner P.C.
       Harry Saul
       John Podesta
       Steve Weiner

From: Sheila Epps

In Advance of Our Meeting Tomorrow. . . Matters to Be Covered. Small Things Can Make for Big Problems if They're Not Taken Care of.

In the spirit of doing what's best for the entire firm, and so that we all get maximum income and continued growth from the accounts I brought in, a number of adjustments have to be made.

They will relieve me of a great deal of anxiety, unnecessarily long hours, and, I should add, dissatisfaction.

While these are small things of minimal expense, only you can get them done.

- My phone system is chaotic. I don't have someone to answer my phone promptly and correctly or to take clear, knowledgeable messages.

- My phone is not equipped with one-touch dialing or memory. I can't continue to punch 14 digits to make a call. I should have pushbutton memory for frequently called numbers and someone to dial for me and get people on the phone when I'm busy.

- I need a secretary to give me priority, even if I share her/him with someone else. I am way low on the totem pole when it comes to getting any cooperation from the secretarial and clerical staff.

- My billing system and income records are not compatible with your financial system. Your accounting department is grudgingly sympathetic, but it is not doing anything about it.

- We have to have a procedure for the continuing development of my client base in order to generate increased income. This isn't on stream yet, and, as it stands now, it doesn't seem likely.

This has to be put into play right away. I must see it starting to happen by next week. Friday, at the latest.

We discussed what had to be done during our merger discussions, but hardly anything has been accomplished. You, not I, must talk to your people about this and see that it gets done. It probably means adding two or three persons to attend to my needs. A small expense when you consider the stakes.

Frankly, I did not come here to work harder, longer, and angrier. The promised state of affairs was to be the reverse of this.

It all adds up to one thing. I am unhappy. I don't intend to continue to be unhappy.

Make me happy!

COUNTER A DAMAGING RUMOR THAT COULD HALT YOUR CAREER.

SITUATION: You were recently appointed a partner at a high-powered law firm and are steadily moving up to the management circle. You supervise an important account, a well-known auto-rental company. Fees are up, and the client is happy.

You get word through the grapevine that a couple of the staff people and perhaps your assistant have whispered in the ear of the top managing partner that you at times denigrate him to your client—that you talk about getting unintelligent advice that hampers you. One snitch said you used the word "stupid."

You have, at times, been carried away in conversations with your client. Remarks such as this were taken out of context and tattled, undoubtedly for self-serving reasons. You are by no means disloyal or disrespectful of the firm's management.

You know that these leaks will mark you for extinction when the timing is right. At the very least, any chance of moving up is now down the drain. You must counteract this bad-mouthing straight out, with absolute certainty. At the same time, use the occasion to climb another rung or two up the ladder.

STRATEGY: Tell your client's top people that it would be good to meet with the firm's managing partner. Set up a lunch date at a classy restaurant, or, if they prefer, their conference room. (They opt for the lunch.) Send a memo to your president saying that your client's brass asked if he would meet with them.

The reason: you had been speaking so highly of your top boss, saying that he comes up with much of the ingenious legal thinking that you present, that they want to ask his advice on certain important issues. This is to be a command performance by your commander-in-chief. Don't indicate any knowledge of the venomous whisperings he has heard.

This will clearly make the bad-mouthing seem ludicrous, an unfounded attack against you for vicious reasons.

September 13, 1997

To: Edgar Ebersol, President
From: Barry Levin

Mr. Ebersol, may I prevail upon you for a favor?

Ravenal's management would very much like to meet with you. May I set
this up? It would be nice to do it as a luncheon meeting, if it is okay
with you.

You see, I get together with them once or twice a week to make sure the
acquisition programs we drafted for them are moving ahead. Naturally, I
give a lot of the credit to you. You are known as the seminal figure
behind the scenes.

Now they are anxious to sit down and chat with you about their upcoming
goals and some business problems that need high-level thinking.

I hope this doesn't put too much of a dent in your time schedule. These
are nice guys, heading up a very nice client. And naturally, I want to
put the firm's best foot forward whenever the chance comes up.

Can you give me two or three dates convenient to you? I'll coordinate it
with their availability. I'll fill you in beforehand on the background
and what will probably come up at the meeting.

Thanks so much.

▌TRY TO PROTECT YOUR COMPANY FROM ADVERSE FINANCIAL SCRUTINY.

SITUATION: You are a senior officer and board member at a real-estate
                investment company which, for the past two years, has
been going through tough times and financial losses. It was decided to
restructure the various operations with consequent accounting adjustments
that will "improve" the balance sheet. This is technically legal, but would it
be considered a fair assessment of financial worth? Would it be credible to the
media and the public?

STRATEGY: The year-end audit and financial report is coming up soon,
                and you have been in long sessions with the partner at the
CPA firm who is doing the job. You explained the need for your corporate
restructuring—which he, among others, took part in—and its impact on your
financial statement.

This is a crucial report, sure to undergo unusual scrutiny by the industry and by the media. You would prefer to have the partner who did your previous audits handle this rather than another partner or another firm.

Your company must come out as being forthright and clean. The accounting partner on your audit said he would cooperate with your financial people while adhering to sound professional standards.

The audit was completed with desired results. The income figures do not cause raised eyebrows. There is no gossip of cooking the books even though a number of adjustments were made.

You will send a thank-you letter to the partner who is responsible for the audit. It puts on record that he did it with objective precision and adherence to the highest professional standards. In other words, the letter confirms that the audit was done in a fair and proper manner, just in case a competitor, the media, or a government bureau asks any questions.

```
Jordan K. Tramiel, Partner
Jensen, Logan Certified Public Accountants


_____

_____


Dear Jordan:

You did an excellent job on our 1993 audit, which will be included in
our 1994 annual report. It warrants a special round of applause because
of the great care you took on the financial adjustments required by our
corporate restructuring, a new acquisition, and a sale of assets.

You handled it with complete objectivity, and the income figures are
reliable in accordance with the highest professional standards, as you
pointed out. Furthermore, it was completed on time. This report will be
the guidepost for our upcoming audits.

Please thank your staff for us.

Best wishes,

Barnet Harris
Senior Vice President,
Lawrence Securities

cc:    Hortense Altshell (Jensen, Logan)
       JoAnn Guilfoyle (Jensen, Logan)
       Lamont Jones (Lawrence Securities)
       Sylvia Roth (Lawrence Securities)
```

▌NOTE OF NECESSARY CAUTION FOR A HIGHLY POPULAR
▌UNDERTAKING—BE A HERO.

SITUATION: You are the VP of Sales at one of the leading home appliance manufacturers. The company is also a player in the automotive field with its air conditioners and heaters.

The company has been in serious negotiations to buy out a large manufacturer of auto and truck tires, Amalgamated Rubber Co. This has been taking place on and off for three months, and it now appears that a deal is coming up. It's been widely covered in the press.

The tire company has a long-standing popular brand, the Road King line, which is number 1 in many markets and number 2 in others, but never less than third.

Amalgamated's conquering hero right now is its X-99 line, recently introduced by costly advertising and wide press coverage. It's a premium-priced high-performance product with a unique safety feature, a patented wet-dry tread.

Your top management and its outside financial and legal experts have been poking through Amalgamated's books, which look okay. Its sales and profits go up and down in this cyclical market, but long range, the revenues are healthy.

Amalgamated is a well-known brand with a good consumer franchise. X-99 looks like a sure success and is expected to give profits a nice push skyward. This is starting to be reflected in the most recent financial data due to heavy introductory shipments.

What has especially excited everyone is the symbiosis of the two companies. Amalgamated has clout with aftermarket retailers, including the big chains, which will help the sales of your company's auto appliances.

STRATEGY: You decided, with the okay of the Marketing VP, to get a quick update on Amalgamated's market status. This is to be an informal check that gets behind the financials and the formal market reports that are put out by Amalgamated in its ebullient style. There were no suspicions of any coverup in its reports; an exploratory check just seemed to be a judicious move.

You personally visited four of the biggest retail auto supply chains that stock Amalgamated. Combined, they do an enormous tire business. Your stature with a major company gave you an entree. Obviously, you didn't reveal the purpose. You were just checking out the tire market, curious about how the various brands were doing, including Amalgamated.

What you found out was startling. You were stunned by the X-99 quality problem in its last two shipments. Also, Amalgamated's bellwether Road King line was starting to slip in market share. This information was given by almost all the key people at the four companies you visited who represent an imposing segment of total U.S. tire sales.

You told the marketing VP about this, and it was decided that you should immediately send a confidential letter to the Chairman/CEO, with a copy to go to the president and, of course, to the marketing VP who is your comrade-in-arms.

The bearer of ill tidings must thoroughly document a case. You prepared a report with the names and verbatim statements of everyone you spoke with. If any are called, you are sure they will confirm the gist of what they had told you. Your findings are incontrovertible.

CONFIDENTIAL

Mr. Richard Hamilton, Chairman & CEO
Harrison Manufacturing, Inc.

From: Arthur Leland, VP Sales

Subject: Important Information in Regard to the Proposed
               Amalgamated Tire Acquisition.

I have discussed with Mr. Turner certain information I found out about Amalgamated, and we decided that I should bring it to your attention as quickly as possible.

I dislike being a fly in the ointment as I know we are in an advanced stage on the Amalgamated buyout, but this could have a material effect on your thinking.

Kathleen Bauman and I felt that I should visit several of Amalgamated's large direct accounts and talk with key people there about what they thought of the company, its products, and any other concerns. I spoke with their merchandise managers, buyers, and retail sales managers. This was to be an informal check to give us an updated reflection of the company's current status.

These are the companies I called on:

> Beelo Stores, Los Angeles
> Barrow Auto Supplies, St. Louis
> Keystone Service, Chicago
> Hildenbrand's, New York

The information from these auto-aftermarket giants certainly gives us a good view of Amalgamated's situation right at the firing line—and precisely now, when it counts.

- The two most recent shipments of its new X-99 line had 5% to 7% defects, which is unacceptable. It consisted of a weakness near the rim which resulted in small fissures. Some were detected before application to wheels, others happened between 50 and 150 miles of use. It's quite possible there will be other such occurrences after 500, 1,000 or 5,000 miles.

As you see, there's a chance there may have to be a recall of some sort. I don't know how many tires are involved but it could be substantial enough to be alarming. I do not know what Amalgamated is doing about this. Suffice it to say, the dealers consider it to be serious.

- These dealers have lost confidence in Amalgamated. They are holding customers off on buying X-99 until this quality problem is fixed.

- Two competitive brands are cutting into Amalgamated's biggest selling line, Road King, due to their somewhat lower retail prices and equal quality. This is because retailers can make better customer deals on these brands due to higher mark-ups and promotional allowances. It's a cutthroat business in which, I believe, Amalgamated is losing market share.

- All these retailers came through with similar comments.

Coming out with caveats at this late stage does not make one popular. But Kathleen and I know this intelligence alert is important for you to have in your pocket as you continue discussions with Amalgamated.

It took me three weeks to get all this and confirm it, which is why I'm bringing it to you now. Obviously, better now than never.

Very truly yours,

Arthur Leland

cc: Leland Nesser, President
        Charles De Wonin, VP & CFO
        Kathleen Bauman, VP Marketing

P.S.   I transcribed the verbatim comments of all the people I spoke
        with. They are in a 31-page report which I'm sending you under
        separate cover.

SENIOR EXECUTIVES DECIDE TO RISE UP AND PRESENT A COMPLAINT ABOUT THEIR COMPANY PRESIDENT TO THE CHAIRMAN.

SITUATION: You are a senior executive at a machine-tool manufacturer.
The president of the company has become insufferable.
His treatment of key executives has deteriorated through the years to where
he is now an abusive martinet. He takes sport in beating down and insulting
people in front of their peers.

Weekend meetings are called on short notice, most often unnecessarily.
He makes dawn and late night calls to employees' homes. The executives
are shaky and afraid to make decisions. It's impossible to do a creditable
job.

The key executives suffering this torture select you as their spokesman to talk
to the Board chairman. You phoned him, and he listened attentively. He then
asked you to specify your complaints in a letter to him.

On the record, the president has been very good for the company. During his
five-year term profits have increased by over 50% and net worth has doubled.
This makes serious denunciations particularly touchy. They could easily be
sloughed off as belly-aching.

The chairman has assured you that whatever you say will not prejudice you
or the executives making this charge, provided it is factual, objective, and free
of passion or invective.

STRATEGY: This situation calls for a businesslike letter stating the ger-
mane points, without specific details. Leave these for a follow-up if and when the chairman asks for it.

You are putting yourself on the line. Reiterate the chairman's pledge that this
will not affect your standing in the company or that of the others in the rebel
group.

PRIVATE AND CONFIDENTIAL

November 22, 1996
Mr. Aubrey C. Hormeyer
Chairman of the Board
Clifton Industries, Inc.

_____

_____

Dear Mr. Hormeyer:

At your request, I am stating, on behalf of myself and the other senior
executives listed on the following page, certain serious complaints about
Mr. Randall Gordon.

They concern the insulting and abusive manner with which he confronts
us, and his inability to clearly guide the direction of this company.
This seriously affects our performance, and we believe is detrimental to
the corporate welfare.

I was selected by the executive staff to be its spokesman in bringing
this to your attention. It is an extremely disturbing task for me personally and, certainly, for all of us. It is acknowledged that during
the five years of Mr. Gordon's tenure Clifton's net profits rose by 56%,
and the stock price doubled.

Mr. Gordon holds a full-scale meeting twice a week to review our activities. We have come to call these meetings "inquisitions." They start
out as business discussions. But, for no reason, Mr. Gordon will often
fly into a rage, with loud outbursts, criticisms, and personal insults.
Most often no significant directives are being made. The result is that
there is no unified corporate policy.

His numerous calls for unnecessary weekend meetings and phone calls to
our homes at all hours are legendary, even outside the company.

This type of treatment is stifling and prevents us from being able to
perform at our best. It is disruptive to the people who report to us.

At this time, I will not go into detail as to specific incidents. We can
furnish these if requested.

We feel it is our duty to bring this information to you. It is in the
spirit of acting to the benefit of Clifton Industries, the Board of
Directors, and our shareholders.

You had assured me that this will not be prejudicial to me or to the others shown below, who have seen this letter and share its conviction.

Thank you for viewing this with interest.

Very truly yours,

Harvey T. Sigler
Vice President, Merchandising

cc: Guy Baxter, VP; Hilda Forrest, VP
        George Maxwell, VP, Audrey Peters, VP

▌RESPONSE TO CRITICISMS.

You were criticized by a management officer because your plan for product improvement had an arbitrary timeframe. There were no facts to support it.

Re: Timeframe for RTZ product improvement.

Your comment on my plan was very well taken, and caused me to reconsider how long it will take for the RTZ product improvement to be successfully completed:

I still think we can stick to my original projection. It was carefully thought through—and admittedly it included a bit of wishfulness. But I think we have to set up a tough target date and try to achieve it.

It makes us work harder, longer and more thoughtfully—which I think is the way to out-distance our competition. Thanks very much for your input and guidance.

Regards,

Jerry Weiss

ANOTHER LETTER

It goes without saying, the questions you raised about achieving our cost-cutting measures in terms of bottom-line results were appropriate and wise.

Those of us who had input into this timeframe target marshalled a lot of facts in coming up with the number we presented. Also a lot of intuition, knowledgeable intuition.

Let's face it—and I'm sure you agree—all big decisions are intuitive . . . . That's how they designed the Mustang.

ANOTHER LETTER

Thank you for bringing up the question of timing and parts availability in producing the needed RTZ product improvement.

It's important enough to rethink this from scratch, using all the data at our command, and put a new, dedicated team on it.

Then let's see what it comes up with. It will take two months.

Let's see what the new team reports, and then we can come to a decision.

ANOTHER LETTER IN THIS VEIN, BUT A SOMEWHAT DIFFERENT TONE— MORE INGRATIATING AS BEFITS THE EGO OF THE CRITIC WHO HAPPENS TO BE THE COO

To: Mr. Cecil McCool, COO

Re: The weak points you noted in the RTZ product-improvement
       project.

Well, it's back to the drawing board to redo the timing projection on this undertaking. Thanks for studying it as thoughtfully as you did, and for putting your finger on the one possibly defective analysis among the many other issues in this comprehensive report.

We'll start over on this one aspect and see if our original results bear up under greater scrutiny. We'll report back to you and the others involved as soon as the data come through.

Respectfully,

You redid certain parts of a planning document after your COO criticized some of the recommendations and projections as not being sufficiently documented. You found some flaws, but you don't want to leave an impression of having bad judgment or acting with insufficient preparation. Your reputation must be unimpaired; you must not admit to a goof.

ANOTHER LETTER

Re: The Advertising Campaign for the BPS Rejuvenation
       Conference

Dear Ms. Richardson:

The comments in the Operations Department memo of May 5 were reckless fingerpointing.

How can you blame a poor showing at this conference on what you called "less than adequate communications," which I understand to mean advertising and publicity. This criticism is categorically wrong, and the fault should be properly placed.

The advertising/publicity campaign was very good—in fact, it could be called superb—in that it attracted as many people as it did to an insufferably dull subject. The conference was badly planned, and the printed program could cause yawns even among people interested in the topic.

It's like a doctor blamed for the death of a terminally ill patient with a hopeless disease.

Very truly,

Bartlett Anderson
On behalf of the Marketing Committee

To: Mr. Peter Care
       Executive VP & Chief Operating Officer
Re: The Encode Software Testing and Evaluation

Thank you for discerning a possible error in our rationale and getting us back to square one.

Guess what? You were right in having us redo some of our testing. We found something that needed to be corrected, although it was very minor. Thus the total results we had reported before do not have to be materially changed. What it amounts to is that, thanks to you, we can launch this product with greater confidence.

Respectfully,

Neil Dietrich

▌YOU MUST GET OUT OF A BAD DEAL.

Your business was acquired by a much larger company, under the terms of a written contract stipulating that you would get certain income, services and perks. It didn't happen and you want out. You have to build up a record of noncompliance with the contract terms, as well as bad faith by the company officers with whom you contracted.

Mr. Perry Allesandro
President
Abacus National Corp.

_____

_____

Dear Perry:

I'm very much disturbed about the way my accounts are being handled, and I have reason to believe that my income is less than it should be. In other words, things aren't the same as what we agreed upon.

Cases in point—

   I received a phone call yesterday from one of my clients, Jack Shapiro, of Shapiro Software, saying he is unhappy about the service he gets. Orders are not being delivered on time, too little attention to his complaints or requests, and other grievances.

   A similar call, and letter, from another client, Libbie Sullivan of Sullivan Realtors. This was more restrained, but it reflected a warning that she might go elsewhere.

Another case:

   Your people weren't able to fulfill a service order from two other clients. How come both these clients were able to get it from another house?

I have more to say about noncompliance with our agreement which I won't bother to state here. In addition, I find it may be necessary to audit your books to check on the income I should receive.

I need assurance from you by August 11 that the above will be rectified and there will be no cause for complaint in the future.

Truly yours,

A BIT SOFTER YET VERY FIRM APPROACH

To: Leonard Zelman
      Marshal Thach

"There's many a slip twixt the cup and the lip."

I guess we both made a slip because there's a disparity between what is said in our contract (as I understand what the intention was) . . . this is the cup . . .

And what is actually taking place. . . the lip. . .

To wit:

> The accounts I brought in are, for the most part, not being serviced well by you.

> Your accounting system is faulty in that I'm not getting all of the commissions I deserve. If there's a computer glitch it always works against me.

I'm not getting the attention from your operating people that I was led to believe I'm entitled to.

I don't think you are personally at fault. But at best it's a matter of sloppy procedure and inadequate instructions and uncaring follow-up of instructions. All of this has to be corrected.

Right away.

Field Burnside

SOFTER STILL

Dear Leonard and Marshal,

Come on—let's get our house in order.

My accounts are, for the most part, badly handled. I am considered a nonentity by your people, and I think some of the income I'm supposed to get is falling between the cracks. And I'm very unhappy. I know you are, too, in reading this. I am also aware that you want to set it straight.

I know you're both very busy—but please, can one or both of you look into this and clear it up. Now! It will make us all a lot happier.

Your comrade in helping this business grow,

Scott Sheldon

A MORE PLEASANT APPROACH—BUT FIRM AND TO THE POINT

Dear Leonard and Marshal,

Make My Business Grow!

Sorry for the bad pun on "let my people go." By the way, I don't want you to "let my people go"—at least not the ones who came with me when you acquired my business.

On a more serious note, I need your help in improving the systems used to service my accounts. And in changing the attitudes of your operating people in addressing my requests.

Let's get together tomorrow or the day after for everyone's good, and more profits for both of us.

Be happy,

Scott

You made a deal and you want to live up to it. It seems the other side doesn't. Start the ball rolling on alerting your opposition to your concerns and grievances. The first step is arranging for a serious discussion.

Dear Todd:

There are a few things on my mind that I think ought to be settled. It may turn out to be of no concern to me—but then again it might.

I hope I'm wrong, but my instincts tell me, from the way I see things happening, or let's say a general attitude here, that some of the conditions under which I joined this company aren't being met. In other words, I'm somewhat disappointed in how our deal is being carried out.

I'm pretty sure things are okay, and you have no second thoughts about our agreeemnt, or me, but let's discuss it. I'll feel better.

Phil

Another approach, to begin a discussion on possible noncompliance with a contract in which a larger company acquired your customer billing assets.

To: Mr. Harold Appleton, CEO

I had a couple of meetings with Ron and Debbie of Customer Service in which they didn't pay any attention to certain terms of our written agreement. It's particularly disconcerting because I'm sure they are aware of our deal—and if so, we are talking violation.

It was probably an oversight, a mistake or whatever, but I need to discuss it with you. I'm sure the matter will be cleared up.

How about Wednesday? The morning would be good for me, but you name the time. I'll call Margaret to let me know what time is good for you.

Best Regards,

Harold Jaffe

ANOTHER LETTER—FRIENDLY. YOU DON'T WANT TO BE TOSSED ASIDE

Dear Eunice—

I came out of our meeting kind of nonplussed as to my role in the marketing planning we'll be doing. In fact, I'm confused since these planning meetings are broad-ranged and very important for the future of our company.

As the Director of Marketing I should have the lead role. It is what I was hired for, yet the duties you assigned to me put me pretty much in a back seat.

Am I reading too much into this, Eunice? Let's take a few minutes to talk about it. I'll call you.

Roger

Friendly, with an ominous threat. It's sometimes good to hint at the possibility of your lawyer getting into the act. The other side will get the message that you are determined to see the matter settled to your satisfaction. Litigation is in no way on your mind—but!

You are the principal of a business, Software Associates, that was merged with a larger company, Communication Dynamics, as a separate division. Upon coming on the scene, you are being given short shrift. It's apparent they want to give you subordinate status and send you off to the sidelines. You don't like it.

You want to work with the other executives at the high status you deserve and you have so notified the owners of the company that acquired you. But you don't have an executive office; the owners have treated you in a cavalier fashion, and have shunted you off to a cubicle away from executive row, unmindful that this has violated the merger agreement.

You met with the CEO/owner and stressed your complaint. The owner acquiesced, however unwillingly.

Send a letter confirming the discussion. No frills or niceties, straightforward. You must act tough because you are dealing with tough people who will try to get away with whatever they can.

March 29, 1997

To: Herbert Segal
From: John Michaels
Re: Follow-up to our meeting on March 26.

This is the agenda as discussed—

1. As an active principal of Communication Dynamics, Inc., I am to occupy a suitable private office acceptable to me. It goes without saying, I will be fulfilling the requirements of my executive duties.

2. All Communication Dynamics mail and memos will be placed on my desk each morning. If I am not in any morning, it will be delivered to Marsha.

3. I will be in on April 8—you suggested 10 o'clock. On that day, I will be given an orientation and be introduced to the Software Associates staff by Jeffrey or Richard. One of the purposes of my introduction to the various departments is to ensure my understanding of the procedures of the vendors. This is to serve best the interests of Communication Dynamics and Software Associates, including the capability of Communication Dynamics to enhance Software Associate's business.

4. Needless to say, I will be apprised of all correspondence, phone calls, etc., and included in all meetings in any way relating to Software Associates business. Likewise, I will have the assistance and full cooperation of the Communication Dynamics staff people.

5. Certain other details of minor consequence but which you surely have in mind:

   a) Door keys.
   b) My name to be listed on all directories.
   c) An assigned parking place, conveniently located.

I will, of course, be working closely with Marsha, who will remain in the same office she now occupies.

Again, Herb, this covers the points set at our meeting, which I'm sure you agree is to both our interests. I'm looking forward to a pleasant and mutually rewarding relationship.

cc: Jerome King
       Marsha Michaels
       Jeffrey Segal
       Richard King

Just a tiny hint of seeking legal redress as to your employment agreement.

To: Herb Zeltner and Steve Marshal

It's now four months since I came here under the terms and conditions of the agreement we both signed. I think some of the things in the agreement have been forgotten—that is, are not being complied with. It disturbs me, as you can imagine.

I mentioned this casually to my wife, and to a good friend of mine, a lawyer, who happened to be there at the time. It was a coincidence that he was present, since having a lawyer involved is in no way on my mind. At any rate I was advised that there is likely no need for concern but I should speak to you about it.

You are undoubtedly not aware of any noncompliance, don't want to change anything in our agreement, and want to clear this matter up to my satisfaction and yours.

I'll call Debbie to arrange a meeting—hopefully tomorrow.

Dave Simmer

You, the head of a division of a large corporation, want to get out of a deal you made to acquire certain assets of another company. You had a handshake agreement, followed by a memo stating the conditions.

Mr. Randall Smith
365 Harbor Drive
Naugatuck, CT 38605

Dear Randall:

We had a flirtation—which was the memo citing the tentative deal we were considering. But before entering into an engagement period I think we both should consider if we want to get married.

Pardon these metaphors. It's another way of saying the time has come to sit down and go over actual terms—the real binding terms. Or if indeed we want to go into a marriage.

Call me to set the date.

Sincerely,

Ben Watkins

PROTECT YOUR COMPANY *FROM OUTSIDE DANGERS—* CLIENTS, VENDORS, ETC.

▌A CHANGE OF COMMAND AT YOUR BEST CUSTOMER.

SITUATION: You are a principal at a TV production company. A large cable TV operator is your best customer by far. It has put in someone new to replace your former contact, a close friend who was fired. You now have a new de facto chief, who okays your bills and can keep you on or dismiss you. Your mission: Get close to this guy.

He is a headstrong catalyst, scurrying about and making sweeping changes. You don't want to be swept out. You've got to meet with him quickly, but he's hard to pin down and difficult to speak with on the phone. What's more, he doesn't know you. Worse: You know he has a favorite production house that he has worked with before and who can ease you out of the picture.

STRATEGY: Send your new client lead-man a letter asking for a meeting. Imply that you had been previously throttled in bringing them creative programming concepts, but that now you'll be able to show them great, trend-setting entertainment ideas.

In order to assure a positive meeting ambience, which will get you off on the right foot, you have to cater to his ego, which you were told is immense. You arrange for an executive of the Cable TV Trade Association to be with you at the meeting. You say in the letter that this trade official wants to be there to

146

get the benefit of your client's thoughts on the future of cable and how the industry can progress more rapidly. Your client's comments will be in the Association Journal and distributed to the news media, which you have arranged through a PR agency.

This is the red herring that will make your client want to see you. By elevating his stature, you will have served him well.

December 16, 1996

Mr. C. Carter Barrow
Executive Vice President
Cable Television Systems, Inc.

_____

_____

Dear Mr. Barrow:

Congratulations on taking the helm! It will be wonderful working for you. You'll now see imaginative programming concepts we previously weren't in a position to present to CTS because of so many inhibiting restrictions.

Depending on your schedule, we want to meet with you as soon as possible to get your thinking on the future direction of CTS. In this way, we'll be better able to target our output. We can be an arm of CTS, an effective tool for carrying out your strategy.

Understandably, you've been extremely busy, so it's been hard to pin you down. The executive VP and another official of Cable TV Trade Association want to join us when we get together. They are anxious to get the benefit of your thinking on the status of the industry and the direction it should take as a trade association.

I believe they want to feature your comments in a news release to the media. Since you are a celebrated spokesperson for the industry, your opinions will have weight.

We, and Cable TV Trade Association, are looking forward to our meeting. I'll call to arrange the date.

Best wishes,

Mel Brown
Production Manager

A FAITHFUL CLIENT IS NOW SPEAKING WITH ANOTHER VENDOR ABOUT COMPETING WITH YOU FOR A LUCRATIVE JOB ASSIGNMENT.

SITUATION: You, a VP at a data-processing firm, have a long and extraordinarily amicable relationship with an important client, a supermarket chain. It is in the habit of handing you assignments, big or small, whenever the need comes up, because you are steady and reliable. Now, suddenly, another company got into the act to present ideas for an assignment. Why?

Your client contact may be doing it to demonstrate to his management that he looks at more than one proposal, more than one bid. That he checks out new suppliers. Did he get pressure from higher up? You are anxious and fearful.

STRATEGY: A letter stating that each one of the client's requests is taken as a new challenge, with completely new thinking. In keeping with this, you are assigning new people in your company to this next assignment. It's your normal procedure.

Some will be freelancers to get entirely new faces and minds into the act. You need these extra bodies to supplement your small staff. The experience and knowledge of your regular account staff is a valuable back up.

In this way, your client will have fresh outside thinking, which is augmented by people with a thorough knowledge of their business—more than a match for your competitor.

You must give this client confidence, both in you personally and in the ideas you present. You don't want the client to become enamored of new flash-in-the-pan spectacular schemes that a competitor may come up with.

April 15, 1996

Ms. Geraldine DeLucas
Vice President
Deserving Supermarkets, Inc.

_____

_____

Re: Limited Network Proposal

Dear Gerrie:

Thanks so much for this latest assignment. You know we've always come through for you before, and I'm sure you're confident we'll do it again.

This letter is not to blow our horn. It's a routine message we send to our valued clients every so often to let them know how we operate. And why you can depend on us to come up with fresh ideas to get your jobs done right. Our ideas are not just flashes. Each one comes about in accordance with a special process we have to make sure it is not just an innovation—but a practical innovation, one that works.

As an example, this new assignment will be put to people here who haven't worked on your business before. Because we rotate the personnel in this way, they are unencumbered by past proposals and past thinking. Their mission is to brainstorm fresh ways of doing this job. The people who regularly handle your account will stay in the background and will not interfere. We don't want to introduce any preconceived notions that may inhibit new thinking.

The regulars are very important, however, because of their experience with your company. They know your policies, industry policies, regulations, the history of what worked well before, what didn't work, and why. And of course they are very capable of fresh thinking.

We'll show you all the new ideas. Some may not be practical, but we want you to look them over anyway. An approach may sound glamorous, fascinatingly innovative, but for a good reason may be a wild-eyed scheme that won't work. Worse, it might cost you time, money, and reputation if you went ahead with it. What we bring to the table is creativity, knowledge, and experience.

Thanks for taking the time to read this, Gerrie. I thought you'd be interested in knowing our policy in handling all your assignments, including, of course, this latest one.

Best regards,

Chance Douglas

FIND OUT THE PECKING ORDER AND SENSORS BEFORE COMMENCING WORK FOR A NEW CLIENT.

SITUATION: You, a partner in a big-time accounting firm, just got a new client. To help assure a smooth start and ease the client's transition from its previous firm, you should know who at the company does what and when, who is in charge of what, etc.

Knowing this will avoid backbiting, turf wars, stepping on toes, and costly frustrations, not to mention excessive overtime. Your client will be happier. You will be successful with the account.

STRATEGY: Write the CFO, your top contact, whom you have known for several years, and tell him your shop has started the wheels turning on his account. But, in order to avoid problems and maximize efficiency, you should know what is not shown on the personnel flow chart, the behind-the-scenes picture.

Do this at dinner, in a pleasant, relaxed ambience, where good food and wine have a way of encouraging candor and good will. In vino veritas.

September 16, 1996

Mr. Timothy Rogers Saunders,
Senior Vice President, Chief Financial Officer
Locus Electronic, Inc.

_____

_____

Dear Tim:

It is the ultimate understatement to tell you we are delighted to have won your business. It was a long, hard road. And I thank you for the part you played.

Now we go to work, and we're looking forward to showing you and your colleagues what we can do.

As a prelude, I think it would be productive to sit down together and put into focus the people and places, aside from you, who will be involved—even peripherally—in what we do. Obviously, you are our boss, but because your time is valuable we don't want to bother you with questions if others could give the answers.

In a nutshell, it would be helpful to know the pecking order. Who has the antennas, where they point, and how far up or sideways they go.

Flow charts are fine, but it's also good to get filled in on what's behind the charts. It's kind of a third dimensional look at the folks in the squares as well as behind and around them—where the egos and alter egos lie.

Tim, let's have dinner next week to go over all of this. Any evening that's right for you is fine with me. If not next week, please give me your next open date.

Thanks so much for your confidence. It's going to be great working for you.

Warm regards,

Bob Carlisle

▌KEEP YOUR CUSTOMERS' LOYALTY WHEN THERE IS A THREAT

SITUATION: You own a reputable insurance brokerage in a wealthy suburb, with a sizeable customer base, acquired throughout 60 years of much sweat and little leisure, in good times and bad. You now have a comfortably profitable operation.

It's time to make things easier. You negotiated with a much larger insurance brokerage to be swept into their operation. Your income directly depends on the retention of your customers, their continuing loyalty.

STRATEGY: Announce the merger to your customers as a good move for them and for you. It will assure the continuation of the excellent service you've provided and even enhance it through a wider range of insurance carriers and more back-up support and expertise. Plus, you'll have a lot more strength in the industry. The bottom line is they'll get the best protection for their needs at the most favorable prices.

Further, as tangible proof that they will get the same personal service from you as before—that they are not being given over to strangers—your key people are moving with you to handle their business. Your customers can call you at the same phone number. Everything is the same, only bigger and better.

February 8, 1996

Mr. Zish Monteveld
Monteveld Restaurant Supplies

_____
_____

Dear Mr. Monteveld:

            WE'RE MOVING . . . WE'RE BIGGER

On May 1, our offices will be relocated to 103 Charter Boulevard, Secaucus, New Jersey. At that time, Schwartz & Michaels will become a major division of Marshall Insurance Counselors, one of the biggest independent insurance brokerage firms on the east coast.

We'll have the same name, the same phone and fax numbers, and the same people will be in charge of your account. The same voices will answer the phone when you call. You will have the same personal service and attention you need and deserve. . .

And, in addition, you will have access to many extra benefits. For example:

- A much broader range of insurance carriers that will enable us to secure the best coverage for all of your insurance needs . . . at the best prices.

- Full service Life, Health, Group, Estate Planning and Employee Benefits departments will be able to handle all of these requirements, *in house*—a cost savings.

- Additional back-up and support from a combined firm with a large professional staff having expertise in all fields of insurance, a firm which has a great deal of clout in the insurance industry today.

The bottom line is that as insurance coverage becomes more varied and complex (and, yes, more confusing to the customer) you will be assured of the best protection for your needs, and the best service. . . at the lowest prices. And again, your account will continue to be handled by the same people, the people you know and can rely on.

We'll be in touch with you shortly. Meanwhile, as always, we're looking forward to your call any time you have a question or need service.

Warm regards,

Larry Schein
President
Schwartz, Michaels & Marshall

THE SECOND-TIER MANAGEMENT AT YOUR CLIENT IS UNDERMINING YOU.

SITUATION: You are a senior management supervisor at an ad agency. Your major responsibility is a big-name package foods company, located 2-1/2 jet hours away. Your influence with your client is beamed right to the top—the corporate chairman, president, and EVP. That's your strength. Your day-to-day dealings, however, are with middle management.

Your power with the ivory tower rankles the members of mid-management. They bitterly resent the greater access you have to their commanders than they enjoy. Their power over you is theoretical. Their authority as "the client to be feared" is subverted. Indeed, you are a threat.

These mid-managers want to make you look bad, to get you off center stage. Their mission is to do everything possible to put traps in your path—-by intention, by impulse, and by instinct, but always with a seemingly earnest desire to help you.

You are in a spot because you have to deal with these people every day. Their job is to give you orders, to certify what you do, and approve your bills for doing it.

You have a distinct disadvantage: they are in day-to-day contact with the powers, in a position to frequently report about your performance. You don't know what they say, and you are not around to defend yourself.

STRATEGY: The time has come to make a move. You have strength with the power center. Use it before you are discredited. Take action before the situation is untenable. As Hugh Walpole stated in one of his writings—"Don't play for safety. It's the most dangerous game in the world."

Call one of your top-brass admirers, the EVP in charge of the entire department you work with. Briefly mention your problem without making a big deal of it on the phone.

Next, send a letter, indicating you are bringing up the same problem you had previously spoken about, one that can eventually hurt her. Give some detail. You want to be helpful. Make a date to see her on other matters and on this one too, when you will spell out all the facts.

This is not a brouhaha. This is guerilla warfare. Map your tactics, then launch your assault.

April 21, 1996

Ms. Annamarie Lucia Alvarez
Executive Vice President, Consumer Marketing
Succulent Foods Corp.

_____

_____

Dear Annamarie:

Annamarie, there is a problem in your marketing department that is caus-ing some turmoil and is costing you money. I touched on it briefly on the phone last week without going into detail.

We've been meeting our assignment deadlines promptly and submitting great work. It seems that most of the deadlines we get are unrealistically and unnecessarily tight. We get last-minute work orders to be completed in a week or two, or even in a few days, that should ordinarily take three or four weeks. We're told there is a dire urgency, so we pull out all stops. Like a fire department, we've been on call from emergency to emer-gency.

That's not all. Sometimes when we deliver the work, it just sits there. Nothing is done about it for two or three weeks. Sometimes never. As in the fire department, there are false alarms.

I don't have to tell you what this costs in overtime and wear and tear on our people and yours. We're coping, admirably well, but I'm afraid that this lack of good organization is going to hurt your business.

Annamarie, we're here to carry out your needs. We submitted plans and we submitted schedules, which everyone agreed on. Naturally, there are last minute urgencies, fires to put out. It's the nature of the business, and what we are good at. But it seems that there could have been more upfront notice on at least some of the "emergencies."

I don't get to see you much since we're 1,000 miles apart. I'd like to hop over next week to go over a number of things. And at the same time, we can discuss what I brought up here. I'll call to set the date.

Warmest Regards,

GETTING BACK INTO THE GOOD GRACES OF A CLIENT, AFTER BEING DECLARED *PERSONA NON GRATA*.

SITUATION: You are a staff writer for a big public-relations agency. Part of your duties is to produce press releases and articles for a valued client.

There was a meeting at the client's offices to present an article you had written for one of its divisions. You were carried away and became a bit too forceful in delivering your work, hinting irritation in your tone and body language when the client voiced some differences with what you had presented. It annoyed the client's division manager so much that she told the agency's VP and Account Director not to have you there again.

It's ironic, because your work was well received, even praised. It was an issue of attitude, not talent. Naturally, it's a shock, a severe blow to your professional pride. Needless to say, your standing in the agency is greatly diminished.

STRATEGY: The first step is to phone the client manager who declared you an out-person. Find out why—you know it's not the quality of your work. Try to set it right. After clearing it within the agency, you made the call. It turned out well. She mentioned the reason for her displeasure—you were out of order by displaying a vexatious attitude. She agreed to withdraw her demand. What a relief!

It's important for you to follow-up with a letter to her. You don't want to grovel or be overly subservient. You must maintain a professional persona and be dignified, yet apologetic.

Ms. Felicia Parker
Division Manager
Hatfield, Morgan Construction, International, Inc.

_____

_____

Dear Felicia:

I was so glad we chatted yesterday. And thanks so much for helping me understand why I irked you to the point of declaring me *persona non grata*.

It was not my work, which you really liked. I feel good about this.

It was my attitude of being too assertive and impatient. I feel very bad about this.

It was an outpouring of zeal, and this time it was displayed too energetically. A bad error. Thank you for forgiving it.

As said by two very wise people:

> *"Zeal is very blind, or badly regulated, when it encroaches upon the rights of others"*
>
> (Quesnel)

> *"To err is human, to forgive divine"*
>
> (Alexander Pope)

It's so good to be working with you.

Best regards,

Hattie Weinberg

▎ YOUR PRESENTATION FOR SOME LUCRATIVE NEW BUSINESS IS DEAD.

SITUATION: You're the head of an insurance-brokerage office that made an all-out pitch for a big new account. It would raise your premium income by 25%, with little extra overhead. Your present staff plus two additional people could handle it.

The scuttlebutt says that you are not getting it. Two other brokers appear to be neck-and-neck in the lead, with you a bit behind. This translates to O-U-T.

STRATEGY: You will not give up. You have nothing to lose by pulling out all the stops and giving it the extra effort. You have to find some way to kindle more interest and give your pitch a new life.

What better way could there be than by reducing the premium by a sizeable amount? It will undercut your competition. You sharpen your pencil and plead with your insurance suppliers. You cut your profits. You desperately want to make this deal. It will give you entree to more of this company's insurance business, which can be lucrative. But you must explain, in a credible way, why you didn't quote this lower premium originally.

Start with an e-mail dispatch to get immediate attention and to halt a commitment with another broker if it is imminent. Follow up with a fax the same day. Then send the fax original as a letter, with a prominent line on top, *Original of Previous Fax.*

You will get the message out quickly and dramatically, and you'll have a document for the record. You've done everything practicable to latch on to this business.

October 4, 1996

E-MAIL MESSAGE

To: Mrs. Helena Packard Estes
        Coalition Real Estate Management, Inc.

From: Manning Tilden, President
        Babcok & Tilden Insurance

A new insurance package came up yesterday. It will save you a great deal of money on your premium—with the same coverage. We have an exclusive on this now. A fax will follow today with details.

October 4, 1996

(By Fax: Original to Follow)

Mrs. Helena Packard Estes
Executive Vice President
Coalition Real Estate Management, Inc.

_____

_____

Dear Mrs. Estes:

Things have changed for the better since we gave you our proposal two weeks ago. Better for you. Much better.

There have been changes in certain insurance rates in the last two weeks that make it possible for us to bring the premium estimate we quoted before down by $42,300 a year—for the same coverage. This means you can have a clear savings of $42,300 a year from what you were previously quoted.

We're never static. We're constantly on the lookout for new insurance packages, new regulations, new coverages, new pricing. This is to make sure our clients always have the right protection at the best prices. They get the benefit of the latest advantages the moment they become available.

We decided to put two executives and a claims technician on your account as their priority responsibility. You will always have an expert on call. In addition, I or my associate will be visiting your office from time to time. As the head of this firm, I assume the responsibility for making sure you get the best possible service. I am available to you anytime.

It would be good for us to come in to discuss this new coverage and the special low rate plan. How about this coming Thursday, October 7th? I'll call you to confirm.

Very truly yours,

THE ODDS ARE STACKED AGAINST YOU ON A CLIENT ACQUISITION PRESENTATION.

SITUATION: You are the sales manager at a communications systems company, eager to get your foot in the door at a dominant cable network. An opportunity comes up: the network is looking for a new communications procedure—just your specialty. Nailing down this project, or at least a part of it, would be a marvelous triumph.

You camped at the doorstep of the decision maker and pleaded/talked your way into a presentation meeting. You got the date, as a courtesy really, due to your persistence and personality.

You worked hard at producing a sterling presentation. Money-saving ideas. Fool-proof back-up systems. This was your chance and you had to make the most of it.

Competing with you are two vendors the decision maker has been working with for years. They are heavy with talent, dependable—the old reliables. Your prospect trusts them. He is comfortable with them. Edging your way in is a tough call.

Your meeting didn't click—you felt it, knew it. Your sales target was polite, even jovial, but he kept looking at his watch. His eyes were glazed, and he stared out the window a couple of times. You were a newcomer, a stranger not being taken seriously.

You gave him the highlights of your outstanding presentation. You caught his interest. But you couldn't get enough time to deliver your entire story. Your full pitch was in a binder that you handed him.

He probably will not review it seriously. All your preparation, your exquisite ideas, and your powerful prose are down the drain. You think. No, you are certain.

STRATEGY: It's crazy to give up, considering all the brains and sweat you put into it. This has to go another round.

Send a letter cajoling him into giving you another meeting date. Tell him you admire his openness in wanting to go beyond the vendors he's used for so long. He will get a gold mine of fresh ideas, a new look, by adding your creative company into his privileged supplier clique. You want to massage his ego without seeming to be gratuitously flattering.

The odds of a second meeting are stacked against you, but you've got to give it a big try.

October 26, 1996

Mr. Jeffrey A. O'Neil
Senior Vice President
FSA Cable Systems

_____

_____

Re: Communications System Revamping

Dear Mr. O'Neil:

> *"Genius. . . Means little more than the faculty of*
> *perceiving in an unhabitual way."*
>
> (William James)

Your having us make our presentation was admirable. Shall I say a flash
of genius?

We're not in your present vendor circle, not one of the people you are
accustomed to have handling your communication needs. Familiarity brings
comfort. It also brings sameness, stodginess, and old ideas being regen-
erated, refurbished, and revamped, but seldom totally replaced. Not
invented from scratch.

You want a new look, another perspective, a new way of solving a problem. I'm sure that's why you agreed to see what we can do. It took boldness, but that's the way you break out of the mold and get innovative
ideas.

Our proposal was put together in our usual careful, deliberate way. It
was thoughtfully conceived and displays a creative concept for carrying
out your assignment with the use of cutting-edge technology. Something
like this was never done before. Think of the extra value this adds to
your network.

Our reputation tells you that you can count on us to do the job above
expectations. We always do what we say we will—and then some—on time and
within the budget.

May we see you again briefly to give you more insight into our previous
proposal? As well as several new thoughts that have come to us as a result
of our meeting? Just a few minutes is all we ask. If we are privileged
to win this business, or any part of it, you will have a refreshingly
new vendor.

Best regards,

Josh Gibson

YOU CAN'T AGREE TO YOUR CLIENT'S UNREASONABLE REQUEST.

SITUATION: You are the president of a marketing-research company
and have just completed a consumer survey, ordered and
paid for by an advertising agency. The purpose was to find out the effectiveness of its current campaign for an important client, a fast-food chain.

The figures show the ads to be somewhat effective. Clearly, there is room for
improvement, and the research data suggest ways to do it.

The agency's supervisor on the account is unhappy about the data in your elegantly bound report and has suggested certain small changes that would mitigate some of the more unpleasant findings. He noted it would help temper "confusion and bias" in the study.

STRATEGY: You obviously cannot accede to this request. The product of your business is truth and objectivity. Let the chips fall where they may. The integrity of your work cannot be compromised. It could mean death to your reputation and your business. Nevertheless, this is a good client, and you are obliged to show a spirit of cooperation.

Send your client a letter pointing out that all you provided are cold figures, which are subject to analysis and interpretation. It can interpret them in its own way to show it is doing an adequate job. You don't have to be brought into this. It's between the agency and its client.

Most importantly, the agency should demonstrate how the research points the way to further improving the advertising. After all, this was the purpose of the research. It couldn't take corrective steps until these findings were available.

Note that you'll be pleased to help the agency in the ad-improvement rationale. Suggest that it should display its ad face-lift to its client at the same time the research is presented. You will be most pleased to be at this meeting as a back-up, if invited.

Mr. Brett Simon
Senior Vice President
Callan, Isprey Advertising Agency, Inc.

_____
_____

Dear Brett:

The conversation we had yesterday reminds me of a saying in one of Aesop's fables—"Every truth has two sides. It is well to look at both, before we commit ourselves to either."

You acquired remarkable information from the consumer survey we delivered last Friday. It shows the agency has been doing a good job, but it also suggests areas of improvement. Let's face it, that's why you did the study. The purpose of the research was to determine how to make the commercial message more effective.

We did very little interpretation in our report. We simply showed the facts as they came out of our tabulations. The hard data can't change, of course. We have no control over that. I know you agree that it's our business to present the findings as they are.

Here's another wise saying, this one by Henry Clay—"Statistics are no substitute for judgment."

As I indicated before, the figures should be interpreted in a way that points to how the ads could be strengthened. I suggest that you make a full-blown presentation of your recommendations to your client at the same time that you display the research. The client is unquestionably much more interested in your creative work than in the cold research facts.

You can count on our full cooperation in backing you up. I'll be glad to consult on your presentation, and I'll attend your client meeting with you, if you wish.

Regards,

Seymour Feinberg
Vice President, Marketing

▌YOU CAN'T MAKE THE DEADLINE ON AN IMPORTANT
▌ASSIGNMENT FOR A NEW CLIENT.

SITUATION: You are a partner in a sales promotion and package design firm and have been aching for years to get in the door of a famous cosmetics company. Finally, you get the call. The company needs a design overhaul of one of its popular lines, plus a trade brochure announcing the change.

There is a three-month deadline. It's extremely tight, but you don't want to blow this chance of finally getting cozy with this company. You feel you can do it with an all-out crash effort.

The time constraint it imposed is necessary to get the designs, plus the brochure copy and layout into the hands of the people who will produce it so as to make a retail store delivery date nine months hence. Everything has to be coordinated with pinpoint timing. You are doing the initial stage and all else that follows depends on your work coming through on time.

You are 2-1/2 months into the job and you see you can't make the three-month deadline. You need two additional weeks. It's not because you fell down on the job; you made the best possible effort. There were just not enough hours in the day.

STRATEGY:　　　　Send a letter. Say that you are doing this work on a crash basis, but without compromising quality. You have to lodge the thought that the schedule will be met even though the final part of the job will be delivered two weeks after the deadline date. The letter must be positive.

Say that you will deliver all the graphics and packaging copy on time for review by the marketing, legal, and lab people. This will include final designs on 90% of the packages. It will take the client's people about two weeks to review all this. And they can then pass it on for the start of production. They will receive the rest two weeks later, so that production will keep moving along without a hitch. The production schedule will not be held up.

For all practical purposes the deadline has been met. No time will be lost. You came through on this very difficult assignment.

```
Ms. Olivia de la Portega
President
Cashmere Cosmetics Associates, Inc.

_____

_____


Dear Olivia:

You gave us the impossible. We are coming through.

More importantly, there is no compromise, not the least bit, on quali-
ty. Not just quality alone, but perfection. Because that's how we do
every assignment. Proof? Your people are seeing it as they follow the
work taking place in our shop. You will soon see it too.

Here is the schedule—

      You want designs and copy ready by February 16, so that it can
      be passed on for your internal review—marketing, legal and the
      lab. This will take two weeks. We'll have 90% of the package
```

designs ready by this date. You can then start sending it to
production on March 3.

On March 2nd, we'll deliver the rest of the packaging and the
brochure designs. This small part can then be reviewed internally and passed on without losing production time.

Your time schedule for getting this revamped line to market is intact,
insofar as our contribution is concerned. Despite the most difficult timing conditions imaginable and the most stringent quality standards, we
made the deadline for getting all the packaging and brochure into production.

Job perfect. Mission accomplished.

Very truly yours,

NEUTRALIZE UNFAVORABLE NEWS WHEN REPORTING IT TO YOUR CLIENT.

SITUATION: You are a VP at an advertising agency, supervising a
                  national fast-foods account. You commissioned a market-
research company to conduct a consumer survey in order to evaluate your
new campaign. The data came in—not bad, but not good. How do you present it to your client?

STRATEGY: After all, the purpose of the research is to indicate how you
                  can strengthen the campaign. You didn't have this con-
sumer information before; you had to shoot from the hip. From this point
of view, your advertising can be considered pretty good under the circumstances. Now, at last, you have the material that will make it a smashing success.

You tell this to your client in a letter, knowing it is anxious to see the research
findings. Mention that the data won't make sense until the client can see what
you are doing about it. That's why, along with this research, you want to present the agency's recommendations for strengthening the advertising based
on this new information.

March 7, 1996

Mr. Harry Sweeney
Vice President, Marketing
Fine & Healthy, Inc.

Dear Harry:

We're sifting through the research findings that are coming. Right now, the data will not make any sense until it is analyzed, enabling us to strengthen the new campaign.

Don't forget, we didn't have the benefit of this information when we built the strategy because we had to get started quickly, in time for your new TV programming. What's running now is the first stage, and it looks like we're on the right track.

Now we can give the advertising the final touches. This will be presented next week with the research. How is Friday, June 23, 11 A.M. in our conference room? Please let me know who will attend. We'll have lunch prepared.

I'm sure you agree it makes sense to show everything at once. The research and the advertising creative work will have more meaning when you see them together.

Regards,

Ben Perez

A VENDOR IS GOING OVER YOUR HEAD. STOP IT DEAD.

SITUATION: You head up an airline's maintenance purchasing department. An equipment company salesman has been showing his wares to you for the past 14 months. Although he's been getting a cordial reception each time, you haven't put him into your inner circle of suppliers. His merchandise is good, but not outstanding enough to take orders away from your coterie of suppliers.

The salesman, looking to crack your account any way he can, served notice he will go directly to the Senior VP of

Maintenance, to whom you report. You are concerned that he will complain about the difficulty of breaking into your supplier network and point out to your boss that an outsider is unable to get a fair hearing.

STRATEGY: Here is a threat to your influence, your strength in the company, your power over your suppliers. He must be blown away, nipped in the bud. His request must be dead on arrival.

Send a memo to your boss warning him of the impending call from a disgruntled salesman who was turned down for good reason. Confirm your policy of purchasing the best products at the best prices and impartially investigating all reliable sources.

This salesperson wants to bypass your appraisal process. Advise your boss not to bother taking the call. It will take up his time needlessly, upset proper business routine, and could foment chaos in the purchasing operation.

```
To:     Mr. Herbert C. Michaels
        Senior V. P.—Maintenance, Alliance Airlines, Inc.
From:   Harry Krackower
        Manager, Maintenance Purchasing Department
```

Dear Mr. Michaels:

This is to alert you to the probability that you may receive a phone call from an equipment distributor, GF Materials, in an attempt to display its product line to you personally.

This is unauthorized by me, and indeed, is in direct violation of what I told this supplier. In short, he is going over my head.

I don't have to tell you, Mr. Michaels, that this office carefully tests and screens each piece of equipment needed and negotiates the best possible price terms. Naturally, we can't buy from everyone. What we purchase, and from whom, is done strictly on merit—in terms of quality, on-time delivery, reliability, financial stability, reputation, etc.

The phone call to you will be from an unhappy salesperson who was turned down here because his products did not measure up to our standards, for various reasons such as were cited before. His contemplated action is disruptive to our entire purchasing system as well as a burden to your office.

In my opinion, it is best not to acknowledge this call. I'm sorry for the need to take up your time on this.

Regards,

Harry

▌YOU WANT TO SHAKE UP A VENDOR.

SITUATION: The people at your PR agency have been looking askance at some of your requests, the ones that are not routine and which require extra effort. It's as if they're being punished. This is not a real problem because they do a good job. But it's unpleasant and has become irritating to you and your staff.

STRATEGY: Send a short letter to the head of the firm. Make it pleasant but pointed. Ruffle him. Let it be known that he'll have to change his employees' attitudes.

October 22, 1996

Ms. Mary Broder Stein
President
Semaphore Public Relations Associates

_____

_____

Dear Ms. Stein:

> *"A smooth sea never made a skillful mariner."*
>
> (English proverb)

It seems that some assignments we give your people are met with complaints. These are the ones that require a little more time and effort. We get such rejoinders as "It's tough to do. It presents a problem," and so on.

Now it has become tiresome and annoying so that my folks are complaining about it.

Mary, we assign you the things that you are in business for. We look to you to take care of our PR needs and problems, period. If they are easy, we don't need you. Our requests are not outlandish. After all, we don't ask you to run a restaurant or build a car factory.

This is not a big deal when you think about it. Your people are good, and we're pleased with your service. Why make it unpleasant at times? I simply think that now is the time to get this off my chest.

Be well,

Audrey

■ A LOCAL ZONING VARIANCE THREATENS YOUR BUSINESS.

Letter to the Zoning Commission

Letter to Nearby Merchants

SITUATION: You own a popular restaurant on a busy shopping thor-
               oughfare in a suburban town. The zoning commission is
planning to authorize a walk-in shelter for the homeless—on your block. This
is a do-good project for the community.

You don't want it on your block or even in the immediate shopping area,
where it will surely affect your patronage. Further, the extra turmoil and traffic will be a significant hazard to the many youngsters who frequent the area.

STRATEGY: Send a letter to the commission stating that although it's a
               commendable move, it would be totally unsuitable for
your block.

Also send a letter to other merchants in the area enlisting their support in
making a formal protest to the commission and the town council.

January 10, 1996

To: Zoning and Variance Commission
       Town of North Haven

From: Barbara Schwartz,
       Owner of Barbara's Cafe, 104 Kennedy Road

Re: Proposal for Converting 128 Kennedy Road to a Walk-In Shelter
       for the Homeless.

I applaud your cooperation with the county in making such a facility
available for homeless people in our area.

Please consider, however, that it would be a serious error to have such
an establishment at this address.

This part of Kennedy Road is a popular shopping promenade, frequented
all day and evening by a great many adults and children, including many
shoppers from outside this community.

This facility will significantly increase traffic on already busy
streets—due to support facilities, staff activities, social services and

so on. It will endanger the many teenagers who gather and shop here. Further, the heavy traffic will put these homeless people at risk.

I urgently ask you to consider placing such a center in a more appropriate location, and avoid the inconvenience and danger it can cause at the location now being considered.

At the very least, I believe you should authorize a research study to determine the pedestrian flow and traffic congestion now and to ascertain the increase if such a facility locates here.

Very truly yours,

Barbara Schwartz

LETTER TO OTHER MERCHANTS ON THE BLOCK

Mr. Frank Martin
Kennedy Eye Glass Emporium

_____

_____

Dear Frank:

This is about the proposed center for the homeless to be established on our block. We talked about it and worried about it, but we never made a serious attempt to stop it because we figured it was some bad news that wouldn't happen.

Now it looks like it's happening. The proposal may very well go through.

I don't have to elaborate on the consequences to us. We all know of the big potential decline in shopper traffic and the reduced property values, of the traffic congestion and further parking problems in the already-scarce spaces. In short, this can be a real threat to our businesses. Business is tough enough now. This could make us go down the drain.

I bit the bullet and wrote the attached letter to the Commission. I'm sure you agree with what I told them.

I've also written this same letter to Country Cheeses and Rosewood Pharmacy. I suggest you talk to other business people here whom you know well. We have to organize the merchants on this block and nearby to formally demand that the zoning commission withdraw this proposal.

Let's get together and talk. Right away, before this gets out of hand.

All the best,

▌YOUR IDEA WAS STOLEN—FIGHT IT!

You are part of a production team that develops ideas and scenarios for TV programs to present to networks, cable companies, and independent producers. You and your partners are dismayed and distraught because a bright program idea you had presented to several broadcasters and agents was stolen. It's being used by a rival producer. Write a note to be put up on the bulletin board where your team works.

```
To:    The entire staff
                 ABOUT OUR STOLEN GEM—

Remember, business is amoral.

It's like a jungle out there. People in our field of work particularly
are like predators. Ever see the face of a leopard or lion up close?
Their eyes are cold and expressionless, no compassion or feeling. They
do what is necessary for survival. . . . They must kill to eat when hun-
gry, or seek protection when threatened, and during mating periods to
have sex so as to breed and enjoy.

Humans in the world of commerce, especially in our industry, are the
same—with the added instincts of selfishness and deceit. Recently it's
become deadlier and more desperate. Cope with it. Fight back to protect
ourselves. We have to in order to survive.

Lindsay
```

A LETTER TO THE HEAD OF THE TV PRODUCTION COMPANY THAT STOLE YOUR PROGRAM IDEA

```
            A PERSONAL NOTE TO SANDY WALLACE

Business is amoral! We both know it. Maybe more so in our business
because the money we try to make all comes from ideas and their creative
applications. They can be easily swiped.

So it might be naive to express my anger at the theft of our idea, which
is what you presented to the CDR production company who bought it.

Sandy, you owe me one! Or maybe four or five because this was an espe-
cially great idea.

By the way, this note is not the end of it.

Judy Alvarez
```

DEFEND YOURSELF UNEQUIVOCALLY

▌COUNTERATTACK A SHARK WHO TRIED TO CHEW YOU UP.

Two Letters for Two Strategies

SITUATION: You are a VP and account executive at a large advertising agency. A big-name executive had been forced to resign from another agency, and your president took him off the beach and hired him as a senior VP. His immediate duties are less than his position and salary can rationalize. Part of his activity is as an adviser on various corporate problems that come up.

He roams about looking for opportunities to enhance his presence and take over important responsibilities. He has targeted you, seizing on a plan you are about to present to your client. He has derided it as fatuous, pedestrian, and said that it could even lose this account. This was in a memo to you with copies to the president and other key executives. His all-out attack shows his confidence in being able to replace you on this business, using this issue as a lever.

You know the account you handle is in good shape; the client likes you. You also know your plan is good. It's well done, and your client already knows the guts of it and is pleased. Mr. Shark obviously didn't check the background of this plan or the account.

TWO STRATEGIES:

  I: *Come Out Swinging*

 II: *Sharp Counterattack*

171

STRATEGY I: You hurry to see the president to inquire about this sudden and unwarranted outpouring of venomous criticism. You take the position that aside from being wrong, it's highly insulting and not good for the business.

The president is clearly simpatico with you. He knows you are on solid ground with this account. The client is happy with you and the agency. Your plan is virtually accepted. It would be nuts to rock the boat.

The president doesn't like this guy anyway. He knows he is getting too bold and disruptive. He gives you carte blanche to go to it. You decide to come out swinging and go for a one-round knockout.

STRATEGY II: A firm, unequivocal, yet slightly tempered counterattack. You have the ammunition to go for the kill, but you use business-like restraint. Sarcasm is in order. You are readying yourself to throw the knockout punch if it goes another round.

(STRATEGY I)

April 26, 1994

To: Harrison C. Rommer

From: Carlo DeLuria

"It is much easier to be critical than to be correct." (Benjamin Disraeli)

I sure didn't expect your crushing criticism of my Augustine plan. WOW! A copy was sent to you as a courtesy, but you certainly didn't show any when you summarily blasted off a castigating memo to me.

First of all, you don't know the background of this account. The plan hits the bullseye of Augustine's objectives beautifully. It's thoughtfully conceived, gets to the heart of the problem, and is skillfully written.

Second, this account is being very well run at our company. Its sales are strong; the client is happy. We're doing an excellent job; It's quite profitable for us.

In the third place, don't you think you should have spoken to me before dashing off this abusive and personally insulting diatribe? With copies to top executives of this company, including the president?

I'll quote another piece of advice by Disraeli, that legendary politician par excellence—

> *"To be conscious that you are ignorant is a great step*
> *to knowledge."*

Truly yours,

cc: Harry Adams   John Garfield, President
      Ginny Carpenter   Seth Gordon
      Bernie Fogel

(STRATEGY II)

April 26, 1994

To: Harrison C. Rommer
From: Carlo DeLuria

> *"It is much easier to be critical than to be correct."*
> (Benjamin Disraeli)

This quote is an understatement in commenting on your memo about my Augustine plan, sent to me and all of the above without warning. I appreciate your comments, since it shows a view that an outside person could have—without knowing the facts.

Without giving you all the facts, which will take several pages and which you can look up in the files, I'll mention these particularly salient points.

First, the client has a certain objective which this plan targets right in the center of the bullseye. It gets to the heart of what it wants done with a skillfully conceived, well-documented operational design. It embodies good thinking on the part of the agency staff.

Second, this account is being very well run here. Our campaigns are successful. The client is happy. The agency is happy. It generates good income for us.

Harrison, I wish you had come to me before sending your memo. It might have been good to talk it over so I could have had the benefit of your comments beforehand and been able to explain the fallacy of your criticism.

And it wouldn't have needlessly created a cause celebre by bringing in all the other people you cc'd. It even might have been helpful, certainly more businesslike. Let's do it this way next time.

Truly yours,

cc: Harry Adams   John Garfield, President
      Ginny Carpenter   Seth Gordon
      Bernie Fogel

A new business presentation went sour. Blame charges are rampant. You and your group made the actual presentation, using the data and rationale produced by other departments, so the blame is being leveled at you—unjustifiably.

LETTER TO THE COO. COPIES TO OTHER DEPARTMENT HEADS

Re: Below the belt scapegoating

Dear Mr. Fiorentino:

There's clamorous backbiting and unpardonable fingerpointing about the LDI presentation debacle. And people who are running for cover are insinuating that I and my group are the villains.

This is unfair, untrue, and is dodging responsibility. (Add a bit of underhanded tactics.)

We had to use the material from other departments (you know which ones by the above names). We had no choice. A play is only as good as the script. The actors need to follow the script. The script was lousy!

This is to set the record straight. Let this matter rest in peace.

Sig Rosenthal

cc: Ralph Sirota
        LaMoyne Carson
        Faith Michaels
        Cele Goldsmith

You are an official in your town government. Word is out that you are controversial. Indeed, certain people are putting this label on you and it has become a monkey on your back. To you this is a virtue because you pose intelligent arguments against unworthy issues. But it affects your standing in the town hall.

A LETTER TO THE TOWN'S PRIME OPINION MAKER

Dear Genevieve:

I have been given the image of being controversial. Some have gone so far as to say argumentative. I have never been preoccupied with what people think about me, but this has gone a bit far and should be put right.

I quote Antoinette Fouque, an active leader in the women's movement over the past quarter of a century. (Does it label her controversial?)—"All that matters is to express an opinion sincerely held. Convincing people is a form of violence."

Did her battles to make changes cause her to be considered congenitally argumentative? My attempts to speak out on what I'm convinced is right, often versus a strongly held opposing opinion, is an expression of a point of view that may be correct and beneficial to our community. Isn't it good to get divergent opinions? Doesn't it lead to better government?

So let's stop this nonsensical name-calling, which has often erupted into vile, personal, cowardly insults behind my back. I rest my case!

Warm regards,

Felicia Jones

ANOTHER LETTER

Subject: Critique of my market-research project

Dear Ron,

"The whole is the sum of its parts". . . A trite expression that's often quoted. More correctly—The whole is more than the sum of its parts.

Whichever way this axiom is stated, the point is: How can you summarize my investigation and then criticize it without reviewing all of its parts? I'm sure if you did so you would come to the same conclusion that I did. It's apparent that you skimmed over the highlights of what you thought were certain key points of my research, and therefore deduced incorrectly.

Ron, I ask that you review this again in depth, giving it the time that I think it deserves. And then let's talk about it.

Regards,

Fred Wardman

You made a bad mistake. You presented a product-research rationale that had an outright error of judgment which was unmercifully pointed out.

To: Ted, Leo, Kaelu,

You pointed out in unequivocal language the error of my reasoning in pursuing my research project—saying that I went down a royal path of failure. Pretty strong!

Did you ever see any leading-edge technological achievement that was done without setbacks? It's called experimentation, testing, development. A magic bullet never came about with one try. It takes dozens, and sometimes many more.

You should know, a discovery has to be preceded by mistakes. My team and I will get there because we know what we are doing!

Christine

P.S.   I'd like to tell you about Thomas Edison.

ANOTHER LETTER

Dear Sedgwick,

I can answer your criticism regarding my "mistake"—which is known as a temporary setback by those who are familiar with the pursuit of new technological breakthroughs—by quoting a statement made by Abraham Lincoln.

"Those who never made a mistake never made a discovery."

It marks the difference between those who discover and those who are happy to loll in sameness and stroll in lethargy.

By the way, my "mistake" was really a temporary setback...which, by the way, happens to everyone who seeks product breakthroughs.

Regards,

Jeff

ANOTHER LETTER

Re: Evaluation of My New Product Idea—(My report of 8/26)

Dear Rudolph,

About my "mistake"—which was not only noted, but also analyzed and reviewed and dissected at length.

This was not a mistake. It was one of the steps on the way to a successful end. As you well know, every innovation, every worthwhile product or program has to be preceded by experimentation. Call it trial and error if you wish. I prefer to call it research and development.

Obviously, we mustn't have too much experimentation without positive results. We have to intelligently build on the experience that was gained to have a successful conclusion.

I assure you this is being done intelligently.

Truly,

Frank

ANOTHER LETTER

Dear Todd,

Your comments and criticisms were quite cogent and definitive; however, the new product ideas in my theses suggested exploratory areas to think about and not clear-cut recommendations. In other words, they were ideas and not intended to be hard and fast R & D efforts to be put into the work hopper.

You also mentioned that the report was "not very good." What do you mean ? Do you mean that it is good but not *very* good? That it is not extraordinary but good? Or is this a euphemism for bad?

To further review this lapse in English (or in your understanding of new product exploration), would your statement saying "not very comfortable" with my ideas suggest being uncomfortable?

What I'm saying is that you are not clear in your writing—or for that matter in your criticism, or thinking. It leads one to say that your critique is not good. You are hedging. I guess it shows you are not sure, have no real opinion.

Let's leave it at that!

Truly,

Monica Travis

You are an investment adviser and made a bad call on a stock that went sour. A customer lost money on her portfolio because you plunged a big amount into it.

**A LETTER TO THE INVESTOR. YOU HAVE TO BUY HER UP SO SHE
WON'T LOSE CONFIDENCE IN YOU.**

Dear Ms. Winchester,

I sit here just as disappointed as you at the slide of Comquit Concepts, and I dare say the company's financial decline was a disappointment to a number of other investors as well. I must emphasize—this is a paper decline. It is not a loss because you will recover this money within the next six months to a year. The only thing that will hold it back is a major market collapse, and then everything and everybody will suffer.

Your other holdings are healthy, which will offset the Comquit downturn to a great extent.

Don't forget, stocks have built-in risk, unlike Treasury bonds for example, but the rewards can be far greater.

Don't be concerned. You are in the best of hands and you will recoup this paper loss in the course of future market trends.

Warm regards,

Philip Luongo

ANOTHER LETTER ON A SIMILAR SITUATION

Dear Dominique,

The stock/bond markets play strange games from week to week, and so do individual holdings. They fluctuate—at times with large swings, sometimes with small ups and downs. Stocks are more volatile than other corporate debts that are traded daily, such as bonds. They also have higher risks.

This didactic discourse doesn't make you feel any better—nor does it cheer me—because I also lost money. You are not alone. But you have outstanding experts advising you. In the long run, we are ahead of the market when it goes up, our loss is less than the market decline on a downward swing. Many on Wall Street refer to us as wizards. This label is well deserved.

Stay healthy, it's all that counts—

Franklin Tood

You've been insulted—blatant personal invectives, snide remarks. It would diminish you to respond in kind, or to each disparaging remark. Your strategy is to disregard particular insults, but rather to scorn, ridicule and impugn the character of the insulter. Send a letter—copies to the people who are witnesses to this attempted vilification.

To: Sherwood Marks

I'm shocked at your maniacal diatribes. They are so offensive to fundamental traditions of proper conduct and honesty as to be considered patently wrongful—as well as rude—and not worthy of comment.

Very truly,

Sara de Palma

cc: Angela Longstreet
      Amelia Weiss
      George Stickles

ANOTHER LETTER

Dear Mr. Bennett,

You asked why I didn't fight back when you made those senseless charges.

Your letter was so offensively personal, baseless and irresponsible that there was nothing else to do but crumple it and throw it away. It was ignored and has been forgotten.

Truly yours,

Jeanine Campbell

ANOTHER LETTER

Dear Harry,

You sounded off to the point of being insulting when you smashed Laura's ideas to little pieces, rebuking each one with cold comments of derision mingled with threats. You flailed away unmercifully.

Did you stop to realize our lack of creative input is your fault? Getting good ideas from people demands open-minded leadership and no intimidation. Another way of saying: you showed a lack of good leadership.

Respectfully,

Mike

You were the victim of a semi-public display of vile criticism regarding your operations plan for your school district.

Dear Mr. Sheridan,

Your vile disparagement of my very sensible plan leads me to believe you are making a political thrust at running the entire program of the school district's finances. This is a pallid effort because the only "good" idea you offered was to run down someone else's ideas.

You can get away with that for only a short time. The day of reckoning has to come when you have to look smart on your own—not by pointing out the deficiencies of other people.

What it means is that you can talk the talk, but can you walk the walk?

Truly,

Jacqueline Malmouth

ANOTHER LETTER

Dear Mary Jane,

I and most of the others on the committee agree. You overreached in trying to come up with a workable funding solution. You overreached and then
tried to put the blame for nonsuccess on us. You then compounded your
mistake by becoming shrill and vindictive.

What language you wrote! What insulting comments! I want to avoid having to defend myself or the committee because it would be unproductive.
I don't want to indulge in recriminations, or to participate in an orgy
of fixing blame.

Mary Jane, stop it ! You are being immature and silly.

Sincerely, and trying to help,

Phyllis

ANOTHER LETTER

Dear Richard:

You know, I feel like Jekyll and Hyde at the same time. Dr. Jekyll because
I want to pronounce a burial of the unwarranted, baseless and insincere
comments you made about my proposal for the gala we are planning. They
are insulting almost to the point of character assassination and unworthy of my comments.

My Mr. Hyde side wants to commend you for the seriousness of your endeav-
or to make this event a truly enjoyable and memorable happening. To have
it be an occasion we will all be proud of.

In short, you must stop your emotional outbursts and be sincerely constructive.

Regards,

Sally

SHOWING THE VALUE OF BOLD, NEW IDEAS

BOOST YOUR CANDIDACY FOR AN IMPORTANT POST AGAINST A FORMIDABLE OPPONENT.

Your rival for a desirable promotion to top management has corraled some potent supporters, because he has been entrenched in his position for a long time. He has written clever arguments about his views and vision for the organization that seem quite persuasive. You must diminish this, and disparage him without appearing to be flared up; no scurrilous insinuations, take the high road. It will also help you gain more allies.

A LETTER TO THE PEOPLE TO WHOM YOUR OPPONENT HAD WRITTEN, PLUS A FEW POTENTIAL ADHERENTS TO YOUR CAUSE

Dear Mr. Lukaitis:

I feel it is my duty to puncture the logic of Barry Langella's contentions as to the steps we should adopt to propel into the next century.

His rhetoric is quite impressive, but the guts of the proposal—namely the strategy—is quite weak. The urgent drive to seek the vertical acquisitions that he proposed should not be the essential focus. It's a sideshow rather than the center ring. Frankly, it's the kind of strategy that was demolished long ago. I feel that Barry is living in the past.

Rather we must concentrate on horizontal expansion, which is a 90-degree digression from what Mr. Langella proposed.

This should be where we concentrate our efforts. This is the way of successful expansion that has evolved and was recently proven. We must adopt a correct growth strategy; otherwise we will fall into a gradual decline.

I will shortly send a memo clarifying my views in more detail.

Very truly

Roberta Rifkin

cc: Jorge Espinosa
      Stephanie Lawes
      Blossom Tavernia
      Robert Xavier

ANOTHER LETTER

Dear Francesca:

Please, for the good of our entire organization, take a good look at my proposal for international expansion before making a decision. Specifically, please do this before adopting the plan that Bradley Strickland proposed.

I have a great deal of admiration for Dr. Strickland. His reputation is beyond criticism, and he has done much good for all of us during his long experience in this industry. I should say his energy and dedication are boundless, and he is a great thinker.

But on this issue I regret to say that Dr. Strickland is wrong. Not necessarily entirely wrong because I believe there are some strong and well thought-out proposals in his thesis. But modern thinking would indicate that he is wrong on the main premise, which could lead to an unfortunate consequence.

Allow me to present my case, which I will do by the end of the week. It just means waiting a few days—a very worthwhile few days, I believe.

Bernardette Costello

A DIFFERENT LETTER FOR A SIMILAR SITUATION

Re: TLB Software System for query responses

To: Mario

I regret that I must take issue with the major premise of Jean Winthrop's technique to stay in compliance with the new codes that were set up. You will find that her solutions are too general and often not directly related to the issues.

My team attacked this problem with a different and more modern technique that will provide greater specificity and reliability. To come to this solution I relied heavily on the technology that Jean's team constructed and took it a couple of steps further.

I want to thank Jean for showing the way, and it would be good—in fact it would be urgent—to have Jean work with me on finalizing this system, and on other projects too. Her talents and long-time experience are indispensable.

Irene

SOMEONE IS DEMEANING YOUR CAREFULLY CRAFTED PLAN
FIGHT BACK

To: Jacki Voorhees
        President

The erudite and well-documented sales plan of the Eddie group is fine in most of its details, but it has a wide-open hole that should be fixed, if possible.

Basically this is a strategy of survival by gradually wearing down the enemy, instead of aggressive forward momentum for a fast and sure conquest. The Eddie strategy is one that has been used by ineffectual army generals: Stand in place and fight, fight. . . The last one left standing wins.

I don't think we can win in this market by attrition: spend, spend, spend . . . and the one that doesn't go broke wins. This was a strategy of 20 and 30 years ago, but it could spell death now.

Marshal Fox

Another piece extolling youthful energy. You are a new computer service company in the running for a big contract. You submitted a pitch in response to a Request for Proposal.

THIS IS A FOLLOW-UP LETTER TO YOUR PROPOSAL SUBMISSION

Dear Fred:

You are hungry for new ideas! So are we!

We are young enough to know we cannot live in the present, because there is too much of the future ahead of us.

In our proposal that you received a few days ago, we kept very much to the specifications in your RFP, but there's a lot more to UNO Computer than you saw in our presentation. We hope you will come see us, and see first-hand our youthful vigor and our years-ahead systems. I'm sure this will strike you as soon as you enter the front door.

There is a lot to be said for youthful ambition in embarking on the quest for the new and the better.

We're looking forward to continuing in this competition.

Truly,

Paul McNulty
President

ANOTHER LETTER

Dear Mr. DiNapoli:

When you are building for the future isn't it best that you hire consultants who have much of the future ahead of them? Who will see 20 and 30 years hence the results of what they are responsible for now?

Rather than engaging people who have a long past history but will not experience much of the future for which their plans are intended?

Mr. DiNapoli, I think these questions answer themselves. Yes, we have studied the past, and know the best of the past, but we are committed to dwell in the future. And so is Alpha Structural Inc.

Best regards,

Stewart Holcomb
Vice President

SHOWING THE VALUE OF EXPERIENCE

The cover letter of a business plan that doesn't chart revolutionary paths but soundly recommends tried-and-true concepts. You are convinced it's better to be safe and sure than daring and wrong when a company's future and fortune are at stake. This is sound, hardheaded logic based on experience.

Dear Morgan:

We are presenting this plan understanding full well the solemn importance of the decision you must make. It is based on a serious investigation of the procedures and the cautions you must exercise.

You must be sure—you can't afford to be sorry. Sorry could easily mean disaster—at best, a bottom-line money loss and a market-share slide.

We are recommending fresh research and aggressive marketing assaults. But these are linked to tried-and-true principles, and only what was experience-proven to work admirably. In other words, we have placed the odds overwhelmingly in your favor.

We also suggest experimenting in small test areas. This is how to win in the long run. We're sure you will find this proposal to be careful and prudent with thoughtful boldness. It's the way to go. It's the way of tried-and-true experience.

Respectfully submitted,

Aaron Weiss

ANOTHER LETTER ALONG THE SAME LINE

Dear Russell:

We are very well regarded for constructing databases for companies in your industry, and in other fields. They all have the same purpose: to develop a tailor-made system for a company's special needs and wants, a marketing tool to propel it into healthy growth in the coming years and decades.

This requires good experience to build on and the talent for developing cutting-edge technology, both of which we have here in abundance. The talent is most effective when it is linked to with a history of inventiveness. Together they breed pragmatic solutions that go to the bottom line.

We very much want you to visit our site—the place where we work and create new technological systems to answer each client's individual requirements.

I'm sure you will find it interesting and well worth your time. I'll call to set a date.

Best regards,

Naomi Tuckman

LETTERS TO TRY TO PERSUADE A CLIENT NOT TO DUMP YOU FOR ANOTHER COMPANY—A NEW KID ON THE BLOCK

(Via Fax)

Dear Mr. Woijowski:

I understand you seem to be leaning toward a new shop comprised of young marketing consultants who broke away from a large company. Without giving unfavorable comments about youth (I greatly admire bright, young newcomers), however successful they previously were as employees in large firms, I request that you hold off on your decision until you talk with us further.

There are two points to consider. . .

> 1. An individual's success in a large company may be—and probably is—due to suggestions, counsel, advice, and orders of seasoned executives at the company.

2. Your business challenges in the years ahead are frightening if you don't have the benefit of historical perspectives that we are able to provide.

These are just thoughts to keep in mind, whether you choose us or someone else.

I'm anxious to meet with you again. I'll contact you tomorrow.

Very truly,

Logan DeMott

OTHER LETTERS—
POINTING OUT THE VALUE OF LONG EXPERIENCE

Dear Morton:

We've served you very well for six years; we have come up with new concepts that worked! We have charted new paths that turned out to be profitable!

Granted, not everything we proposed resulted in earth-shaking successes, and a couple, including the latest one, didn't work.

But the sum total is that your profits and net worth increased during our tenure, while some of your competitors' fortunes went downhill. Think about this before making a change.

Let's meet at lunch, just the two of us. I want to bounce off some new technology concepts that will blow your mind.

Regards,

Perry Flora

You are an officer of an advertising agency. A prospective account that you anticipated getting looks like it is leaning toward an agency that's been publicized for its youthful vigor.

Mr. James Simpson
President & CEO
Acorn Technology Services

Dear Mr. Simpson:

You are getting ready to make a tremendous decision: hiring an ad agency that will create campaigns for the new products you will be launching.

An innovative advertising approach, plus its smooth, error-free execution, will have a great deal of impact on your bottom line next year, not to say many years ahead. Insufficient insight into what provokes a buying decision and/or poor execution will be a setback, likely a serious one.

Who would you put in charge of this task? Do you want a wet-behind-the-ears group that scurries ahead with offbeat advertising on the excuse of being "creative"? That may or may not be what you need—and could well fall flat on its face. You have too much at stake for that, Mr. Simpson.

By all means, we believe in creativity, in charting new ways, seeking out your most likely customers and convincing them to buy your brand. We also have the seasoning, the wisdom, to intuitively understand what will work and what won't. Moreover, we have a track record that documents how we go about it...successfully.

Who do you want to take a chance with?

Truly,

Mary Cleary
President

ANOTHER LETTER

Dear Ms. Leigh:

I guess it has boiled down to a choice between impetuous youth and us, who have been ridiculously described as old-timers by our competition.

Don't pay attention to this slanderous misrepresentation. We are known as seasoned professionals. We carefully research and test, and do more testing. That's why we are successful. That's why we come up with out-of-the-ordinary promotion campaigns that get extraordinary results.

We have some great new campaign themes to show you that will back up what I'm saying here. We walk the walk, we don't just talk the talk!

I'll call you to arrange a meeting.

Best regards,

Jessica Swenson

ANOTHER LETTER

Dear Ms Kahoori:

Allow me to smash into little pieces the fallacy that we are stuck in a stereotype of being ordinary and hackneyed because some of us have a few gray hairs.

We have young, wet-behind-the-ears, four years out of college, unrepressed engineers who have been doing fine work. Most often, however, what sees the light of day is tempered by the hard-bitten experience of others around here.

What would make you feel better. . . Having impetuous youthful ardor or youthful ardor buttressed by the wisdom and polish that comes from experience?

I'm sure you'll see it as an easy choice. Grasping the best logical solutions is why you are running a successful business.

Best wishes,

Harry Slocum

You are doing scattered projects for a client, but, of course, you want to win the entire account. This client assigned you to create some sales promotion literature for its company—which you think could lead to a new marketing approach and more business. You do it by taking advantage of past experience—what worked well before, what failed, building on past successes and learning from past mistakes. This is a pragmatic, common-sense approach which has the best chance of succeeding.

A few people at this client's major supplier saw a rough draft, listened to an explanation of how you are proceeding and then spread the word that you are just dredging up old ideas. You must negate this.

LETTER TO THE CLIENT'S DIRECTOR OF MARKETING WHO IS RESPONSIBLE FOR IMPLEMENTING THE PROGRAM

You must explain that your experience is a necessary ingredient for a creative solution.

Dear Hortense:

I'm approaching your project in a very creative way, and also in a businesslike fashion. The two must go together so that your campaign is not merely successful, but a sky-high blockbuster that will help you out-distance your competition.

A lot is at stake for your company—and for you and me personally. This has to work superlatively well; therefore it has to be the ultimate, not just good.

The best strategy, to my mind, and I'm certain you agree, is to draw on what was most successful in the past and give it a contemporary and exciting approach. In other words, we're doing what could be sure-fire successful and giving it a modern, even futuristic look that will propel it further. We don't want to take chances by traipsing through the unknown. And neither do you.

I'll show you a preliminary review of what we've done and I'll ask for your thoughts on how to finalize it. Let's keep in mind, we will succeed by drawing on the past so as to better chart the future.

All the best,

Seth Berger

ANOTHER LETTER FOR A SIMILAR SITUATION

Dear Dr. Langbaum:

In moving forward on your project, we're pulling out all stops as to futuristic thinking. We're creatively charting next generation ideas.
But. . .

We are also taking full advantage of history—

> *"History is a better guide than good intentions"*
>
> (Jeanne J. Kirkpatrick)

As a service company, we approach assignments in this business-like manner, yet we don't hold back on far-out creativity. That is why our success record is a standout in the industry. I'll call you about setting up a progress report meeting.

Cordially,

Kim Toon

ANOTHER LETTER TO ADDRESS A SIMILAR PROBLEM

Dear Debra:

We believe that one of the important reasons for our company's growth in the 20 years we've been in business is sticking to a certain discipline in creating solutions for our clients, to explore the past while charting the future.

Our company has a reputation in the industry for technology breakthroughs—and innovative solutions to marketing problems.

There are other standout reasons for our success, including impeccable client service, and a clear understanding of our clients' needs. But, again, new ideas—that is, new ideas that are practical, forthright, solidly based—are a big feature in our forward momentum.

Thank you for your assignment. We take this as a special challenge, namely, a platform for obtaining more of your business later on.

Norm Langella

ANOTHER LETTER

Dear Mr. Ostermark:

In moving forward on your project we came up with a wonderful, forward-thinking idea. It's an entirely new approach. It encompasses a previous theme but gives it a contemporary look and feel. In other words, we took the best part of history and gave it a fresh twist.

Isn't this a more certain formula for success than an untried approach?

We have an outstanding record in innovative technological solutions—i.e. solutions that work. It doesn't mean we summarily cast aside what has been done. We go on the premise that the challenges ahead are more frightening if you have no historical perspective.

We urge you to look on our presentation with this in mind.

Best regards,

Gene Freedman

OTHER LETTERS

Dear Morgan:

How would you like to be on a plane in which the pilot has only 200 hours flying time? This is when most accidents occur due to pilot error. If seasoned pilots didn't watch over them they would be killing a lot more people.

You get the point, Morgan. The analogy holds for your marketing plan. Regardless of what I believe some people are telling you, you're in good hands because we have a good mix of experience and fresh thinking. It holds your best chance of success—to again use the airplane metaphor—of not crashing and getting killed. It's because we don't go off in the wild blue yonder and come up with wild schemes that wind up in a tailspin, that won't work.

By the way, we have some ideas you'll find fresh and timely. They are great because they are built on a bedrock of creative thinking and the knowledge of what moves people to buy.

I'll call you to review this in its preliminary stage.

Warm regards,

Sven Hansen

ANOTHER LETTER

Dear Otto:

> *Experience is a great moderator.*
> *It can also save money by discarding nutty ideas.*

The purpose of this letter is to let you know that we did our homework, very thoroughly, in coming up with our recommendation on your b-to-b sales catalog.

Please dispel any notion that we went for the tried-and-true and didn't introduce new concepts. You'll find our total recommendation to be a new concept—it is brimming with fresh ideas. . . *that will work.* It is built on sure-thing concepts that succeeded before which we filtered through our thinking. They are spiced with new twists, new excitement and new kinds of words and graphics.

I'll call you about lunch. I know of a new restaurant that serves great food. You'll like it a lot.

Regards,

Andy

RECOVERING FROM MISTAKES THAT COULD UNDO YOU

GLOSS OVER A SERIOUS BLUNDER THAT HURTS YOUR CLIENT, AND MAKE A FAST COMEBACK FROM POTENTIAL DISASTER.

SITUATION: You are a middle-management VP at a Wall Street financial powerhouse, McCool & Co., on a zoom track to the top, marked by your smart, effective stewardship of an important client, Largesse Data Processing. Now you are sitting at your desk in shock, distraught and scared.

You were just informed of a high-visibility goof in an important and innovative financial plan you presented to this client. It underestimated the profit picture by 8%. Quite damaging, but not fatal, it nevertheless cast a dark shadow on the veracity of the entire presentation. To make matters worse, the client caught the error, and its Marketing VP phoned you with the bitter news.

You see your brilliant reputation and sure-fire ascent to top management being shredded, your career eroding like a storm-ravaged beach. You must pull yourself together for rescue and rehabilitation. NOW.

STRATEGY: Don't trivialize the error so as to seem uncaring.

Make it look like a small glitch. Stress that this was known before the client called, and it's been fixed.

It won't affect results to any big extent. The program's viability is beyond question.

The schedule must continue as before, even accelerated for a fast-as-possible start. Once the program is in the works, it will create its own momentum, and the goof will soon be forgotten.

The glitch is due to a supplier's error, but you, the team leader, accept responsibility. The buck stops here.

Massage the egos of the client's people. They'll enjoy personal accolades when this industry-shaking program is introduced.

Make corrections by tonight. Early tomorrow morning replace the tainted pages with corrected ones, at the client and internally.

You must come out looking good, even a hero, your top-seed reputation untarnished.

Tomorrow morning deliver a letter to the client's Marketing VP that buttresses this strategy—all in a page and a half, single spaced—plus a short private P.S. to the same guy, on a separate page.

October 15, 1996

Mr. Gordon F. Chandler,
Senior Vice President, Marketing
Largesse Data Processing, Inc.

Re: 11/12/96 Launch—
        Asset Marketing Program

Dear Gordon:

Sometimes two minds go into sync at about the same time. The day before you called me on the cost figure, we had been going through the process of double and triple checking all the numbers and found this glitch. We then revised the estimate, and I was within an hour of calling you when I got your ring.

You'll be glad to know, however, that we expect to come close, or even hit the profit we had previously projected because of savings in other parts of the program. As always, we've been conservative in our cost estimates and figured on the high side to allow a margin for contingencies.

Most importantly, Largesse is set to achieve—and may well exceed—the business and financial objectives you have established.

Additionally, this trailblazing program will further enhance, in a big way, Largesse's reputation as the industry's pacesetter. It will certainly reflect on the people who are involved in this program.

Gordon, just think how the entire financial community and the big players in information processing—not to say the investing public and the print and broadcast media—will sit up and take notice when this hits the public, just four weeks from now. Our staff has been working around the clock to smooth along this launch date. All systems are in place; we'll start on schedule.

As an afterthought, everything is hush-hush here, and we're taking pains, as you are, to avoid any leaks. The PR gurus are starting to get the publicity juices flowing, so we expect a media blast a few days prior to the launch. Those in the media who, of necessity, have a hint of what will happen are keeping it under wraps.

Please be prepared for requests from the press and broadcast media titans for statements from you, your top management, and your associates. It would be good to have someone in your PR department keep it under control, and I'll work with you on this. Any media requests that come to us will be checked out with you, of course.

Best ever,

Michael M. Hemming,
Vice President

MMH/jr

P.S. to Gordon

By the way, the cost glitch was due to a misplaced figure by one of our suppliers, but obviously, the responsibility rests with me.

The McCool people have the revised pages of the plan presentation and will be inserting them in all the copies at your offices. I'm sure that you and Largesse's management directors will be pleased.

Gordon, if you are available for lunch tomorrow, let's do it, and we can talk about implementing the details—the guts of which are neatly covered in the plan. Who does what and when. If not lunch, let's do this in the morning. I think we should also discuss setting up a meeting of our respective staffs.

M.M.H.

▌A CARELESS MISCUE MAKES YOU LOOK BAD.

Two Situations, Two Letters

SITUATION I: You are a partner in an accounting firm. A report contain-
ing some financial information was supposed to be faxed
to your client. Instead, it went to an unknown company because your secretary transposed two digits in the phone number incorrectly. The recipient
was good enough to look up the correct number and relayed the fax to the
right party. Fortunately, the information made no sense to the people who
mistakenly received it.

Your client was incensed, expressed it loudly, and asked for an explanation.

STRATEGY II: How do you explain a dumb, careless error? There is no
excuse. Try to toss it off without appearing to make light of
it, and assure the client it will never happen again.

From now on you have to check every fax, every letter, every message to this
company. It's little things like this that could make you look stupid and alien-
ate a client.

```
November 16, 1996

Mr. Charles Claypool,
Vice President
Regent Technologies, Inc.

_____

_____


Dear Chuck:

Thanks for letting us know about our error in dispatching a fax intend-
ed for you to another company we don't even know. It was unpardonable.
It will never happen again.

It had private information, as you pointed out. Something you don't want
your competitors to know.

But, fortunately, the information was not really confidential. If it had
been, we obviously would not have sent it by fax. The people who got it
and were good enough to look you up and call you had no inkling whatso-
ever of what it meant. It could have been a foreign language to them.
```

Don't get me wrong. This is not an excuse.

One of our secretaries, who has been extremely reliable, transposed two of the digits in the phone number. It was human error combined with the unforeseen perils of technology.

Even though this hasn't caused any harm, we're by no means taking it lightly. Some day I'll tell you about the ugly repercussions around here, with my taking most of the beating because it was my letter. You know— the buck stops here.

Chuck, thank you for your understanding. It will not happen again. Of this you can be sure.

Best regards,

cc: Ms. Jill Harrison
      V.P. & Chief Financial Officer

SITUATION II: You are in charge of a testing lab that is researching the efficacy of a weight-reduction drug formulated by your client, a health-systems company. You sent early top-line results, which had a "bonehead" ridiculous error: figures for the test product and the placebo were reversed. It was caught the next day, and you have to report the correction.

STRATEGY II: No harm done. Thankfully, you caught the error before your client brought it to your attention. It could have been a *cause celebre* with embarrassing implications if not discovered quickly.

Fax the correction right away, then mail the original. Give it a light touch. Have them smile instead of frown.

October 18, 1996

Dr. Michael Pryor, President
Leander Health Systems

_____

_____

(By Fax)

Dear Mike:

There was a typo error in the figures we sent you yesterday morning on the top-line G45 results. The results on the test panel and the placebo panel were reversed, and we caught it pretty quickly.

Here is the weight loss after the first 90 days of usage.

> Average % weight loss
> After 30 days
> Test 5.8%
> Placebo 4.7

As you see, it looks like the new weight-reduction formula is on the right track. According to the evidence so far, there are no adverse reactions of any consequence.

For some reason there is a smaller, although fairly significant, weight reduction with the placebo group at this early stage. This is likely a matter of the panel, early results, or halo effect.

Mike, when we first looked at the wrong figures we sent yesterday, we thought we had a wondrous new discovery in the placebo. We started to analyze what was in it. You've heard of great scientific breakthroughs from fortuitous accidents. No such luck here.

At any rate, it's good to give you this information. I'm sorry I can't report a new discovery. However, we can say that your test formulation is working well so far. Don't forget, however, that it's at an early stage.

Best wishes,

EXCUSE A BAD ERROR BY BLAMING ANOTHER PARTY (THE GOVERNMENT IN THIS CASE).

SITUATION: You are the chief executive of a waste-management company that has a choice contract with a large national construction company. In a waste cleanup at one of its sites, your office was careless about checking thoroughly with the EPA as to environmental problems and special rules at this location. You okayed this operation, assuming, from similar cleanup jobs, there was nothing to be concerned about.

Wrong! Your employees were two days into the work when the client's site manager said you were violating the rules. You checked and found he was correct.

You had to stop the work and regroup. Your men had to undo the damage before proceeding. It cost money, but luckily no summons had been issued and no charges were filed. Think of the horror if the site manager hadn't told you. He informed his boss that you were about to cause an emergency, but he averted it with his good thinking.

STRATEGY: Your company, an outstanding name in waste management, is in a bad spot, and so are you—humbled and humiliated. There is no reasonable explanation. But you must try.

One excuse is to blame the government; most people have empathy with this. Even so, you must admit the mistake and note that you faced it, solved it, and saw to it that your client was not harmed. Here's more proof of the reliability of your company. You also have to give a nod of thanks to the site manager who saved you. Fortunately, you didn't lose a good customer. You might have.

Mr. Janusz Sowinski
Vice President
Harrison Construction Co.

_____

_____

Dear Mr. Sowinski:

What follows is an example of how hard it is at times to get proper information from the government, which is crucial in our business. The printed rules are often difficult to understand, even for experts in this industry such as us. Further, the regulations change and the interpretations change. This one certainly changed from what they told us, which we were using as a guideline.

It all boils down to the fact that what we told you about the EPA rule on the waste cleanup at your Stockton site was incorrect, even though we checked with the Washington office in advance and were assured of being in compliance with the regulations.

To his credit, your site manager informed us about it. I thanked him then, and I thank him now. I thank you for your understanding.

We have taken care of it. There is no harm done. No need to be concerned about any penalties or any bad reaction.

As I said, it's so difficult to make sure of regulation compliance, with the EPA as well as with so many other agencies.

We are scrupulous about avoiding any problems, but an unintentional mistake can creep through.

It shows that even a dominant company in this industry can make a mistake when it comes to untangling the regulations of the government bureaucracies—federal, state, and local.

Fortunately, we have damage-control procedures for this highly unlikely chance. We protect you against untoward circumstances that are not your doing, and this is what was important in this episode.

Best wishes,

Patrick Murphy

A CUSTOMER CAUGHT YOUR OVERCHARGE AND NOW QUESTIONS YOUR INTEGRITY.

SITUATION: You run a trucking company. A customer's credit allowance was misstated, to your benefit. You knew it when it happened, but you were too busy putting out fires and figured you would get to it eventually. The customer caught it and raised a fuss. He indicated you were less than honest and threatened to dump you.

STRATEGY: A letter of sincere regret and repentence. You plead innocent. It's a computer mishap. Display embarrassment and outrage at your computer maestros who made the mistake, albeit an honest one.

It will never happen again. Your damage-doers have been chastised. Your information system is now error-proof. Guaranteed.

Mr. Jack Schultz
Warehouse Manager
Maritime Cargo Warehousing, Inc.

Dear Jack:

There's a lot to be said for computer technology and management information systems (MIS). But they sometimes replace human error with computer error.

Yes, despite the up-to-date data-processing technology we have installed at enormous expense, sometimes errors occur. My technicians can tell you how this could happen. I can't really decipher all of their technical lingo.

Yes, it was a computer error that caused us to understate the value of your merchandise returns. To put it mildly, it's extremely embarrassing.

I apologize for this mistake, and I'm sending you the amount we owe you. I raised hell with my technical people, and it won't happen again.

If it does, I'll double any money due you because of an error. I'm making this bet to show you how certain I am that from now on we will be error-free on your account.

All the best,

Jennifer Cummings

cc: Mr. John C. Aubrey, Jr.
       Comptroller

IMPROVE YOUR STATUS

| A ROUGH, TOUGH NEW GROUP TOOK OVER YOUR COMPANY. THEY DON'T SEE YOU FITTING IN.

SITUATION: Your company, a giant food processor and marketer with traditional brands that are in almost every household pantry, merged into another dominant consumer-products company.

The other side took over. Five of their top people, the new president and four of his cronies, are now running the combined operation—their way. They had a big hand in making the merger deal, with the help of financiers, bankers, lawyers, and accountants.

The new culture is a sea change from your former polite, staid surroundings. Now it is blood and guts. These guys are bold, brash, witty, and profane. They ridicule policies and rules and are certain of their invincibility.

Their great success so far baffles you, except that they've been in the right place at the right time, and are experts in the arena of corporate politics. Nice guys, but rough and tumble.

You are the VP head of the Special Markets Division, responsible for non-retail sales. A tidy spot, and important, but out of touch with the glamour of the business.

Your patrician appearance and manner and your semi-British way of speaking, a product of your youthful upbringing in an area of eastern Canada, is a sorry handicap in this new environment.

202

They look on you as a plodding bureaucrat, necessary but merely a good behind-the-lines logistics officer. This new management clique and their wives socialize together constantly; in the workplace they continually toss shoot-from-the-hip business ideas at each other. Some good, some fair, but mostly lousy.

The president, the leader of the pack, is a country-club type who is on a first-name basis with various show-biz celebrities.

Your new chief is riding a high road to glory as long as the business continues to thrive. His macho coterie is riding along with him. You want to ride behind. First of all, to secure your job. Second, to take even a baby step into the high road.

You are a consummate survivor. You are also smart. You'll find a way.

STRATEGY: Send the president a provocative memo—and send copies to the clique members. Display your brilliance. Tell them about the deals you've made with boldness and panache that are bringing wealth and stature to the company. Whet their appetites. Don't give the names of the famous companies and institutions you made deals with or any of the details. You must fire up their curiosity. Make them want to ask for more. Have them include you in their scheme of things.

Your writing has to be down-to-earth, brusque, pithy, and informal, in line with the life-style this group proudly flaunts.

You have to turn your image around. You are not a bland, ponderous, dull-as-crabgrass, back-room cipher. You are au courant, sharp, and audacious—like them.

```
To:     Joseph Reynolds, President
        Harry Abelson
        Jim Harrigan
        Barry McIntyre
        Neil Peters

From:   G. Carter Hedrick

Re:     A Turn-on Message from the Guy in Charge of Special Markets

Being a veteran here (eight years), and as the head of the Special
Markets Department, I want to give you an overview of what I've been
doing—the deals that are in the works, and those I have pending. I think
you'll find them exciting.
```

It Will Get Your Creative Juices Flowing

I'm sure you will see ways in which you can fit these things in to what your fertile minds are planning. By the way, it would help me to know what your plans are so that I can tilt my thinking (for future deals) to fit in with what you want to do.

I Need Your Ideas

Along these lines, it will be a big help to put my proposals and ideas up front for your finishing touches and your comments. Tell me which are lousy, which are great, which are strokes of genius, which are like an angel tapped my shoulder. It will be so satisfying and pleasant to get this kind of input at last, sort of like sipping Johnnie Walker Black, neat.

Here's A Taste (No Pun Intended)

This is some of what I've being doing. I'll make it short and to the point. The complete descriptions, details, cost figures, and so on, are buttoned down in good-looking, bound reports.

- Harvard Business School would be proud of the way it's done. You can read these reports anytime you want to. I'll tell you now that all these programs are cost-effective and are good for our business or they wouldn't be around.

- Our Delightful Grains brand is now on the menu at school lunchrooms in 83 school districts in 30 markets, with a total population of 48 million, including 10 million school kids.

  I'm working on getting this into more schools nationwide.

  Also, many of the kids are being given samples to take home.

  It was tough to crack this market, but we've done it.

- Tasty Bran and Macaroni n' Cheese are now on the meal trays of three major U.S. airlines and two foreign ones. We'll be getting more airlines soon as well as cruise ships.

- We've always done well with the hospital-nursing home trade, and our sales are getting heftier there. I have some great contacts, which solidify our position in this market with a good chance for further penetration.

- Think of this. The White House commissary is stocking six of our brands—so far. Yes, the President's White House in D.C. We can even flaunt this in our PR.

- We had to do a lot—like make food donations for flood and hurricane victims (tax deductible). We also sent three of our nutritionists into disaster areas.

I don't know why this hasn't been hyped to the media, but it may not be too late. It shows how we have sometimes not been able to exploit things to the maximum.

When Can We Get Together and Talk?

Now that you've gotten a nibble, how about putting your imagination into orbit? Give me direction so I can be side-by-side with what you have in mind on the overall scheme. I'm sure I can help with many of the things you are planning to do.

I'll drop by your offices.

Standing by,

G. Carter Hedrick,
VP, Special Markets

▌BREAK INTO THE POWER EPICENTER.

Two Situations

Two Strategies

SITUATION: Everyone in the company knows who the superstars are. The smart, sophisticated, articulate, witty, and charming few—the decision makers. Grouped together in their private circle both at work and at play, they enjoy being at the center of power. They are on the inside track of shaping their individual destinies.

You crave to get accepted into this policy-making elite.

It may take a deliberate yet disingenuous campaign to eventually break in— if you are worthy and the right material.

STRATEGY I: Do it slowly and choose the opportunity carefully. You see a start—a business plan that one of the power-core leaders has produced. Throw bouquets at it and praise the author without seeming to kow-tow.

You can't be obvious or odious. In a very short memo, you must project cleverness, urbanity, sophistication—without affectation. Go for it.

```
To:    Millicent Vandexter
From:  Michael O'Hara
```

Dear Millicent:

I happened to see the document you put together—*Report and Plan of Action—Marketplace Development.*

Even though this topic is not in my specific province, and even at the risk of seeming to patronize you, I must make one point.

It is great, a matter of pride for the company. Of ultimate importance, the bottom line is that it will work.

Your piece brought to mind a sequel that might make sense. Sort of a gratuity to this excellent plan. When you have some time, I'd like to share this thought with you to see what you think.

Millicent, you came up with a first-rate idea. Equally outstanding is your way of implementing it. You're great at transforming a concept into first-class action.

Regards,

Bernie Samuels

SITUATION II: The ruling council at the organization where you work—a quasi-government entity to help our legislators bring government closer to the people—consists of polished individuals from prestige, big-name universities. You, a product of lesser known academe and of plain social background, are just as smart, just as ambitious, and just as able and qualified. Mission: Get into this elite club. Be one with the shapers of policy. You are convinced you have as much or more to offer as any of them.

STRATEGY II: Send a letter to the chairman of the association.

Bring to her attention that the fortunate people in the power circle seem to all have the same appearance, act the same, and have the same outlook in facing problems.

A few came from humble beginnings but were assimilated into the ranks of the rulers. Having been at the top of the influence structure for many years, they are out of touch with the habits, hopes and thinking of ordinary people, the vast 95% whom they lead.

Focus on your image of the common touch. You are as well educated, as sophisticated, and as smart as the ruling clique. And you know how to get to the heart and mind of Joe and Jo Citizen.

Ms. Johanna Wilson
Chairperson
Governmental Structuring Association
110 Connecticut Avenue
Washington, D.C.

Dear Ms. Wilson:

As a GSA administrator in the Chicago office, may I make a suggestion that I know will put our organization closer to the public pulse and make us more effective in addressing people's needs. It should greatly expand our ability to influence the vast heterogeneous public.

It's obvious to me that those in the ruling circle at our D.C. head-quarters are products of pretty much the same privileges and educational backgrounds. Some came from advantaged families, others were born into humble households, but all have been out of touch for most of their adult lives with what's taking place with American families today.

How many had to take out second mortgages to make ends meet? How many had the dark rigor of having to find work when there was no work to be found? How many went without essentials in order to build a business? How many had to search for a loan when it meant survival and money was exceedingly tight? How many had to go to public clinics when their children were ill? Very few, if any, really.

All are brilliant scholars, truly. They received their education at elite power universities and then on to the most acclaimed graduate schools.

Other people, and I include myself, of humble backgrounds, and with less prestigious but very creditable educational credentials are out of the loop here. We have a tremendous handicap in getting into the top crust of this organization.

I say with deference, Ms. Wilson, that we need more diversity in the selection of policy-making managers. Diversity of family, work experience, and education, as well as gender, race, and age. This is what will make us more closely attuned to mainstream America.

Further, we, the not so fortunate, also want the challenge and the opportunity. We are also ambitious and capable.

Thank you so much for your time.

Respectfully,

Joseph DiCrescenti

THERE'S A SPECTACULAR CAREER-BOOSTING OPPORTUNITY THAT YOU CAN ONLY ACCESS BY BEING GENTLE AND HUMBLE.

SITUATION: You are a human-resources associate at an aircraft manufacturer for the military and civilian markets. It's a
junior executive job. An ad hoc corporate committee was set up, at the
request of the Defense Department, to advise it on the conversion of
military personnel skills to civilian uses. The purpose is to develop concrete proposals to help the Pentagon outplace inactivated military people.

This is a great coup for the company. The PR drumbeaters have been
hyping it for days. You must get involved. Even if it's in an unimportant
way, even on the periphery, as long as your name can be identified with
this project. It would be a spectacular entry on your resume. Here is your
big chance to stand out from the ordinary plodders in your next career
move.

STRATEGY: Write to the committee chairman. Plead with him to get
you into the loop, just so you can say you were part of this
program. Tell him of your deep-rooted interest, your academic background in
the subject, and how useful you can be. You are willing to help in any way, however menial, even if he chooses to use you for as little as a couple of hours a
week.

Imagine the distinguished people you'll be rubbing elbows with. Think of the
important contacts you'll be making. Make it almost impossible to get a total
refusal. When you are in, you can then look for ways to pirouette up the line
to a meaningful position.

Mr. Jeremy T. Martin
Vice President
Kendor Aircraft Company

_____

_____

Re: Military Personnel
       Conversion Committee

Dear Mr. Martin:

Please consider my exceptional background in the work your committee is assigned to accomplish, and my sincere interest in its mission.

Although my plate is quite full as a member of Kendor's Human Resources Department, I am eager to help, even after hours, if need be, because I know I can make a meaningful contribution.

My college courses in human resources included many hours of study in retraining and personnel allocation, and I've done original research in this sub-specialty. My work at Kendor has received high ratings, and I continually upgrade my abilities through extensive reading.

Specifically, I will be useful in doing research, editing, correspondence, and in meeting and conference details. I am even willing to do secretarial or clerical duties, or work in whatever capacity you see fit to use me at this time.

Regardless of the amount of time I put in, even if it's as little as two hours a week, there is one thing that is certain: you'll find me to be productive.

May we please meet to discuss this? I'll drop by your secretary's desk to find out when you will be available. All I ask is just a few minutes of your time.

Very truly yours,

Elizabeth McDonald

YOUR BOSS SCREWED UP. YOU DECIDE TO TAKE THE HEAT. NOW HE OWES YOU ONE.

SITUATION: You are a marketing manager at a long-distance phone company. Your job is customer procurement, for which you conduct tie-in promotions with other companies.

Your boss, the VP of marketing, thought up an idea for a promotional offer on packages of high-turnover food products sold in supermarkets. He nego-tiated a deal with Happy Bakers for its popular priced, widely distributed brand of cakes and cookies. He was head-high proud at having pulled this off. Top management was equally enthusiastic, for we were getting into bed with a great consumer-brand franchise.

Right from the beginning you had reservations about the kind of offer being made. Further, the people who buy Happy Bakers products are mainly blue-collar, middle and low income, which is not your market.

You told this to your boss, but he shut you up fast. You had to go along. Your job is to dutifully carry through on projects once they are approved. You can't be an unimaginative doomsayer.

First, you did a test in two markets. The test had flaws in that it was difficult to segregate the baked-goods distribution to two small areas. Results were okay, maybe, but not really conclusive. However, the optimistic fervor of the key executives caused them to be seen as good. The order from your boss was, let's go—now we roll-out to the whole country.

This had to be done in stages, because of Happy Bakers' distribution pattern. You are now in 30% of the country and moving ahead.

The promotion bombed. Badly. How do you spread this news? Who is to blame?

STRATEGY: If you let the chips fall as they deservedly should (your boss made a deplorable judgment call) your boss will hate you. If you protect your boss from blame, even at your own expense, he'll love you for your loyalty. He'll protect you from harm now, and you can expect your just reward sometime later.

You believe the latter option is the smarter thing to do. You send a memo to your boss about the sad news. You take the blame because you convinced him to do it, noting that the fault is yours.

Your boss will be able to show this memo to his management colleagues so they will know that his underling is the one who fell down. It will take the sting off him. Keep the documents handy that show your boss' faulty judgment, such as his directives to you, his flash of inspiration, asking for your input, etc.

Unless your boss has become insane, he is fully aware of the true story. Your devotion is inscribed, and he will respect you for shouldering the burden of responsibility in true executive style. He now owes you a reward or two sometime later.

```
To:    Seth
From:  Jason
```

I got more figures on our joint promotion with Happy Bakers. I'm sorry to report it hasn't changed for the better from last week.

The downside. . . The response to our offer is continuing to decline. At this level of sales we're losing money on every customer we get, even if the figures project out to a normal level of ongoing call volume. We're also losing money on store displays, flyers, etc.

The upside. . . So far we only have exposure in 30% of the country. We can pull the plug now and stop the roll-out before it goes any further.

Everyone was excited about this deal. They were sure it was going to be a winner. The two-market test we did showed good promise and gave us the signal to move ahead. But the roll-out didn't live up to test indications.

I firmly recommend that we cut our losses. If you agree, I will inform Happy Bakers and the suppliers who are involved.

I'll have to take the responsibility on this. I handled it all the way. You sold it to management on the test results and on my assessment as well as my recommendation, which I believed was logical at the time.

The ball game isn't over. There will be more product promotions this year. So far our batting average is good, even with this miscue.

▌GOING OVER YOUR BOSS' HEAD FOR A TRANSFER ▌AND MORE MONEY.

SITUATION: Your immediate supervisor is very hard to work with. He's abusive and humiliates you if you don't adhere to his poorly stated instructions. Others have the same problem. He refuses to transfer you, and you haven't gotten a raise in two years.

You are ambitious, you want to move up and make more money. To do this, you feel you have to get out from under your boss and transfer to another division in the company. The company as a whole is a fine place in which to work, with good benefits and room for advancement.

STRATEGY: You have to go up the chain of command to the chief offi-
                 cer of the division.

You must get his attention and make him aware of your problem with a
respectful appeal to his sense of duty as overseer of all employees in his division. As such, he is responsible for efficiency and productivity, which
involves good employee relations.

You can't appear to be insubordinate or a trouble-maker. You must convince
this top man of your loyalty to the company.

Don't make grave personal charges against your boss. You might be called
upon to prove them, which could cause a problem and rebound against you.
Nor should you involve others at this stage.

The chief will ask to see you so that he can have more details. Tell him without censuring your boss, overtly diminishing his value to the company, or
interjecting your personal feelings. Make sure what you say is credible, and
keep your demeanor businesslike.

You don't want to be dismissed or have your future at the company compromised.

To: Mr. Scott Pilney
        Vice President, Information Services
        Regency Data Processing, Inc.

From: Harriet Rosner

Dear Mr. Pilney:

I have been administrative assistant in the MIS section for the past
three years. After reading further you'll understand why I am writing
directly to you.

I admire my supervisor, Mr. Ralph Jonas, for his technical competence
and his dedication in carrying out his assignments. However, I find him
very difficult to work for, with the result that I'm not able to perform
to my potential. This has become intolerable and is causing me a great
deal of anguish.

I made a formal request to Mr. Jonas for a transfer to another department, which he refused to sanction. Further, I haven't received a raise
in two years.

I am very conscientious. I know my duties well, and I want to do the best possible job for Regency Data Processing. But I'm in a stressful situation with apparently no chance of advancement.

I urge you to consider my request for a transfer so that I can better exercise my abilities. All I ask for is this opportunity. I'm proud and happy to be working for Regency, and I want to make this company my career. It's my goal to do well here.

You should know that I am writing this on my own and do not suggest that this troubling situation occurs with any other people in my department.

Thank you so much, Mr. Pilney, and please understand my need to contact you directly. As you see, I have no choice.

Respectfully yours,

Rebecca Lieber

THORNY JOB ISSUES

GET RID OF A PROBLEM ASSISTANT WITH A SMOKE SCREEN OF MAGNANIMITY.

SITUATION: You are a division chief in a data-communications company heading up its business-networks department. Your assistant is brilliant, resourceful, ambitious and headstrong, not to mention impatient in scurrying up the ladder.

He upstages you in meetings as a tacit demonstration of his superior abilities. Cunningly, he avoids any outward indication of disloyalty; in fact, he even puts on a display of die-hard allegiance.

Simply put, he is a threat to your job. You have to get rid of him. But how do you do it to someone who is bright, gifted, hard working, and has made everyone aware of the superb job he is doing? The rest of the staff consider you lucky to have him working for you.

STRATEGY: Voila! A job has opened up in another department. It's a nice step up from your deputy's current rank, a good promotion for him.

Recommend him for the position. You hate to lose him but why hold a good man down? Management should give him a break. He has earned it. This clearly unselfish gesture, for the corporate good, demonstrates to all your outstanding executive posture.

You won't be left in the lurch. You already have a replacement on tap.

214

```
To:    Mr. Frank DiClemente
       Vice President, Marketing and Planning
       PCI Data Networks Inc.

From:  Ted Zimmermann
```

LET'S NOT HOLD A GOOD PERSON DOWN

I'm talking about my assistant, Tony Rivers. It regards the position that is open as New Products Manager.

Tony has been doing a great job for me, as we all know, and I would really hate to lose him. But he is ready for an upward move, and I know he yearns for it.

It would be good for the company to give Tony a chance to prove himself in this spot, and I'm confident he'll make it. It goes without saying that we have to move our good people along and up when an opportunity arises.

It would ordinarily be tough for me to find a replacement. However, I have someone in mind who is ready and able. I'm sure he'll be able to fill Tony's shoes with no lost motion.

Why not give Tony a break when he is ready for it? And importantly, when he has earned it.

YOU HAVE TO FIRE THE RELATIVE OF AN IMPORTANT CLIENT.

SITUATION: The executive VP of one of your big-time clients asked if you would give his nephew a job in your company, a large food wholesaler. You put the lad to work in client and customer relations. He is capable, but nowhere near a world-beater, and you cannot have him take on more responsibilities without upsetting other, more deserving people.

He has to be let go. But very, very carefully so as not to make waves with his uncle.

STRATEGY: Send a private memo to him in which you laud his performance and note that letting him go is intended to further his career advancement. You'll try to help him find another spot that will be more suitable for his talents and ambition.

You can be sure he will show your memo to his uncle.

PRIVATE AND CONFIDENTIAL

To: Jim Ambrose

From: G. Clark Walker

This won't make you feel good now, but in the long run you'll look back and be very happy I did it.

As you can see when you look around, we're reorganizing our entire staff. What it comes to is that there is really no room for advancement for people at your level. The people above you are well ensconced, and at their ages they'll be around here many years.

Jim, you're too good a guy, too talented, too smart, and have too much potential to be locked into a static position like this.

We really hate to lose you. But we want you to be in a place where you can now start to blossom. Your next move should be a bigger job than you have here. Look on this as an opportunity for career development.

You have the run of all the facilities here if necessary—your office, the phone service, typing help and so on. We'll do all we can to help you connect with the right spot. I personally will get in touch with friends in the business.

This is a push to help you achieve bigger and better things. The timing is now, when you are ready for it. Stay here as long as necessary to find a spot. It's important that you pick your new post carefully. Let's get together and talk. Give me a call.

Best wishes,

▌FIRING A VENDOR WITHOUT INCURRING ILL WILL.

SITUATION: You are a principal at a car-rental franchise. You hired two sales-representative companies for commercial accounts. One of these is incurring higher expenses (which are billable to you) than the other, but its sales aren't any better. Your overall business has slowed down lately, which requires one of these reps to be let go. The finger points to the least productive one.

STRATEGY: It's a fine, reputable company, with good resources, and its people have contributed good thinking on your commercial business. You don't want any bad feelings, and you want to maintain friendly relations. There may be a need to call on it in the future. Express these thoughts in a letter and follow up by phone.

Ms. Kathy Loughran
National Sales Manager
AGA Sales Representatives

_____

_____

Dear Kathy:

I'm sure you realize that the amount of orders we've been getting from AGA in relation to expenses has caused us to review our relationship. We are, regrettably, obliged to terminate our association.

I say "regrettably" because you and your staff have been so helpful in developing our sales strategy. The currently slow sales activity is certainly not the fault of the AGA staff on our account. We're continuing with our other representative on a basis that, I believe, may not be practical for AGA at the present flow of business.

We certainly hope the time will come when we can call on you again. Our people have often spoken about you and your staff's professionalism and business judgment. You have a lot of admirers here.

You may be less one customer (not as profitable as it had been), but you have retained a large number of friends and solid boosters.

I'm looking forward to working with you again.

Best regards,

Reggie Thomason

HAVE THE ACCOUNT EXECUTIVE ON YOUR ACCOUNT REPLACED WITHOUT HURTING HIM.

SITUATION: You are a marketing group head at a long-distance phone company. The account executive at your ad agency is not a super performer, thus not quite the kind of person you want. The agency is top notch, and you believe you could get better service if someone more capable handled your account.

You want him replaced. However, he happens to be a nice guy. You have a rapport, and you don't want to hurt him. Above all, you don't want him to lose his job.

STRATEGY: You must state your wish to the group head the account man reports to. It would be too harsh to spring it on the phone; your intent might be misunderstood. A letter, followed by a phone call, is the least harmful way.

The letter should salute the agency's work and praise the account executive. Give a convincing reason for the need to change without stigmatizing him. Why cause bad feelings? Why not make everyone happy?

Ms. Leonore Schram
Executive Vice President
Arrow Advertising Inc.

_____

_____

Dear Leonore:

This is a thank-you note, well deserved. At the same time, I'm taking this opportunity to make a request. Well, not so much a request as throwing out a suggestion for you to consider.

The staff on our account has been doing a remarkable job, sometimes under tough conditions. I want you to know firsthand how we feel about it. Jeff has spearheaded the group in a first-rate, professional manner. You supported him when he needed it.

I thank you, and I thank Jeff.

Now for the request, rather suggestion, which I don't want misunderstood. You see, we have a policy here of rotating personnel. It's a way of making sure that an individual doesn't get into rigid habits in handling any particular segment of our business. It brings a more diversified talent stream into the problem-solving complex. I think this is good management. I'm sure you do, too.

Jeff has been the lead person on our account for two years now. And he's very good. We all like him, and we will hate to lose him. But I think the time has come for a change of command. It's done in the military for good reason. For the same reason, it's good in business.

Please explain this to Jeff. I will too. Naturally, we want him to be close at hand to guide the new person, especially at the beginning. His acute sense of our business is invaluable.

Let's talk about this, Leonore. Naturally, I'll want to see Jeff's replacement before there is an official assignment.

Best wishes,

Nina Migorsky

UPLIFT THE SPIRITS OF ONE OF YOUR EMPLOYEES, AFTER YOU PROMOTED HIS ASSISTANT TO BE HIS NEW BOSS.

SITUATION: Your VP of purchasing left for another job, and you have to fill the spot in a hurry. A logical choice is the purchasing manager, Stan. He's been with the company for 24 years. He is dedicated, honest, reliable, and knows his job from A to Z. But he is not quite officer material. You want an executive-style individual, and one with fresher thinking.

Stan's assistant is sharp, youthful, college-educated, and has been well groomed by Stan for an upward move. She can handle the VP position for less money than you would have to pay an outsider. What you save will allow you to give Stan a "feel good" raise and still come out ahead. He is due for a raise anyway in about three months.

How do you handle Stan?

STRATEGY: Send Stan a personal note telling him how well he is thought of and the wonderful job he's doing. Thank him for taking his assistant under his wing and teaching her the ropes so that she is now ready for an upward move.

This is no reflection on Stan. Being in this new spot would bore him. Besides, the money isn't much more than what he's making. He is being considered for more interesting things, both inside and outside of purchasing.

Stan will see a 4% raise next payday.

On a personal level, ask him to relate your best wishes to his wife and kids.

To: Stan Weinberg

From: Otto Stritch

Stan, you may have heard rumors, but I want to personally tell you that Greta Nielsen is being promoted to VP purchasing, starting November 16th.

I also want to take this opportunity to tell you how much we appreciate the extraordinary way you do your job. It hasn't gone unnoticed. Furthermore, your marvelous tutelage of Greta and your bringing her along to more and more responsibilities, have made it possible for her to be selected for this spot. You will have a good friend there.

You are probably wondering why you didn't get the position.

Stan, you've spent so many years in purchasing that moving a notch higher would mean no new challenge for you. You would be doing the same thing, only under more pressure. There is little difference in pay. We have you in mind for other important assignments both within and outside the purchasing department.

Financially, you'll be doing well too. You've been here a long time and have accumulated a nice retirement nest egg. And you can expect a 4% raise in your next paycheck as an expression of our appreciation of your work.

I know you'll cooperate with Greta all the way in this transition.

Please give my best wishes to Ethel and your children, Peter and Mary.

With best wishes,

YOU WERE HIRED ON A SINCERE (?) HANDSHAKE, AND PUSHED ASIDE AT THE LAST MINUTE FOR SOMEONE ELSE.

TWO SITUATIONS:

 I.   *You Have a Job and Were Going to Switch*

 II.   *You Are Unemployed and Are Looking*

SITUATION I: A headhunter tapped you, a civil engineer, for a promising career jump to a well-known engineering firm. It means leaving the somewhat smaller establishment where you now work.

You had a right to assume the deal was final. The senior engineers promised that the job was yours. They said a written statement noting job responsibilities, salary, etc. was on the way.

Out of the blue, they had a change of mind. Another engineer got the job. You were informed quite hastily, six business days after their solemn verbal "commitment."

STRATEGY I: Why be timid and let it slide by, chalking it up to the fortunes of the marketplace? You went through the maze of scrutiny, hand-holding, negotiating, and staying awake nights conjecturing the move in your mind. You and your family had become psyched about your new status.

You had started going-away preparations at your present shop.

Fortunately, senior management wasn't officially notified, although you discreetly passed along the news to a couple of your associates. You feel humiliated.

Your dignity and professional credibility, not to mention your own sense of self-worth call for not taking it lying down. You can't change the company's last-minute decision, but send them a letter stating the discomfiture, indeed the harm, this has caused you. The indication is that considering the way the engineers conducted themselves, you don't want the job anyway.

Mr. C. Howard Ross
Executive Vice President
Gatley & Rogers Engineering Associates, Ltd.

_____

_____

Dear Howard:

Being left at the altar has put me in an embarrassing fix.

By no means am I suggesting that you reverse your decision, nor am I even questioning it. The fact is, in view of what has happened, I do not want the position. This letter is merely intended to point out the harm your sudden shift caused me.

I accepted your verbal commitment in good faith, in advance, as you put it, of a written hiring agreement. You told me to report three weeks hence.

Since you wanted me to start in this short time, I had to make preparations immediately for terminating my current job. This meant hurrying up my work load, shifting responsibilities to others, and so on. And I couldn't avoid indicating the move to some of my colleagues and my immediate supervisor. You have caused me much embarrassment.

I should add that Sanders & Stevens are most happy to have me remain here.

In the interest of your company's reputation, I am due a better apology than I was given on the phone by your associate.

Very truly yours,

Samuel T. Bishop

cc: Betty Ann Schomer
       Dean & Sherwood
       Personnel Consultants

SITUATION II: You are a professional civil engineer, out of work due to a business reversal at your former employer. Economic conditions bode ill for out-of-work civil engineers. Finding a job is a gloomy prospect.

A headhunter put you in touch with a wonderful opening at a well-known firm. There were intense meetings and get-to-know-you sessions, and you came out on top—(for a few days, that is). Actually, the firm told you, with much praise, that the job was yours. You were to start in two weeks.

You and your family were euphoric. Then, five days later, like the Chernobyl blast, your world was shattered. You were told it was off. Someone else the firm had previously negotiated with agreed to accept the job. You are back to a desperate square one.

STRATEGY II: Send a letter noting that you had good reason to conclude that you had been hired. The serious discussions you had during the past two months precluded you from actively pursuing other opportunities.

Make management feel guilty, but be gracious. You are in no position to show pique; what's more, it won't do you any good. Why not keep up a positive relationship? It's silly to burn bridges. The firm may keep you in mind for something else later on.

Mr. Howard C. Ross
Executive Vice President
Gatley & Rogers Engineering Associates, Ltd.

———————————————

———————————————

Dear Howard:

I must say it was a sudden jolt getting the news, so soon after your verbal commitment. I guess things like this sometimes happen.

It set me back quite a bit, because I had informed another company that was interested in me that I was no longer available. Furthermore, during the two months in which we held meetings and negotiations, it was difficult for me to pursue other opportunities. At any rate, I wish you luck with your "new" appointee. I respect your decision, even though I believe it is not the right one.

It's a small world in our profession, and we may again have reason to get together. I would look forward to it.

Best regards,

Samuel T. Bishop

TURNING DOWN A JOB CANDIDATE AFTER HE WAS ASSURED HE WAS HIRED ON A HANDSHAKE COMMITMENT.

SITUATION: A world-famous academic institution conducted a highly publicized search for dean of its school of business administration. You are a professor and head of the search committee for the nominating board. After interviewing many candidates, the committee zeroed in on a distinguished business professor at another well-regarded university.

You told him the position was likely his at that point in our search. He went home with an understanding that this was a done deal and so informed his family and several confidantes.

Then something happened. Another candidate, a newcomer to the selection process, came into view and swept the nominating board off its collective feet. He was their last-minute choice. By dint of personality and academic credentials he became the individual they concluded they had to have for this important post.

Now the news must be given to the person who was previously informed that he had been selected. Concern must be given to his sensitivity and reputation. But, however it is said or done, the university's reputation must not be blemished.

STRATEGY: Do not call him initially. First send a letter to his home. Then call him.

Let him down as gracefully as possible, extolling his credentials. Try to convince him that it is to his advantage not to take the post, which was a factor in the board's decision. Propose the thought of working together on future projects.

```
Clarence Van Clemens, Ph.D.
3 Apple Tree Lane
Ukiah, CA 41302
```

Dear Dr. Van Clemens:

You may at first consider this to be an unfortunate piece of news. But I'm sure that in the long run you will think of it as a fortuitous message. The Board has decided to appoint another candidate to be Dean of the Thorndike Business School. This came about after very painstaking deliberations.

Throughout all of our discussions, your name came up as being extraordinarily qualified, which is the reason we had so many sessions with you and invited you to meet with several of our faculty members. And why we said you were at the top level in our considerations of candidates.

However, we came to the conclusion that the academic philosophy you display at your present institution and in your writings would not blend with the direction we take here. We don't, by any means, disagree with your school of thought. It is just a difference of cultures, which would put you at a disadvantage.

This eleventh-hour decision took much soul-searching. We kept coming back to the point that you wouldn't care to adjust to the academic concepts at Thorndike. Nor would we expect you to do so. Your achievements are greatly admired by everyone here. You have our best wishes on your future endeavors.

By all means, let's stay in touch now that we've gotten to know each other so well. We hope you will give us the privilege of keeping you in mind for joint pursuits on projects that may come up in the future.

With kindest regards,

```
Clara Fine Kleinman, Ph.D.
Chairman, Search Committee
```

P.S.   We have set aside a budget, maximum of $5,000, to compensate you
        for any direct out-of-pocket expenses you incurred in the course
        of our discussions. We'll be happy to pay an itemized bill.

LETTING SOMEONE DOWN EASY WHEN AN EXPECTED PROMOTION DIDN'T COME THROUGH.

SITUATION: You are on the board of an investment brokerage firm. A
              department manager, who has been with you for many
years, didn't get a coveted promotion. He thought he was in line for it, but
the board felt he may have reached his peak where he is. To make the situation worse, a young outsider was hired.

You don't want to lose him, and you don't want to shred his morale. He's very good at what he is doing, and it would be hard to replace him right now. Further, a disgruntled employee can be a problem.

STRATEGY: Send a personal letter to his home. Tell him he is so indispensable in his current slot that the board couldn't see its
way clear to move him. It was a decision it made reluctantly because it knew it meant a lot to him. But his value to the business as a whole had to be uppermost. You want him to know he could be in line for good things in the future. Give him a raise.

Mr. Oscar Fite
421 Poplar Drive

Dear Oscar:

The hardest thing in the world for me to do is to disappoint you on the investment director spot. You are just doing too good a job running the municipal department, and we can't spare you in this important position. The directors said it would be too difficult to get another person to fill your shoes.

We therefore tapped an outsider, Harry Bishop, of Harper Securities, for director. Keep in mind, your job is just as important to the company as Harry's. The directors all agree with me on this. Your future here is better than ever. You can be assured that there will be other opportunities for promotion around here.

To convey our appreciation for the great job you've been doing we are
giving you a salary increase. The amount will be shown in a separate
note. In addition to putting more money into your bank account each
month, I hope it will help assuage any let down you may feel.

Keep up the good work, Oscar. You are an important part of the team.

My warmest regards to Phyllis.

Best wishes,

Lou

MOLLIFY YOUR FRIEND'S DISAPPOINTMENT. YOU PUT HIM IN THE RUNNING FOR A VENDOR CONTRACT AT YOUR COMPANY. HE LOST OUT.

SITUATION: You are a sales manager at a proprietary drug manufacturer. A new merchandising program was developed which
required letters to be mailed weekly to a large number of doctors and phar-
macists nationally.

Your friend is a principal at a direct-mail company, and you invited him to
go after this business. You know his work and that his company is well-
regarded. You would like him to have this assignment. You asked your colleagues to consider him.

He made an all-out presentation that ate up quite a bit of his company's
money. It was competent and professional, but another company wound up
with the business. You argued with your colleagues on your friend's behalf,
but it did no good. The winner had previously done good work for the company and had proven itself.

STRATEGY: You told your friend on the phone, but you want to follow
up with a letter to assuage his disappointment—and to rec-
ognize the solid effort he made.

You also want to mitigate your embarrassment and console your friend by
assuring him a preferred hearing on the next piece of business that comes
along. You don't want this incident to stand in the way of your relationship.

Larry O'Hara
President
Active Mail Marketing

‾‾‾‾‾‾‾‾‾‾‾‾‾‾‾‾‾‾‾‾

‾‾‾‾‾‾‾‾‾‾‾‾‾‾‾‾‾‾‾‾

Dear Larry:

As in a ball game, one team wins, and the other loses. It was very close. It went into extra innings and, unfortunately, the other guy scored the winning run.

I want you to know that you had my support all the way, but I lost by one vote in a knock-down stormy session. What finally tilted the scale was that PNO had done business with us before and had done a good job.

Larry, I know this doesn't do you any good now and that it's small consolation, but everyone here was impressed with your presentation. The amount of work, and the smart thinking you put into it, were obvious to us all. You did a great job of showing what you and your company can do.

That's why, in a way, you won. That is, if you want to consider the seeds you planted for the future. You are assured of a crack at any other project that comes up. And, when it does, you'll be in a preferred position because the people here now know you and like you. Sometimes it takes a couple of shots to hit the bullseye.

Warm regards,

A JOB RECOMMENDATION FOR SOMEONE YOU FIRED. YOU WANT TO HELP THE PERSON WITHOUT LYING.

SITUATION: As director of lab research at a pharmaceutical company you had to fire one of the research scientists. He was not entirely effective on his own, needing more supervision than his rank called for. He also botched up a research procedure. He's a nice guy, a willing worker, and likeable, but couldn't cut the mustard.

A prospective employer of this scientist asks you for a written evaluation.

STRATEGY: Be careful about what you say as there could be repercussions. At the most, you should give a barely noticeable hint of your exresearcher not measuring up under his own power and that he needed an undue amount of supervision. Besides, you want him to land a job.

C. Raj Hadeema, Ph.D
Vice President, Director of Research
Caspar Pharmaceuticals, Inc.

_____

_____

Dear Dr. Hadeema:

You asked me for my evaluation of Dr. Wilson Rogers, which I am most pleased to provide you.

Dr. Rogers was a fine presence in our diagnostic medicine lab as a Senior Research Associate for the past five years. He is a learned scientist who works tirelessly and with great effort on his assigned projects. He adheres to established scientific principles.

I don't have to tell you that not all research leads to a commercial triumph, by any means. Most do not pan out or are marginally successful. Dr. Rogers was a member of the team that developed several successful formulations, but the endeavor he was put in charge of during the past 18 months did not result in an acceptable product. However, he performed to the best of his ability.

Due to a restructuring of priorities, we abandoned the research concept that he had headed up. This concurred with a corporate staff reduction; thus Dr. Rogers was not transferred to another division.

This, regrettably, caused his departure. We wish him well.

Very truly yours,

Mary Wang, Ph.D.,
Vice President, Director of Research

MW:jr

A REFERENCE LETTER FOR A WORKER WHO WAS FIRED FOR OUT-AND-OUT INCOMPETENCE

A production manager at a packaging company was fired after 10 months on the job—for grossly unsatisfactory performance. You are the VP he reported to, and are asked to send a written reference to a company considering him for a job. Basically, he was badly organized and a faulty production planner. He made some costly mistakes.

STRATEGY: Discretion is the watchword. There must be no damaging statements, even though he was fired for cause.

Have the letter come from the human-resources department or a minor executive. Short, formal, safe, innocuous, without anything outwardly undermining his chance to be hired.

```
Ms. Agatha Enright
Vice President
Dual Delivery Systems, Inc.

_____

_____

Dear Ms. Enright:

This is in response to a letter you sent to Mr. Theodore Sherman request-
ing our evaluation of Jackson Miller, who worked here from August 9, 1996
to May 11, 1997.

Mr. Miller was generally liked as an individual by his fellow executives
and other people who came in contact with him in the course of his activ-
ities here. He brought a pleasant and cordial atmosphere in his work area
and he attended to his assignments with enthusiasm and a desire to do a
good job.

It is difficult for me to provide further information about Mr. Miller,
except that there were no specifically negative statements in his per-
sonnel record.

Very truly yours,

Leonore Malkowitz,
Assistant Director, Human Services

LM:jr
```

▌HOW TO FIRE YOUR LAWYER.

TWO STRATEGIES:

I.   Friendly

II.   Unfriendly

SITUATION: You are the plaintiff in a law suit, seeking sizeable damages. Your attorney told you that you have a good case. He assured you that the law was on your side.

It's now in the midst of discoveries, depositions, filings, and so on. You don't believe your lawyer is handling it well. He is giving you evasive answers or nonanswers to your questions. It's a reason to worry.

A friend recommended another lawyer, better suited to this kind of case, and with an impressive track record. You met and liked him. You decided to switch.

STRATEGY I: You don't want to show your displeasure at the careless way your lawyer is handling your case. Tell him who is taking over, a big-time lawyer. Tell him, as well, that the new attorney will call on him for help, and you hope he'll be available. You had previously asked his opinion, in an offhanded way, on the feasibility of such a move, so it's not a complete surprise.

You don't want to cause any rancor. Alienating your former attorney may hurt you. You want to keep his good will.

```
Mr. Jackson Schwardon
O'Hara, Schwardon & Harris
```

_____

_____

```
Re:    Perry vs. Doctrino
```

Dear Jack:

I'm sure you'll agree with me on the move I'm now making in the case. After a lot of deliberation, I have decided that this suit should continue with another lead attorney. In fact, I touched on it with you a couple of times and got the notion that you were in agreement, which is why I'm doing this.

You have done a wonderful job in setting up the case so far. You've established a firm bedrock of documents. Now, for the next stage of litigation, I decided to engage Arnold Spiro of Spiro & Partners. I'm sure you know of him and that you'll agree with this choice. Please let me know if you have any misgivings.

I hope you will get involved when called upon. Arnold made it very clear he wants to be able to look to you for help.

Please be good enough to transfer all documents to Spiro & Partners within the next week. Mr. Spiro has a list of what to expect.

Send me an up-to-date bill as of November 26, 1993. There are to be no charges after this date.

Jack, I want your talents to be on hand when any other legal problem arises. Let's talk further—I'll call you for lunch.

Best ever,

Joanna Perry

STRATEGY II: You don't have to be deferential or spare your lawyer's feelings. He's been sloppy on an important matter in your life that is causing loads of worry. You are bitter.

Professional ethics call for him to turn over all your records to your new attorney. You don't have qualms because the new lawyer will stay on top of the transfer. Besides, you have the originals of everything. Your exlawyer has copies.

Mr. Jackson Schwardon
O'Hara, Schwardon & Harris

_____

_____

Re: Perry vs. Doctrino

Dear Jack:

I came away from our meeting on Wednesday, March 14, dismayed at the inadequacy of your preparation in answering the latest series of inquiries. Very little has been done since my previous meeting with you on October 12.

In fact, I've been displeased all along with the way your firm is handling this case. My unhappiness has now turned to serious misgivings.

I have therefore engaged another law firm, Spiro & Partners, for this matter. Arnold Spiro has a list of all documents and will call you in a few days to arrange a transfer. He expects your cooperation which I'm sure you will not withhold.

Send me a bill for all outstanding charges through November 26, 1993. There are to be no charges after this date.

I'm sorry I had to take this step, Jack.

Very truly yours,

Joanna Perry

REVIVE YOUR CHANCES FOR A BIG JOB. YOU SENSE YOUR INTERVIEW FLOPPED.

SITUATION: You were interviewed for a top job at a high-powered financial services company. When you walked out you knew in your gut that it didn't click. The job is a big plum. You desperately want to redeem your chances.

STRATEGY: Send a letter to the person who led the interview. Give him a few relevant tidbits that you didn't say at your meeting, things that might add another perspective. It must be brief. Make a heroic effort. It's a bold shot, the odds may be against you, but it's certainly worth the effort.

Maxwell Perez
Senior Vice President
Bulwark Investment Management, Inc.

_____
_____

Dear Mr. Perez:

Thank you so much for the opportunity of meeting with you and your colleagues. There were a couple of questions you asked me which I then was-
n't free to answer since I had to make certain that I wouldn't divulge
anything confidential.

After checking, I found that I am now able to give you the information
you wanted.

> The Succulent Foods stock offering, which I shepherded along
> every inch of the way for my firm, amounted to $1.2 billion.
> It was successfully concluded in four weeks. This was a big
> coup for the firm, and I got a great deal of praise for it.

> I am assured I will be free to draw on my contacts in the finan-
> cial community, which will make me a valuable asset in your New
> Offering Department and likely in other divisions as well.

Needless to say, I'll be delighted to provide other information you wish
to know and that I'm free to disclose.

It was a real pleasure seeing you. Please think more about how I will fit in; I will, too. Regardless of what happens, we shouldn't let our relationship lapse. Let's get together soon. I'll call you.

Best regards,

Drew Warren

FIND OUT WHERE YOU STAND ON A PROSPECTIVE JOB OFFER.

SITUATION: You are among the top ranks at an investment banking empire. Your major responsibility for the past five years was supervision of the various loan-acquisition and funding activities of a world-wide conglomerate that specializes in communications equipment and software.

You developed a close relationship with the client-person you take orders from, the chief financial officer. You are buddies. Your strength with this account draws the resentment of your company's chairman and the chief executive officer, which predestines you for the trash heap at the opportune time. You know it, for sure.

Pow! The time arrived. Protocol at your company is to change the guard on a big account every five years so as to avoid any talk of possible ethical transgressions. It's usually adhered to. Your client couldn't save you because it's an established policy. You were even in the anomalous position of recommending your successor.

You are now without any duties, waiting and hoping for a decent severance package. A year ago, you had known this would happen. Your ace in the hole is that your client told you he would give you a job when the time was ripe. The time is now very ripe.

Your exclient is somewhat vague. He hasn't said no, but he hasn't said yes. You think it's in the works. Should you count on it? Two meetings were scheduled with him, but he called them off at the last minute. Your phone calls have not been returned lately.

Jobs are scarce, if available at all, at your level. Is something you counted on for the past year now a mirage? Your nerves are piano-wire tight.

STRATEGY: Send your client-friend a letter to his office. Mark the envelope—*Private. Open Personally, Please.*

Ask him not to keep you in the dark. You will soon be ousted from your office, and you need a job. Note that the height of your ambition is to work for your ex-client. You would like to know one way or another.

Tell him that whatever comes of it, your friendship remains intact.

PRIVATE—Open Personally, Please.

Mr. Richard Ebersol
Executive Vice President
Paragon Enterprises, Inc.

_____
_____

Dear Dick:

As you can imagine, I'm in an uncomfortable on-the-shelf position right now. There is no mention of having to leave Ingram's premises and pay-roll—so far anyway—but clearly, the day is coming up.

At any rate, I have to make a move. Hopefully, the right one.

We had been talking for some time about my coming aboard at Paragon. Personally, I would like nothing better than to work for you in my next and final career move.

I know you, I know the company, I know the people there. And you, above all, know me. After all, I've been working with your company for many years.

You are obviously extremely busy, especially now, with your new acqui-sition, which is why it's been so hard to get to talk with you. I called a few times but you were tied up and haven't had a chance to get back.

I just wonder how it now stands. Should I consider myself slated for Paragon? If so, when do you think it will happen? Is it in the cards, but there's a temporary holdup? Is it doubtful? Is it something that's not now doable?

I'd appreciate hearing from you as soon as you have a few minutes. It would be good if we could get together for dinner to talk about this.

Whatever happens, Dick, it will certainly have nothing to do with our friendship.

Best regards,

Timothy Dodge

█ A CAREER WIPE-OUT. OUTRIGHT SEXUAL HARASSMENT.

- ■ Letter A . . . Accuse Your Supervisor Of Sexual Harassment.
- ■ Letter B . . . Supervisor Retorts—Defends His Job, Reputation, and Future.
- ■ Letter C . . . Response To Supervisor's Retort—You Deny His Story.

SITUATION: You are a senior salesperson in ladies sportswear at a local branch of Harrison's, a large department-store chain. A woman, 33, ambitious, you've been there four years, and were recently promoted from sales clerk.

Your department supervisor, a fiftyish married man, the father of three, has been coming on to you the past four months. In private only, with no witnesses. He speaks to you with sexy innuendoes. He tells dirty jokes and uses obscene expressions to make a point. He touches you "accidentally."

There is the hint, spoken indirectly and innocently, that he likes your work, and you would have the ability to advance, if only you would loosen up. He says you are too aloof and too rigid in dealing with people.

He maintains a proper outward demeanor, which increases your frustration and misery. You repeatedly try to get your supervisor to stop, but he persists. Is this the way to get ahead in the company? You are in a trap.

STRATEGY: You can't let this frustrate your career goal. Why toss away four years of hard work and good future prospects? In time, perhaps you'll advance to buyer.

You send a confidential memo to the store manager, a man. Factual, unemotional. You note that you are trying to keep this private, and within the store.

You would be terribly embarrassed if it got out. You also want to protect the store's reputation.

The Denial:

The accused supervisor is confronted with the damaging memo and is asked for a written response. He categorically denies the accusation, eschewing any sense of worry. This is unbelievable. He has an impeccable record at the store and has always conducted himself with rectitude. He has a fine future ahead of him.

And after all, he's been married for 22 years. He is a model husband with a loving wife and three children.

He doesn't go into detail at this point about the accuser and avoids personal criticism. He does not want to say too much. He remembers: Anything he says can be held against him.

Response to Denial:

As the victim and the accuser, you must respond to your harasser's denial. Why would you put your career, your reputation, and your whole future on the line? You still want to keep this within the company walls. You can get tough, but not now. Try hard to avoid a public furor; it might backfire. Even if you win, you could lose.

LETTER OF ACCUSATION

PRIVATE AND CONFIDENTIAL

To: Mr. Nikola Copernicos
        Vice President, Store Manager
        Harrison's

From: Fleur Delaura

It is with much pain that I must report an ongoing episode of sexual harassment, over the past four months, by my department manager, Mr. Peter DeMentes. I very much wish to keep this a private matter.

Mr. DeMentes has been making subtle but explicit advances towards me throughout this four-month period. They are in the form of sexual innu-endoes, dirty jokes, obscene remarks, and "accidentally" brushing against me. All this has taken place in his office or the stock room when there is no one else present.

I've been strongly discouraging these advances and making it explicitly clear that I find his actions reprehensible. Despite this, they persist.

Mr. DeMentes pointedly implied that my refusal to be "friendly," my "attitude," may be blocking my advancement in the company.

I prefer not to go into further detail in this letter. You can be sure I would not make this serious charge without justification. It was a painful decision to write this. I agonized over it for a long time.

Thank you for giving this your attention. I leave it in your hands.

Respectfully yours,

Fleur Delaura

RESPONSE TO ACCUSATION—TOTAL DENIAL

To: Mr. Nikola Copernicos
       Vice President, Store Manager
       Harrison's

From: Peter DeMentes

I categorically deny Miss Delaura's unsubstantiated and ridiculous charge. It is completely without foundation.

Frankly, this is a shocking surprise, for I regarded Miss Delaura as a good employee. All of my contacts with her have been for business purposes only, and we have both maintained a strictly formal demeanor.

After all, Mr. Copernicos, I am a devoted family man. I have a loving wife, two daughters, and a son. I would not treat any woman in a way that I would not want someone to treat my wife and daughters.

I find the actions Miss Delaura describes as repugnant. It is inconceivable to connect this with me, especially considering my nature, my religious beliefs, my reputation, and my family values. The manner in which I have conducted myself in the store has always been at the highest level of executive rectitude.

It is for others to presume what caused Miss Delaura to make this charge. I am writing this letter with compassion in my heart for her.

Very truly yours,

```
To:     Mr. Nikola Copernicos
        Vice President, Store Manager
        Harrison's

From:   Fleur Delaura
```

The letter you showed me that Mr. DeMentes addressed to you was naturally no surprise.

I can only say that what I told you previously is the truth. I'm not a trouble-maker. It hurts me greatly to bring harm to anybody.

Now I'm forced to bear the extra burden of having my integrity questioned. Everyone who has had any contact with me, in the store or elsewhere, will say this is absurd. My reputation, my uprightness, and my good sense speak for themselves.

I had my choice of keeping quiet, quitting my job, and going elsewhere. But I value my position at Harrison's. I don't want to throw away four years of conscientious effort, recently rewarded with a promotion, not to mention the prospect of a good career at this fine company. All I want is a fair chance to advance on my merits alone.

As I said before, I want to avoid any public exposure, if at all possible. The turmoil and embarrassment, which might lead to the involvement of legal authorities, would devastate me.

May I respectfully suggest that Mr. DeMentes be reprimanded and cautioned, which should obviate the need for carrying this matter further.

```
Sincerely,
```

▌SUBTLE SEXUAL HARASSMENT. STOP IT

SITUATION: You are a secretary in the purchasing office of a transportation company. You are 23, outgoing, and ambitious. A co-worker in his late thirties takes a fancy to you and constantly tries to engage you in cozy talk. His conversation when you are alone is peppered with off-color humor and suggestive remarks.

You are uncomfortable. You feel vulnerable.

He is careful. There is nothing explicitly indecent that you can pin on him, but his intention is clear. And it has to stop.

You spoke to him about it, judiciously so as not to put a big dent in his self-image, but he apparently didn't get it. You want to avoid any backlash against you.

STRATEGY: Put it to him in writing. A short letter, more chummy than
                hostile, explaining your discomfort and declaring without
reservation that his innuendoes and overtures are unwelcome and must stop.
You enjoy his company as a co-worker, and would like to be office friends.
That's all.

You add that you don't want to cause any trouble, implying that you might
have to take the next step if he continues.

```
PRIVATE

Jim Thornton
Supervisor, Purchasing Department
and Fellow Laborer

Dear Jim:

I know we get along well, and I like working with you. I also know you
enjoy working with me. Shall I say a bit too much?

Being a proper young lady, I find that the way you talk to me at times,
the way you get "friendly," is disturbing. It's not right, and it has to
stop.

I see you as an attractive man, Jim, and you are a lot of fun. But I am
definitely off-limits.

I hope you take this in the amiable spirit in which I intended. I don't
want to have to make waves.

Your office buddy (that's all),

Lucille D'Amato
```

▌DISCREET RACIAL BIAS IS HOLDING YOU DOWN.

SITUATION: You are an African-American woman, a brand manager in
                a famous packaged goods, toiletries and cosmetics compa-
ny. You are type cast, assigned ethnic products rather than big-volume, high
profile brands that can get you noticed—the brands that can send a career
soaring.

You are well liked, admired for your bright, quick marketing sense and your
keen intellect. There is no overt sign of racial bias. It is an attitude of your
being apart, of having a "different" background. This abstract pall hangs

over you and you have to fix the problem of being shunted away from the fast track.

STRATEGY: Send a memo to the top person in marketing in a sealed envelope marked "private." Make no waves whatsoever. State that you believe there is no intentional prejudice, but you are being subtly yet strikingly thwarted from pursuing your career enhancement. All you want is a chance to prove your mettle in the corporate mainstream.

```
To:    Mr. Marcus Silverman
       Senior Vice President, Marketing
       Sanders & Pratt Products Company

From:  Betty Ann Watson
```

Dear Mr. Silverman:

I had to muster up a lot of courage to send this memo. I trust it will have no adverse bearing on my status in the company.

As you know, I'm a product manager in the Beauty Products Division, having been here four years. I am the only African-American product manager in this division.

It seems I have a unique place here as a specialist for this ethnic market. The two brands that were developed for the black market were assigned to me. This has been great experience, but it is now time for me to move on to an area where I am not typecast.

Please understand that this is not a racial issue. Indeed, I'm sure my supervisors have no bias whatsoever. I value their friendship and their counsel.

There just seems to be a condition where I am singled out as being a representative of the African-American community. The general understanding is that I know this consumer group better than anyone here and, therefore, I am the logical manager to head up these ethnic brands.

My professor at Wharton, where I received my MBA, said this could happen. I didn't think it would happen here because of the company's reputation for fairness and tolerance, which is in no way the issue here. It's a matter of a glass ceiling that I have to penetrate.

I'm honored to be working at S&P. It was—and is—a wonderful career choice. May I please be judged on my ability, without any regard to ethnicity? All I want is the opportunity to advance on my merits in the corporate mainstream.

Respectfully,

Betty Ann Watson

▋ GENDER BIAS . . . A STOP SIGN ON YOUR CAREER PATH.

SITUATION: You've held mid-management positions with an impeccable record for the past 16 years at one of the world's outstanding hotel-management companies. You are one of the few female assistant managers at a major property. Despite an outstanding performance in these significant mid-management assignments you haven't risen to become the general manager of a hotel.

Whisperings have it that the chairman doesn't consider women to be appropriate hotel general-manager material. "Let's face it," he is reported to have said, "the top bosses at our hotels have to socialize and have a close rapport with the leading figures in their communities. They must have a cordial relationship with the corporate big-wigs, the politicians, the influentials, and they are mostly men. They have to drink with them, entertain them, amuse them, and a woman doesn't fit this role. Furthermore, a woman's child-care responsibilities have first call on her time and energy, and she can't give 100% to her job." This is the chairman's prevailing position.

You have reached your zenith, strapped and frustrated. This is not what you diligently trained and sacrificed for in academia and on the job.

STRATEGY: Send a letter to the Executive VP, who handles operational matters, including personnel policies. He is also the chairman's top aide. He parrots the chairman's wishes, but can also advise him on what may be prudent and wise.

Bring ivory-tower management up-to-date, into the modern world and into acknowledging that superior job performance and management skills are gender-blind, even considering the taxing duties of the hospitality industry.

Realistically, you may not change the chairman's antiquated notions very much, but he has to be made to realize that he is way out-of-step with reality and has an unfounded, unacceptable bias that could hurt the business.

In terms of hard-headed practicality, you know that justice and the law, science, cold facts, and predominant public sentiment is on your side. The chairman and his aides are aware of it. You can be sure the executive you address will thoroughly check out your personnel record which is very commendable.

You will likely give a nudge that puts your name up front for bigger things. You are a showcase candidate to shatter the glass ceiling of gender block.

Mr. Ernest R. Sommers
Executive Vice President
Hospitality Management International, Inc.

_____

_____

Dear Mr. Sommers:

May I ask you to consider a matter of utmost concern to me, and, I'm certain, to quite a number of other people in our company.

There appears to be a formidable barrier that is preventing me from being promoted to general manager. To my knowledge, no woman has ever been appointed general manager of an HMI property, or for that matter attained any senior-management post. I believe my academic training, experience and performance equal or possibly exceed those of several of my male colleagues who have passed me by and have risen to higher positions.

For the past 4 years I've served as the assistant manager in our Chicago property. Prior to this I held assistant manager posts in Costa Rica for 3 years, and for 4 years in San Antonio.

Before that I spent 5 years as an executive below the assistant-manager level in San Juan. So you see, I've been with HMI for 16 years—11 years as an assistant manager, and currently at one of our choice properties. My personnel ratings have been in the top 10% wherever I served.

This frustrating situation understandably discourages me, and, I assume, other women in this organization. You can help maximize our profit-making potential by taking full advantage of all of the wonderful talent we have here.

It gives me great pride to be a part of HMI. My uppermost ambition is to succeed in this company, and to further contribute to its outstanding reputation in the hospitality industry. I am willing to be transferred to any location which offers greater rank and responsibilities.

I am asking only for the opportunity to maximize my potential worth to HMI.

Most respectfully,

Dolores Fernandez
DF:jr

▌ YOUR COMPANY IS LEAVING YOU TWISTING IN THE WIND.

SITUATION: You are a regional sales and marketing manager at a major airline. The FBI is probing around on a rumor of price-fixing with another large carrier. The finger is on you because you have occasionally been seen socializing with your counterpart at this competitor.

There is no hard evidence of any wrongdoing on your part. But your company is getting ready to make you the sacrificial lamb if something bad comes up so as to get it behind them with the least damage.

You will not be the patsy, and you don't want to hire a lawyer at this point. It would be very expensive and even possibly imply that the Justice Department is on the right track. A publicized allegation of wrongdoing could destroy your career, even if it is eventually found to have no merit.

STRATEGY: A letter to the Senior VP of Marketing, with a copy to the President categorically stating your complete innocence. From where you stand, the Feds will not be able to find any credible evidence of your complicity in anything like this. It's a fishing expedition, and you are unequivocally clean.

Your company must give you full support in dispensing with this. You will not be out front all alone.

Mr. Peter G. Travis
Senior Vice President, Marketing
Worldwide Airlines, Inc.

_____

_____

Dear Mr. Travis:

I want to briefly review here the situation in which the FBI is checking on the possibility of a price-fixing scheme with Ajax Airlines.

Charges were apparently made by what we understand is an anonymous source, likely a vindictive competitor. Rumors are rife, and it is far from pleasant.

I'm in the middle, along with Ben Thompson at Ajax Airlines. We're the so-called "suspected culprits." And why? The FBI found nothing on me, but I head the department that supposedly conspired with Ajax.

Mr. Travis, I categorically deny that I ever engaged in any price-fixing plot, with Ajax or anyone else. As for Ben Thompson, if he did it with anyone, it was not with me. Nor did I ever violate any law or regulation or any company policy or rule.

If Worldwide had pricing similar to that of another airline, it was never planned in advance. You're well aware, Mr. Travis, that we constantly monitor what our competition is doing, as they do to us. Indeed, you have emphasized many times that we have to match or be below our competitors' fares on similar routes. That's how we survive as well as we do.

Ben Thompson and I are acquaintances. We sometimes lunch together and we socialize occasionally, but I assiduously avoid giving him any inside information whatsoever. I follow this same policy with anyone outside this company. To my knowledge, no one in my department has leaked any information about pending fares.

I expect Worldwide to stand fast and fully support me in this inquiry, whether it involves the Justice Department, the FAA, Congress or anyone else. I am perfectly clean. My reputation, my future employment and advancement, and the well-being of my family must not in any way be compromised.

I don't see how anything can come of this, except, unfortunately, some groundless publicity. Naturally, you can count on me to elaborate on the statements I've made here with government authorities or anyone else. Based on what I now know, I will defend the company with a clear conscience.

Truly yours,

Lawrence DeAngelo
Western Regional Manager, Sales & Marketing

cc: Mr. F. Scott Curtis
       President & CEO

YOU GOT TURNED DOWN FOR A HIGHLY PUBLICIZED TOP JOB.

SITUATION: A financial colossus was looking to fill a top spot. It was well publicized. You, a senior-level investment manager at another well-known firm, were named in the press as one of the four candidates on the short list.

You didn't get the job—a highly visible turndown, embarrassing and demeaning. You are concerned that you may now be considered glued to your level, not equipped as an out-front policymaker.

STRATEGY: You have to recoup your dignity with your peers in the industry. Send them each a letter to spread a favorable story for public consumption. You didn't want the job and actually turned it down. Be gracious and statesmanlike.

Mr. Larry Burton
President
Bulwark Assets Corporation

_____

_____

Dear Larry:

You must have read in the papers that I was on the short list for the CFO's slot at Dexter Securities. Mary Roth took the job, and I wish her well. To my mind it's good for both Dexter and Mary.

I think you'll be interested in knowing the inside story of why I didn't take it, without revealing any privileged information.

Jerry Evans, the board member who headed the search committee, got in touch with me through a headhunter. I didn't want to pursue it, and said so. Why should someone start something like this when he is happy where he is? Especially at a place like Ashton, Crawford. I'm getting what I want and doing what I want—what anyone could want, really. I am told the sky's the limit for me here.

The headhunter said they just wanted my advice and asked if he could set up a meeting with Evans. Naturally, I told Cap here what was happening and he said, "See them, but be careful. Don't let them talk you into anything that's not right."

Evans introduced me to George MacTavish, the chairman, and some of the other Board members, and we chatted about what the job required and who would be good for it. Ostensibly this was the reason they wanted to see me. I mentioned a few names.

Afterwards they asked me to consider it, but I took Cap's advice. I wouldn't have been interested, even if Cap hadn't said anything, for good reasons that I mentioned before as well as other things that I'm not free to talk about. It has nothing to do with Dexter as a company, or the people I saw. It's a wonderful company and a great bunch of people.

I thought you'd want to know what really went on, what with all the rumors bouncing around and the reports in the press.

Call me when you get into town and we'll break bread. Give my best to Edith.

Warm regards,

Bob Carpenter

HANDLING EMPLOYEE CONCERNS, COMPLAINTS.

FORMAT MEMOS

April 8, 1997

To: The Staff

From: Michael Moran

I heard you!

Some people expressed concerns about safety in our parking area. I certainly understand what you are saying.

Without delay, I'm doing something about it. Here's what's going to happen.

- There will be more lighting in our parking area.
- The dumpsters that hinder some views of the parking area will be removed to other locations.
- If you parked far from the entrance door, you will be given time to move your car closer as space becomes available.
- More visible video-monitoring equipment.

I am very pleased that you informed me about this. I and others will continue to look at this issue, and please let me know what you think about these steps—or any others ideas you may want to give me. Constructive ideas are always welcome.

REGISTERING A COMPLAINT WITH YOUR BOSS

Re: A Safety Concern

Dear Mr. Kelly:

May I request that you look into this matter. I'm one voice among several, and I guess I'm unhappily in the role of spokesperson.

It's about the parking lot.

It gets quite dark there when we leave after work and a little scary, especially for the women, when we walk to our cars. Can something be done about this, please? Better lighting, removing obstructions which can serve as hiding places for predators.

We know you want to be informed of this, and will no doubt take action. Thank you so much, Mr. Kelly, for hearing us out on this important matter.

Very truly,

Samantha Nordquist

ANOTHER LETTER OF COMPLAINT TO YOUR BOSS

Dear Mr. D'Amato:

May I respectfully tell you about a practice of job assignments that seems quite unfair. I am writing you because once you know of this issue, you will want to investigate it and then set it right.

Some of us get a lot more assignments than other employees. In fact, a number are inundated with a very heavy work load, while others are allowed to coast at an even pace.

As you can see, this is unfair and has created a sense of ill will as well as a morale problem. Everyone that I speak with is delighted, and proud, to be working for GRG. Straightening out this disparity will make for an even more pleasant work environment which you have done so much to foster.

Thank you for your attention to this, Mr. D'Amato. I hope it has made a contribution to company morale—and to productivity.

Sincerely,

Charles Abrams
Supervisor, Computer Services

STOPPING BAD RUMORS FROM FLOATING AROUND

To: Keston Carpenter
        Jenny Barrett
        Serena Fuller
        Lew Hammond

From: John Severn

Re: False Rumors

The scuttlebutt has it that some people are concerned about the future of this company, and their jobs. This is apparently caused by newspaper reports which are not corroborated, not checked out fully, and attributed to some rumor mongers who apparently are not friendly.

THIS IS FALSE! We're in fine shape.

Things like this happen when a company has discussions about an acquisition or some reorganization, or moving its site, or whatever. You know how it is—the news media see something to speculate about and pursue it in their quest for sensationalism. Again, there's nothing to these poison pen intimations.

What you have to do is get all your people together and quash this ugly misinformation. We're in good shape, and they are in good shape.

Please let me know what happens. And let's take steps to stop in its tracks anything else like this before the poison spreads.

▪ YOU NEED TO REPRIMAND A GOOD CUSTOMER.

SITUATION: You are the adminstrive secretary of a country club. One of the members, a very generous contributor, uses the club as a summer camp for his 17-year-old son. He drops him off several mornings a week and picks him up in the late afternoon.

The kid is brash, boorish, and breaks the rules. He speaks loudly and profanely to the employees and even to some of the members. The dress code is nonexistent insofar as it concerns him. A number of members want the kid tossed out.

STRATEGY: Write to the father and explain the problem, noting that his son faces suspension if he doesn't change.

Don't beat up too much on the youth. Note that this is typical of so many energetic young men today. You are sure the father can take care of it and will consider it an amusing incident later on.

Mr. Clarence T.L. Galbraith
Chairman of the Board
Johnspoker Publications, Inc.

———————————————

———————————————

Dear Mr. Galbraith:

It is with a sense of disquietude that I write this letter. It regards the behavior of your son, Jonathan. It is not a terribly serious problem, but it has to be corrected. I'm sure you will be able to handle it in your own wise way.

As you know, Jonathan is being dropped off here several times a week this summer. He has the run of the place, as it should be. However, he violates club rules and has made himself unpleasant to many of our members.

To be specific, your son refuses to abide by the dress code in the dining room and on the tennis courts. He talks loudly and uses profanity when addressing employees or even other members and their guests. He grossly insulted one of our members.

It's gotten to the point where members have formally complained, some quite vigorously, requesting that Jonathan be suspended. We will be forced to do so if his behavior here continues to be objectionable.

I'm sure you understand our position. You, above all, want this club to be a distinguished haven for gentlemen and their ladies, a model of taste, gentility, and decorum.

Jonathan is a fun-loving young man who sometimes gets out of hand and must be reined in, which is typical of so many youths today. I think of

my young days—and I at times have to discipline my children for unso-
ciable behavior. I'm certain you will straighten this out and will look
on it later in terms of an amusing anecdote.

I'm taking this opportunity to say that we are most pleased and honored
having you as a member. All of us here very much enjoy the company of
you and Mrs. Galbraith.

By the way, you are registered in our club golf tournament which starts
next month, as is Mrs. Galbraith. In the meantime, I'd love to have you
and Mrs. Galbraith as my guests at dinner. Would you please let me know
when you will be available?

My kindest regards,

Jonathan Wheatley

PROVIDE A NEGATIVE RATING OF YOUR ASSISTANT'S JOB PERFORMANCE.

CONFIDENTIAL
JOB-PERFORMANCE EVALUATION

Mr. Gregory Hooper
President

Re: My evaluation of Bob Rector's fitness for an advanced position
      as Supervisor of Customer Service—an executive position. This
      is in advance of my discussion with Mr. Rector.

I am making this evaluation with full consideration that the position
touches on the extremely important matter of dealing firsthand with our
customers. It includes the very sensitive duty of handling complaints and
rectifying real and surmised malfunctions, often with irate and demanding individuals. As such this position requires a high level of people
skills.

With this in mind, my opinion is that Bob isn't ready for this promotion. He would be advancing from a capable official mulling the jots and
titles of administration rules to a broad-spectrum executive.

I urge that we try to give Mr. Rector more seasoning by broadening his
responsibilities and determining how he adjusts. He is a valued employee and we should bring him along as best we can.

I will tactfully inform Bob of our decision on this particular position, and tell him we are grooming him for future advances.

Regards,

Matthew O'Donnell

▌ DISAGREEING WITH YOUR BOSS.

Your boss has a fixed opinion on a new corporate logo. You feel it may be wrong. Your boss picked it and loves it. You want to get your concern on the record.

MEMO TO THE BOSS, NO COPIES

To: Hal Buckley

From: Pete Lopater

I feel it my duty to voice a concern about our new corporate logo. I agree with you that it symbolizes high tech, connotes progress and is very attractive. I realize there is tremendous support for it in this company.

As a manager, I think I should bring up this objection. It seems to my untrained eye that it bears a close resemblance to Magnum's logo. Perhaps our enthusiasm causes us to dismiss this caveat.

We're relatively small; Magnum is overwhelmingly huge. Will Magnum have grounds to say we copied it, or that its logo is where we got our design idea?

Some Magnum mid-manager wanting to make a name for her/himself may get nasty and cause us grief and pain.

I fully agree with you that the new logo is wonderful. But I'm bringing this up as something to think about. If you disagree, or think it's not an issue, I certainly bow to your judgment.

ANOTHER LETTER—CRITICISM OF THE SLOGAN THE BOSS CONCEIVED

Dear Mr. Samuels:

Subject: About our slogan

Certainly your judgment prevails—but I think there may be problem.

Our new slogan tends to be misinterpreted by enough people to be of concern. I checked fifteen people in the office; four gave it a meaning different from what is intended, and two didn't understand it at all.

Obviously, this is not a scientific survey, but enough people got the wrong impression to note that we should stand back and give it a cold, new appraisal. Don't forget, the people I canvassed are close to the company and are more likely to get the meaning we want than the public at large.

Should we do a small-scale survey among a sample of our customer market? If even a small percentage doesn't get what we want to convey, it is a problem.

The bearer of bad tidings often gets killed. Nevertheless, I thought I should mention this. . . and hope that I survive.

Best regards,

Jay Medwick

MONEY MATTERS

A GOOD CUSTOMER WANTS TO DRASTICALLY CUT YOUR BILL.

TWO LETTERS:

Long and Short Form

SITUATION: You are the chairman of an industrial-engineering company that designs and produces manufacturing tools and
machinery. The president of a valuable client wants to deep-cut a bill that was
mutually agreed to in writing. His staff told him that the job, though well
done, was completed in far less time than was anticipated. He sent you a letter stating this. This client has muscle because it is a good source of future
income.

If need be, you are willing to reduce the bill somewhat to preserve the amicable bond you have developed—but not by the amount the client noted. You
want to get as much money as possible without compromising the relationship and, at the same time, solidify the good will of this client.

Answer the client's letter by asking for a meeting to settle the matter. It's
important to talk face-to-face, top-executive to top-executive. The issue and
the money involved are important, and it can only be resolved at the top.

The letter is to show a sincere willingness to cooperate. It's been a rewarding
relationship, and, as always, you want to act in the client's interest.

At the same time, you want to invoke the client's sense of fairness and understanding when he learns the facts. The meeting will clarify this. His staff probably gave him half-truths so as to be heroes by saving a lot of money.

Two letters are shown. One expresses your good will and desire to cooperate and includes some of the key details that buttress your case. This way, the client knows the guts of the issue prior to your meeting.

The other is a short form, not giving any details but expressing a strong desire to be cooperative. And it notes that the client will be fair and understanding when he's apprised of the facts. In this version, you want to conserve all your ammunition for the personal meeting.

Both letters proclaim your willingness to bend over backwards to do what's good for your client.

LETTER #1

Mr. Timothy Georgeson
President
Communications Specialties, Inc.

———————————————

———————————————

Dear Tim:

This is to respond to the points raised in your letter of April 15. I am doing this in the spirit of working for the benefit of CSI. Throughout our relationship, your interests have been of primary importance to us. As such, we will be guided by your budget constraints and will give you our best possible cooperation.

Please consider my position, Tim. When you know all the facts, I'm sure you'll look at this with your usual sense of fairness. Below are the issues that I want to clarify—

Although your R&D staff came to us with the Telesphere specifications and product archetype, we had to start from scratch to develop the manufacturing process. This entailed a great deal of original thinking, much research on tool design, and countless episodes of trial and error. Not to mention frequent 18-hour days and weekends.

The result was a practical way of getting your product to market at a competitive cost and at a normal profit margin for CSI.

We came through for you before, and this time we did it again—successfully and within your time frame. But now your people say that the time we devoted to this job was less than is warranted by the fee—and that the fee should be cut in half!

Tim, bear in mind that the $300,000 fee was a fixed amount for this assignment, mutually agreed upon. The fact that we completed the job faster than anticipated attests to our engineering skills, originality, efficiency, and our experience in tackling this kind of problem. Also, as noted before, we put a vast amount of overtime into it.

Should we be penalized for knowledge, efficiency, and devotion to the task you gave us? If it took longer than anticipated, would we have asked for more money? Of course not.

The important thing is that the assignment was accomplished successfully, meeting all specifications with total satisfaction on the part of your staff.

Let's have a meeting to discuss this. I'm confident we can resolve it in a way that is right for both of us.

Best regards,

C. Winthrop Edmunds
President
Cycle Engineering Ltd.

LETTER #2

Mr. Timothy Georgeson
President
Communications Specialties, Inc.

Dear Tim:

You raised certain points in your letter of April 15, and I'd like to have the opportunity to review them with you. It has to do with our agreed-upon fee for designing the Telesphere manufacturing process.

Please understand that this is in the spirit of working for the benefit of CSI. We will be guided by your budget constraints and are prepared to give you the best cooperation possible.

Tim, when you know all the facts I'm sure you'll look at this with your usual sense of fairness. Let's have a meeting and we'll be able to resolve it in a way that is right for both of us.

Best regards,

C. Winthrop Edmunds
President
Cycle Engineering Ltd.

▌ A GOOD CLIENT IS "SLOW PAY," BUT YOU CAN'T AFFORD ALIENATION.

SITUATION: You are a sales VP at a telemarketing company. One of your accounts is a heavyweight magazine publisher who is responsible for about 30% of your income.

Unfortunately, it has a nagging flaw. It is slow-pay on your company's invoices—60 to 90 days. You are told to get it to a 30-day-cycle because a lot of money is involved each month, and the delay causes problems.

The last thing you want to do is rock the boat with this account, but you are compelled to follow orders and straighten out its lackadaisical way of paying bills.

STRATEGY: Send this client an almost apologetic letter pointing out the problem. Ask for its assistance. Make it seem like you didn't want to bring it up, but you were pushed to the wall by your company's comptroller. This hard-nosed bean counter is the heavy—it's not your doing.

Mr. Dennis O'Toole, Treasurer
Acme Publications, Inc.

Dear Dennis:

I had a really hard time writing this letter. I had refused to do it, because I felt it was out of order. But our comptroller and head bean counter, Joe Spurno, put my feet to the fire. I'm sure, when you read this, you won't see a problem, but I nevertheless feel lousy sending it.

It seems that our bills get paid in 60 to 90 days or more at times, which has become the pattern. This is a long time for us, because it means putting out a lot of money over two to three months to service your business. For example, at this point you are $185,000 past due 60 days or more. As the schedule now stands, it could be as much as $250,000 by next month.

You see, we are obliged to pay our suppliers' bills in 30 to 45 days, and our internal expense outlays, which are basically salaries and office overhead, have to be current.

Although I realize you generally pay your vendors on a normal 60 day cycle, which sometimes stretches to 90 days, could you please see your way clear to push payments through to us in 30 days, which may at times overlap to 45 days?

Even though our company has the resources and creditworthiness to back up these finances for you when necessary, it comes to big numbers on a continuing basis, which makes a problem for Joe.

I don't have to elaborate on what a marvelous relationship we have, and that we've been doing inspired work for Acme Publications. I'm sure you're aware of it. It makes me feel so good to know that our work has generated profits for you during the entire time we've been privileged to handle your account.

Please understand Joe's position—and again, take note, if you will, of my personal aversion to writing this letter. Please let me know if there's a problem.

Sincerely,

Frank Hooper
Vice President

A CLIENT ISN'T PAYING YOUR BILLS. LOTS OF MONEY IS WAY PAST DUE.

TWO LETTERS:

Request Client Pay Past Due Bills and Stay Current

Resign the Account If Client Doesn't Comply

SITUATION: You are a senior executive at an ad agency, overseeing a major electronic client. The people are charming to work for, but with one defect. This client is a slow-payer—often agonizingly slow—past due many months. You hate to dump it and sue, because it represents good income and you know it is far from broke. The money is good, eventually. But you can't afford to play banker.

At any rate, if you sue, there will be legal costs. And it will take months, maybe years to get your money—perhaps not all of it.

You don't want to blow this account, and you don't want to say anything that will diminish your chances of getting it current.

STRATEGY:

Letter 1:

A firm letter, but as pleasant as possible under the circumstances. You can't go on this way and must stop your services until they are current. But you emphasize that you want to continue, if at all possible. Register the point that your work has been excellent and that there's no reason to hold up payments.

Letter 2:

Time passed and they didn't pay up. You now send a letter resigning the account. Next step: sue them; you have no choice.

LETTER #1

(By Registered Mail)

Break-A-Way Electronics Inc.

_____

_____

Attention: Mr. C. David Benson
              Executive Vice President, Marketing

Dear Dave:

I was given strict orders to write this letter.

It has to do with your overdue bills, going back as far as eight months. A schedule is enclosed.

The bills amount to $658,000 past due, of which $212,000 is delinquent six months or longer. Much of this is out-of-pocket expenses, which we have paid. And we're currently working on assignments which call for additional expenditures.

All of these bills were well-documented and approved by you and your staff. Your people are happy with our work, which is still in use. Our previous requests for payments were acknowledged, but nothing of substance has been received.

Our finance department told our account group to discontinue all work on your account until you become current. It stands to reason, we can't continue as bankers for Break-A-Way. Quite frankly, it's beyond comprehension that a company of such distinction as Break-A-Way could be so unmindful of its financial obligations. Our comptroller said he needs an answer within the next four weeks.

I hope you understand that we are taking this action with much regret. We have no choice. Our people have been knocking themselves out on your account and the work is exceptional, as you have remarked many times.

Dave, sending this is painful to me personally, and I hope we will be able to continue working together. We are so well experienced in your business, and we have so many new ideas to help keep Break-A-Way growing. We feel we can still have a wonderful future together.

Truly yours,

Bill Kayson,
Senior Vice President

cc: Mr. Angelo Fortunato, President
       Ms. Elizabeth Doherty, CFO
       Mr. Gerald Martin, Comptroller

LETTER # 2

(By Registered Mail)

Mr. C. David Benson,
Executive Vice President, Marketing
Break-A-Way Electronics, Inc.

_____

_____

We have not received a satisfactory response to the issues raised in our letter of April 13 regarding delinquent bills. We are therefore obliged to resign your account, effective June 10, 1994. Your payments are due for all unpaid invoices and for all work in progress as of this date.

Upon receipt of your payments in full we will transfer all art work, materials, and copy files.

We're doing this with much sorrow. We all liked working with you and are proud of the results you've been getting. We've been very effective for Break-A-Way.

I'll be pleased to have our paths cross again under better circumstances.

Regretfully,

Bill Kayson
Senior Vice President

cc: Mr. Angelo Fortunato, President
       Ms. Elizabeth Doherty, CFO
       Mr. Gerald Martin, Comptroller

▌BREAK THROUGH BUREAUCRATIC STALLING AND GO TO THE TOP TO GET THE MONEY OWED YOU.

SITUATION: You are the owner of a wholesale stationery company, and you purchased some office equipment on a bank credit card. The merchandise was stolen. The bank is obliged to cancel the charge in accordance with a special promotion to card customers that they've been advertising for months.

You are getting stalled by the bank's middle management. You called and wrote the marketing director, but there is still no action.

STRATEGY: Write a letter to the marketing director again, but this time make sure copies also go to the bank's top brass. Technically, you are not bypassing the director, but he knows you are letting his boss of bosses know of his intransigence. It also serves notice of the obligation of the bank's top management.

You want to show your know-how and determination by citing the government agencies that have jurisdiction in these matters. If you complain to them, the bank may well have a problem, with its management bearing responsibility. This will shake up the bank and get you action.

Send it by certified (or registered) mail, return receipt, for greater impact.

The copies to the big-wigs should be addressed to each of them personally in separate envelopes, but not certified or registered.

(By Certified Mail)

Mr. Barry T. Joonow
Vice President, Director of Credit Card Marketing
Assured Bank

_____

_____

Mr. Louis Lewin, Chairman & CEO
Ms. Rona T. Mapery, Sr. VP & General Counsel

On September 21, 1997, I wrote to you about $3,497.10 Assured Bank owes us because office items purchased on my credit card had been stolen. Your advertising states that you will cancel a card charge if such a situation occurs.

I spoke to your customer-service representative about this, and at her request I mailed a copy of the sales slip and a statement of what happened, together with a police report.

To date, I have not received this refund on my credit card account. When I called your office, I was told it was being reviewed, and there may be a question as to the validity of my claim.

I then wrote to you on the above date, and so far you have not responded. Nor have I been able to get through to you personally by phone. I have already paid for phone calls and correspondence, not to mention the time I spent on this.

I can't believe that Assured Bank would engage in misleading advertising.

Mr. Joonow, if this is not resolved within the next 30 days—i.e. by February 22, 1997—I will be obliged to contact the State Banking Department, the Attorney General's Office, and the FTC to obtain what is rightfully owed me.

Very truly yours,

Samuel Herbert, President
Enclosures with supporting documents.

A CARELESS GOOF BY A FINANCIAL MANAGER COST YOU MONEY. YOU WANT TO BE REIMBURSED.

SITUATION: You informed the investment broker who had handled your bond fund that you have selected another money management house. You instructed the broker to make the transfer. However, the transfer went to the wrong money-management company, a firm you didn't even know. It took three weeks for it to be straightened out—and only after you made a lot of noise. Your fund was in limbo all this time.

It couldn't be traded or sold, and you lost money because the price fell day by day and you weren't able to sell. This is a clear case of broker incompetence and carelessness, perhaps because of pique at losing this business.

STRATEGY: Send a registered letter to the president of the company that goofed. Give the facts and state you want to be paid for the money lost, which your accountant and financial manager are determining. This alerts the president to start another financial analysis.

Allow 10 days for a response following your statement of loss, after which you'll seek restitution through the proper authorities.

February 22, 1997

(By Registered Mail)

Mr. T. Roger Quinn
President & C.E.O.
Shelby, Leonard Investment Brokers

_____

_____

Dear Mr. Quinn:

Enough! This comedy of errors has got to stop.

This has cost me money. Plus insufferable anxiety and an inordinate amount of time trying to get it straightened out.

Here is the Situation:

Shelby has managed my fund since Feb. 1987. On January 27, 1997, at 2 P.M. I specified that it be transferred to Washburn Bank & Trust. This was confirmed in writing the same day.

By mistake, the fund was transferred to the Parleau Fund. The reason for choosing Parleau is convoluted, and I will not discuss it here. Suffice it to say, it was an inexcusable blunder.

This fiasco was not discovered until seven days later when I inquired of Washburn why they hadn't received my bond holdings.

>   Shelby kept dodging the problem, saying Parleau should make the
>   correction. Parleau threw it back to Shelby, and so on.
>
>   I prevailed upon Washburn to act as referee and to effectuate
>   the transfer, which they are doing. I think my fund is now
>   finally where I want it to be.

The issue is not cleared up by any means. During the three weeks my bond fund was in limbo, the price started to go down. I wasn't able to sell, but I watched the price fall, to my dismay and financial loss.

I don't have to remind you of your responsibility in this. My investment manager and my accountant are now ascertaining Shelby's liability, which will be forthcoming in the next few days.

Needless to say, I have complete documentation for all the statements mentioned here.

Very truly yours,

Elizabeth Pryor Gibson

P.S.   If I don't hear from you within 10 days after I send you the financial report of my loss, I will be obliged to act through official means of redress.

A BANK IS TRYING TO SQUIRM OUT OF A MORTGAGE COMMITMENT.

SITUATION: The bank accepted your application for refinancing a second mortgage on your new office condo at a very good rate, which it was promoting at the time. Since then, the rates have gone up.

The bank keeps losing your application. It stalls, it misplaces your documents, and then it puts you off. With gnashing teeth, you are determined to inch it forward.

Finally, the bank acknowledges the application. But it imposes an impossible condition, not brought up before, that will effectively kill the deal. Thus it won't have to live with the low rate.

If you start all over, at this or any other bank, it will be at a higher rate.

STRATEGY: Write a certified letter to the VP in charge of the mortgage department. Make it factual and restrained. Point out the problem and indicate the bank's obligation to honor its commitment.

You wish to maintain pleasant relations with the bank, so it's best to avoid a nasty or threatening attitude. On the other hand, you are determined to pressure the bank to honor this mortgage loan.

January 20, 1997

(By Certified Mail)

Ms. Regina Harper Greene
Vice President, Mortgage Lending
Upstream National Bank, International, Inc.

_____
_____

Dear Ms. Greene:

We're sorry to have to call on you for help. But it's come to the point where it is important for you to clear up our predicament with your department—specifically, that your department is not fulfilling the bank's legal obligation on our application to refinance the second mortgage on our office condo in Franklin Park, Illinois. What follows is a summary of the circumstances.

> Our application (No. 30217) was filed on August 17, 1996. We locked in the special rate you offered at the time and paid a fee of $450, which the bank is still holding.

> Every time we called to expedite this, a new person was in charge. We successively dealt with five different people. Each one said there was no record of the filing and asked us to fax the documents. So far we've faxed this material five times. Whenever we tried to talk to an individual, we were put through an obstacle course. The bank records are obviously disorganized.

> Finally, we got approval. But it was subject to a new condition that wasn't in effect, or even discussed or hinted at when we filed. It is an impossible condition. Anyone could be led to believe the bank imposed it in order to renege on the refinancing deal.

> The new condition is that the condo committee has to give up the right of refusal to the resale of this property. In other words, in the case of foreclosure the bank can sell it to whomever it chooses, at whatever price it chooses.

> There is no way the condo committee would ever agree to this. It is contrary to its charter, contrary to its rights, and contrary to any normal condo conditions.

The rates have gone up since the filing, at Upstream and other banks. It would be burdensome for us to refinance at the present rate.

We cannot tolerate the egregious condition the bank imposed on this loan, done summarily and after the fact. We are fixed on the rate that the bank advertised and agreed to, under the conditions that were in effect at the time. The bank accepted our application in good faith, and we don't believe you can walk away from it.

Thank you for your time in reviewing this. We're sure you will see to it that Upstream honors its commitment.

Very truly yours,

Lucinda Cannon

P.S.   We have long been Upstream customers. The bank holds the first mortgage on this office complex and has serviced us on a number of other loans. We have enjoyed our relationship, and we would like to continue doing business with Upstream.

▌YOUR BILL TO A CUSTOMER IS MORE THAN THE CONTRACT ▌CALLED FOR.

SITUATION: You, as the owner of a printing company, finally got a chance to bid on a big job for a new customer who contracts out a lot of printing, and whom you have been courting for a long time.

The specifications are tough as to quality and deadline. You lowball your bid so as to be sure you get the assignment, hoping for the best.

Three-quarters of the way to completion, you find you can't finish the work for nearly what you quoted. It would mean a sizeable loss, which you can't afford to absorb even if you wanted to. You have to ask for more money.

STRATEGY: A letter explaining the higher charge must be plausible, so that the price will be acceptable without much protest.

Your contention is that the customer is to blame. It made changes beyond anything that could be reasonably anticipated, and you want to make an on-time delivery without sacrificing quality. Say that you are eating a big part of the additional cost.

Furthermore, point out that the printed piece will be superb—work that it will be proud to show within its organization and outside. You will make the customer look good. Isn't this what's most important, when all is said and done?

```
Mr. Herbert H. Rothman
Vice President, Credit Card Marketing
2nd National Bank

_____

_____


Dear Herb:

It took a lot of doing, but we made the recent changes on the mechani-
cals that you and Tim ordered, and we're on track in getting the work
done on time. This caused a lot of extra expense because the visuals and
some of the type had to be completely redone.

We probably could have squeezed through without making all this extra
effort, but it wouldn't have come out right. That is, it wouldn't have
been perfect. You said you wanted perfection, and that's what you're get-
ting. No compromises, no kidding.

Your staff had previously asked for other changes that turned out to be
time-consuming. Frankly, we put a lot of overtime into your job to meet your
due date and specs. We did not want to let you down on quality or timing.

All of these production changes have added 19% to the cost over what is
shown in the production order. It went from $50,000 to $59,500.

We're able to bring it in at this price because we're eating a big part
of the overtime cost. In addition, our paper supplier raised the price
of the stock after we gave you the quote, and we're not charging you for
this additional cost. If we charged you for all the extras, the price
would be over $68,000.

As it stands, you are getting a terrific bargain. But, more impor-
tantly, you are getting wonderful paper stock and the highest quality
printing. You will have flyers you will be proud to show your chairman
and president. A beautiful piece like this is sure to increase your con-
sumer response—the extra expense will more than pay for itself.

Thanks so much, Herb, for the opportunity to serve you.

Best regards,

Urbana Gibbons
President

PS.    Let's have lunch or dinner next week. I'll call your secretary
       for a convenient date.
```

DUNNING A CLOSE FRIEND FOR A BUSINESS LOAN OWED YOU.

SITUATION: You came through for someone close to you when he needed money for his business. It was three years ago, and he had been courting you at the time. The relationship cooled, but the tender feeling didn't. You are still good friends.

It was not a small sum. He asked for $60,000, which you lent him. All you got back was $30,000, which was a year and a half ago. He seems to be taking advantage of the relationship and hasn't made a move to pay back the rest.

Too much time has passed without bringing it up. And you are now in urgent need of the money for your business. His business is doing fine, and he can afford to pay up.

STRATEGY: A chummy letter with affectionate undertones. The debt won't stand in the way of friendship, but there is a pointed reminder that the money is due and that you need it. Include a veiled reference that legal persuasion would work but is not necessarily on your mind. That is, not yet.

Mr. Harry Camanakis, President
Desiree Beauty Care

_____

_____

Good morning, Harry,

It's come to pass . . . I have to quote James Baldwin, the author. . .

"Money . . . is exactly like sex; you think of nothing else if you don't have it, and think of other things if you do."

You thought of money (not sex) three years ago because you needed it (the money). Now I'm thinking about money for the same reason.

In other words, I need the rest of the money I lent you—$30,000 plus $1,500 interest. A total of $31,500. I still have your loan note.

I understand your business has been quite good and that you should be able to pay, so this is not an unrealistic request. (Among friends we don't use the awful word, demand.)

If need be, you can pay me $10,000 now, and $7,000 a month for 2 months, with $7,500 in the third month. Naturally, it would be great if you rob a bank and pay the whole thing at once. I'll be in touch with you next week.

Honest, Harry, if I didn't need the money for my business I wouldn't press you. But I do and I must. That's how important it is.

Thanks so much, Harry. I know you'll complete your obligation as you had promised. We'll always be friends.

Truly,

Sandi Michaels

▌A LAW FIRM UPPED ITS BILL OVER ITS ESTIMATE.

SITUATION: The bill came in much higher than the law firm indicated it would. More time was charged, and more copies of documents had to be made, creating additional charges which hadn't been specified in advance.

Professionals sometimes eat up more time than expected when they get into a project, and they are extremely reluctant to agree to a cap. At $200 to $300 an hour, it mounts up quickly to big numbers when the meter starts to run.

STRATEGY: *Caution:* Be nice. Try to avoid getting rough with lawyers. Remember: It costs them hardly anything to sue you, but it costs you a bundle to defend it. Ask to settle for the original estimate because you can't afford to pay the extra amount. Note that you will need more legal help in the future, at which time more money will be available. Good luck.

Mr. Oliver T. Golden
Darwin, Golden, & Meister
Counselors At Law

_____
_____

Dear Mr. Golden:

Thank you for the information you provided and for your advice. This will help in formulating our immediate decision, although we will need more legal assistance when we get to the next stage in this new business venture.

We decided to take this piecemeal approach in seeking legal guidance because we don't want to go beyond a $10,000 charge at this time, which is the outside limit of what you said it would be. That's why we were surprised and shocked when we received your bill for $16,440. It is much more than we are in a position to pay at this early stage.

Your bill noted, among other things, extra research costs over what we had discussed in order to have auxiliary back-up. You didn't tell us you were going ahead on this, and, truly, we didn't think we needed this extra assurance for our current purposes. If you had asked us in advance, we would have told you not to go over the $10,000 charge.

Mr. Golden, we value your expertise and legal judgment, and we certainly want to continue with your firm as this project grows to what is considered to be a major enterprise. But for the present, we ask your cooperation in keeping our bill at $10,000, which had been agreed to, and which, as I mentioned before, is the absolute limit of what we are able to pay now. It goes without saying, our legal budget will be higher in our next stage.

Thank you so much for your consideration.

Cordially,

Mario D'Amato

YOU WERE FLOORED BY THE BILL A LAW FIRM SENT, WITH NO ADVANCE ESTIMATE.

Letter to the Attorney

Letter to the Other Defendants in the Case

SITUATION: You were employed by an engineering company and left for another job at a company in the same industry. Six fellow employees at the same level also switched to various competitors—all of these job changes taking place within a six-month period. You all have stock options in your former company.

Your former company instituted a blanket suit, naming the seven of you as codefendants. The purpose of the suit was to recover your stock options at no cost due to what they consider to be a legitimate loophole in the issuing document. They cited collusion because all of you left within a short time of each other. There was no collusion—it was coincidental.

They also charge that you use your excompany's privileged information at your new locations, and you all have to answer the charges.

The seven of you banded together and hired a law firm for a common defense. You had given the firm's partner on your case a retainer and asked her to let you know of impending expenses before she proceeded to pile them up at the rate of $200 to $300 per hour plus expenses. She went to work on the legal chores, however, without providing an estimate of expenses, as you had requested.

Without warning, she sent each of you a bill for $6,500, covering the first four weeks, with a description of the legal work that was done. She also sent an agreement form to sign, authorizing her to continue her work and be able to bill for it on an ongoing basis.

STRATEGY: Draft a letter to the attorney which expresses your feelings, and documents your request for the information you want—a detailed accounting of ongoing expenses and an agreeable cap.

Send a copy of this to the other defendants along with a letter to them, relating your displeasure with the lawyer's conduct and expressing your attitude on legal expenses. You will all have to arrive at a common understanding on how to proceed.

```
December 10, 1997
Ms. Sara Sobolev
Connors, Melnik Law Firm

_____

_____


Re:    Your Letter and Bill of November 3, 1997.
       Casvit Production Engineering Ltd.

Dear Ms. Sobolev:

Your letter and accompanying bill came as a distinct surprise—and an
unnerving jolt.
```

    A. First of all, we had agreed that you were to let me know in advance of any activity you would undertake that would result in a major expense. I consider this amount a major expense.

    B. There is no indication as to how long this will take and the amount of legal effort and bills. Signing your fee agreement on a going-forward basis amounts to a blank check.

       I'm sure it is not your intention to seek approval to move ahead without some kind of cap or protection device to guard against outlandish payments in terms of what the case is worth. It may get to the point where it doesn't make sense to proceed.

    C. I am asking for an opinion from you as to the worthiness of our case, how much is at stake, and what our chances are.

       I know you can't predict what a judge and jury will do, but you do know, from your experience and knowledge, the strength of our legal position, the odds of the plaintiff winning, and the advisability of making a countersuit. In other words, is it worthwhile to pursue this at the level on which you are proceeding?

Please let me know so I can decide how I want to proceed.

Respectfully,

Cynthia Fuller

December 10, 1997

To the Parties Defending the Lawsuit of
Casuist Production Engineering Ltd.

    Janice Bomar   Linda Sue Hager
    Paul Caplitsky   Perry Mitchell
    Drew Reynolds   Paula Herbert

Dear Friends:

This is about the letter from our law firm, Connors, Melnik, which I assume you received. I was nonplussed—shall I say shocked?—by the size of its bill, which came without warning. And also by its request for an open fee agreement on ongoing activities. It amounts to signing a blank check, which, frankly, is against my nature. I'm sure you feel the same way.

I'm enclosing a copy of the letter I am about to send to C.M. I'd like to get your opinions. Did I reflect your attitudes? What do you think about this whole matter? Do you have any other questions that should be put to C.M.?

I think we should have a meeting of the minds as to what we want to do and how much money we should put towards it. I also think we have to marshal our forces to rein in C.M. without impairing our position.

Let's get together or have a phone conference.

Warm regards to all,

Cynthia Fuller

YOU ARE BEING MISTAKENLY BILLED AND IT CONTINUES UNCORRECTED.

SITUATION: You returned office supplies that were bought through a catalog. The catalog company didn't record the return and keeps sending you bills, with interest added on every month because it is in the "past due" format on its computer.

You phoned and were asked to send a letter with a copy of your return receipt. You did, twice. Later phone calls produced pleasant replies, apologies, and assurances that it was being fixed. The bill continues to come in, every month, and the interest keeps piling up.

STRATEGY: A letter to the sales manager expressing your annoyance. Report the facts. Refrain from any invectives or insults, but do let her know that you will charge for your time and expenses if this dialogue continues. It's a good way to free you from its correspondence and stir up some action.

Ms. Sheila Hammerman
Catalog Manager
Newman's Office Supplies, Inc.

_____
_____

Dear Ms. Hammerman:

It's been said that patience is a virtue.

Does running out of it mean not being virtuous?

My patience and virtue (and perseverance) are being tested by Newman's catalog. I am now calling on you to finally put an end to it. I'm sure it can be done very easily, now that it's in your hands.

On January 10th, we placed an order for equipment, chairs, and supplies amounting to $2,878.41, billed to our account. Part of the order totalling $1,260.08 was returned because it was not the color ordered. I have the return receipt for this. No replacement was requested.

Then it started. I've been getting a bill for the original sum every month for the past four months, which includes a 1-1/2% monthly interest charge.

I called and wrote several times. Each time I get a prompt letter in response, but these are stock letters taken off the shelf. Your people just fill in the blanks. Newman's, it seems, has a generic letter to fit every possible contingency.

We don't have the advantage of stock letters. I have to compose a new letter every time I write. I and my associates have already spent much too much time writing and phoning. Ms. Hammerman, you must put an end to this.

This is to serve notice that if it is necessary for us to do anything more on this matter, we will bill Newman's for time and expenses, as follows—

Composing letters:	$50 Per Hour
Typing and phone calls:	$10 Per Hour
Postage, stationery, phone charges:	To be billed at cost.

My previous activities on this matter, including this letter, will not be billed, since I had not informed you in advance of my rates.

Thank you, Ms. Hammerman. I anticipate your prompt attention to this.

Very truly yours,

Mrs. Rebecca Sloane
President, Hudson Real Estate Brokers

UNAFFORDABLE EXTRA CHARGES ON REPAIRS AND EQUIPMENT.

Two Situations:

I: *No Written Confirmation of Cost Overrun*

II: *Written Confirmation of the Extra Cost*

SITUATION I: A contractor bumped up his bill for shelving, rigging, and
                office furniture due to modifications he had not anticipat-
ed. The issue of extra charges was specified on the phone, but not confirmed
in writing. The price hike was considerably more than was verbally cited—a
real shocker.

STRATEGY I: Send the contractor a letter noting your surprise and cha-
               grin, and say you can't afford the cost overrun. Tell him
that, if need be, he will have to take back the furniture and equipment.

Offer to settle. The contractor has little leverage. Removing the merchandise, particularly the shelving and rigging, would be costly, and, besides, it
was modified for your premises. He may not accept your first offer, but
you'll probably be able to settle for less than the total overrun that was
billed.

Note that you want to do business in the future, but from now on every cost
must be specified in advance in writing.

SITUATION II: A contractor increased his bill above the original estimate.
                An overage that was confirmed was exceeded. The addi-
tional cost is a distinct financial burden.

STRATEGY II: You offer to pay the original estimated amount at once,
               with the additional sum to be paid three to four months later.

You want to avoid having the contractor go the legal route to get the full payment. You simply need more time to pay it all off.

STRATEGY I

January 25, 1996

Super D Office Equipment Service

_____

_____

Attention: Ms. Edwina Sherman, Vice President, Sales

Dear Ms. Sherman:

I say this with agitation as well as concern. When your bill came in (No.
11030, copy attached), it floored us. Literally.

The shelving, rigging, and furniture were originally priced at $138,275 which was confirmed by our purchase order. We grant that you had to make modifications on the merchandise, which you told us about. However, you didn't specify the full amount of the cost overrun. We had no idea the extra charge would be $33,050, which brought your bill total to $171,325.

Regretfully, we are not in a position to pay this additional money. Further, we believe the modifications are in large part your responsibility since you did not have merchandise that fit our space needs, and you agreed to alter what you had in stock.

It is your option to take back the merchandise, which, understandably, would be costly for you and inconvenient for both of us. We certainly don't look on this with any favor.

We are willing to settle the bill for $15,000 over the original quote, for a total of $153,275. There is really no way we are able to go above this figure.

Since we both want to resolve this quickly, we ask that you let us know your position in writing at your earliest convenience.

Please, next time we do business together, let's pin all charges and extras down on paper before they take place. Everything, so there are no surprises. You have a good shop and good people, and we would be pleased to have you supply our needs in the future.

Sincerely,

Leander Williams
President

STRATEGY II

January 25, 1996

William Quinn
Senior Vice President
X3 Computer Resource Ltd.

_____

_____

Attention: Accounts Receivable   Re: Your Invoice No. 34772
               Oscar Steuben

Dear Mr. Steuben:

We received the software we had ordered, together with your bill for new peripherals. The total is $22,370, of which the peripherals portion is $20,000.

We value this equipment and your people did a fine job of installing and testing. Our monitors are working satisfactorily and up to expectations. However, your original estimate was $14,000, which we set aside for payment. We acknowledge that we had later authorized additional components at the extra cost.

The cold fact remains, however, that we are not prepared to pay the additional $6,000 at this particular time. We are confronted with a tax surcharge that hadn't been predicted, and which has to be paid at once.

Please bear with us. We will be able to comfortably pay you the $6,000 difference in the next 90 to 120 days. And then we also want to talk about additional equipment to take care of expanded business volume.

We value your service and want to maintain a good relationship. Be assured, this bill will be paid in full.

Very truly,

William Quinn, Sr. Vice President

A COMPANY WANTS TO PAY YOU. BUT YOUR CHECK IS TRAPPED IN ITS DATA FILE.

SITUATION: You were laid off (i.e., fired), and several thousand dollars are owed you for severance and vacation pay—actually, over $20,000. The amount is beyond question and is not challenged. Nevertheless, it is trapped in a bureaucratic maze. You cannot decipher or even understand the problem when it's explained to you.

Time drags, bills are due, and you need the money. You can't afford to start a lawsuit. The company can easily afford to defend it, and a legal fracas would drag on and on.

STRATEGY: Send a letter to the company chairman. Say that if you don't get your money shortly, which is a cut-and-dried expense on its part and is not in contention, you will have to alert the proper government agencies, albeit unwillingly. Appeal to his sense of compassion. You are a poor lone person versus a rich giant. This letter will be a good document if and when you seek legal help.

September 10, 1997

(By Certified Mail)

Mr. David H. Solomon
President and C.E.O.
Manor Hotel Supply

_____

_____

Re: My letters and documents forwarded 7/1, 7/13, 8/17

Dear Mr. Solomon:

The whole issue boils down to this . . .

> When I was dismissed on July 29, 1993, the company owed me
> $20,628.00 in severance and vacation pay and unreimbursed
> expenses.
>
> I should add that this experience caused me to have anxiety,
> depression, and physical suffering, which a doctor can verify.

Your legal and accounting departments have confirmed this amount due me,
but no one I called has any inkling of where it stands.

My intuition says this is mired in your accounting files or in your computer memory. My common sense says if I don't get a positive notification of payment by September 30, I will have to reluctantly start the
legal machine rolling with the appropriate government agencies.

Why not be fair to an exemployee and pay what you unquestionably owe?
I'm looking for a job and need the money. My pay check has stopped, but
my bills haven't. Unemployment insurance hardly covers it. Please, Mr.
Solomon, don't keep me waiting any longer.

Very truly yours,

Debra Potemkin

PROTECT YOUR COMMISSION AS A BROKER WHEN THERE IS NO WRITTEN AGREEMENT.

SITUATION: A company in another state wants your printing company
to produce its brochures. You find you can't handle it with
your equipment and are subcontracting the job to another printer—i.e., a
third party.

The third party asked you to sign an agreement guaranteeing payment. In effect, you would be guaranteeing your customer's payment. You don't want to take this risk.

STRATEGY:

Two Letters:

NOTIFICATION TO YOUR CLIENT.

NOTIFY THE THIRD-PARTY SUPPLIER.

Send the guarantee statement to your customer. He now knows you are using an outside supplier and who it is. You previously asked for a broker's commission on this job, and he approved with a verbal agreement. However, he could now deal with the third party directly and squeeze you out, neatly preventing your commission.

If you ask your customer to sign a broker's agreement now, he might stall or refuse, which could sanction his not paying. Therefore, send him a letter confirming your verbal agreement. It gives you some protection, which is better than none.

At the same time, let the third party know in writing that you have a right to the broker's commission, which he may have to pay by increasing his bill to include it.

You've done what you can. It sounds convoluted, but this paper trail is the way to go in this situation.

This exercise is not nearly as good as a written agreement prior to starting the work, but it provides a basis for getting tough if you don't get paid. Anyway, it's worth the effort.

```
(By Certified Mail)

Victor Stepanian, Senior VP
Coup Promotions, Inc.

_____

_____


Dear Victor:

As we had agreed, I got an outside source to produce the 500,000 print-
ed flyers you need for your client's promotion. We weren't able to adhere
to your specs for the precise die cut with our equipment.
```

Anytime Graphics is doing the job. I understand that you have previously done business with this firm directly. You should understand that I negotiated with Anytime to bring its price down $10 per 1,000 from its quote—from $35 to $25 per 1,000. This took a lot of negotiating, particularly in view of your tight schedule. You had originally said you were in a position to pay as much as $35.

Anytime wants a signed commitment guaranteeing the price and payment terms, which I'm not in a position to give. I'm enclosing it for you to sign and forward to Anytime, with a copy to me.

As the broker on this deal, my commission is a flat $5 per 1,000 pieces, which is what we agreed to. It is to be paid to me at the same time you send payment to Anytime. This comes to $2,500 for this 500,000 print run, and $5 per 1,000 for later print production with Anytime or any other printer.

I will handle the set-up details with Anytime and will keep this job moving.

We're delighted to be serving you, and I'm looking ahead to a boom promotion.

Truly yours,

Sidney Lebow

Mr. Ferde Carew, President
Anytime Graphics, Inc.

_____

_____

Dear Ferde:

I sent your agreement to my client, Coup Promotions, for signature, since it is not in my province to assume this obligation.

I realize you had done business with Coup directly, but I am the broker in this project and am to receive a flat commission fee of $5 per 1,000 pieces for this 500,000 run and all subsequent runs.

As it stands now, I'm to get this payment from Coup. But this could change, and I'll advise you whether to add the $5 to your bill and send me the commission.

Truly yours,

Sid Lebow

▮ STAY IN THE BEST OF GRACES WITH YOUR EX-EMPLOYER.

SITUATION: You just left a giant media conglomerate for a top spot at a
                competitor. A BIG going-away severance payment is due
you—on paper. Your ex-employer, the company president, got his back up
about your departure and threatens not to pay you. "Sue me," he says.

STRATEGY: It would be dumb to burn your bridges. It's smart to keep
               up a friendly connection with the head honcho of the com-
pany you left. You never know when the connection can pay off, only that it
probably will. Show him your admiration. Every executive loves flattery,
regardless of how he/she may toss it aside.

Send a letter of regret that you'll miss his guidance, his counsel, and his company. Indicate that staying close will pay off for both of you. There's a small
circle of top players in this industry, and your paths are sure to cross. You'll
be making deals together.

The issue of the severance package is left unsaid. But it's in the wind, and this
letter is intended to quell resistance.

January 18, 1997

Mr. Donald T. Degraw, President
Data Connection Corporation

_____

_____

Dear Don:

As I look out my office window here in the suburbs, what do you think
is on my mind?

It's how I liked working with you, which I'll really miss.

Mostly,it was the valuable guidance you gave me. It was great tossing
around ideas with you. How you seized on strategies to make the business
thrive, and how we made competition sit up and take notice. The decisions we made on the run. I don't think I'll ever forget the drag-out
sessions we had in your office. But we sure got things done.

The lessons I learned—shall I say the training I got—at DCC no doubt got
me ready for the big challenges I have here. There's so much to do to
grow this business and they gave me much leeway to do it.

The new technology that will soon be available to consumers will be mind-boggling. No one company can avail themselves of all of it. Part of my mission here is to set up partnerships, joint ventures, and parallel marketing for exciting new consumer services—entertainment, shopping, politics, investments, and personal counseling. You name it.

I'm sure we will be able to work and invest jointly, get a big jump on the industry, and make a lot of money together. We often talked about it. Don, that's the future, and it's coming up fast. In fact, it's here, staring us in the face. I can see our working together in the future. I'd like nothing better, because I know what you can do.

Give my love to Theresa. Jacki sends warm regards to both of you.

Have a great day,

Pat Shamahan

YOU CAN'T MAKE BANK PAYMENTS THAT ARE DUE ON A BUSINESS LOAN.

SITUATION: You are the owner of a temporary-worker franchise. Your company is financially strapped and can't continue making installment payments on a $100,000 bank loan. It's a three-year loan, and half of the payments have been made.

You need more time to straighten things out. You may be able to resume payments in six months or so.

STRATEGY: Be candid and sincere in your desire to make good on your debt and maintain your reputation.

It's caused by a temporary setback. Your condition looks viable and you should soon be in a position to pay. You need time.

You want to appear intelligent, responsible, and worthy of confidence and trust.

You value the relationship with the bank and with the executive you're addressing, with whom you'll be doing business for a long time.

You will be liable for interest being accrued during the hiatus, which will increase your total interest on the loan. But you need a break for now on monthly payments for principal and interest.

The underlying factor: actually, the bank has little choice but to grant a hiatus, so long as it believes you are sincere and good for the money.

```
Mr. Roger McDevitt, Vice President
Standard Bank and Trust

_____

_____


Dear Mr. McDevitt:

May I prevail upon you for help in a special situation? It's about
our installment loan for $100,000 (#82351), which calls for 36 month-
ly payments, and on which we've been making payments for the past 18
months.

As you know, we have been punctual in our payments to date, as with all
our other financial responsibilities. We very much value our reputation
and credit standing. However, a problem has now arisen.

We're undergoing unexpected expenses for emergency office repairs. In
addition, there has been unusual difficulty in collecting a substantial
payment from one of our customers. This customer has had a business set-
back which will soon be alleviated, and it has assured us of payment
shortly.

This is a temporary condition caused by these two one-time occurrences.
Our business is viable, which is certainly a good record considering the
state of the economy. We've cut expenses to continue an ongoing profit
situation while still maintaining our normally high standards of customer
service.

Mr. McDevitt, may we request that you suspend our loan payments for the
next six months? We will then resume on schedule. As you know, we have
been customers of Standard Bank and Trust for the past four years, and
we expect to continue for many more years. We've had a pleasant rela-
tionship with you personally as well as a fine business relationship with
the bank. We value both of these greatly.

Thank you so much for your cooperation.

Sincerely yours,

Jack O'Doul, President

JO:xx
```

YOUR COMPANY WAS SHORTCHANGED ON AN INSURANCE CLAIM.

SITUATION: There was storm damage to your commercial building and adjoining parking lot. The insurance adjuster put your loss at $238,000. Your actual cost of repairs is $53,000 additional, after your deductible.

STRATEGY: Point out the error in a registered (or certified) letter, return receipt, to the head of claims at the company, and send copies to your broker. Attach a complete list of damages and the cost of each item of repair and compare it with the amount the company allowed. You already spoke to your broker, and it is agreed that you will write to the company directly.

Be amicable and assume it has made an honest mistake. Invite company representatives to come back and reassess the damage, although, understandably, repairs are in progress.

This is a lot of money. You have to be prepared to pursue this if the insurance company doesn't make good. Enclose the facts and figures with the letter. However, write with the assurance that the issue is cut-and-dried and that the company will pay the extra money.

(By Registered Letter)
September 27, 1997

Mr. Roger Andrews
Vice President
Angelou Insurance Corp.

Re: Claim No. 30542, 32 Westminster Drive

Dear Mr. Andrews:

This is to report a sizeable miscalculation in the adjustment of damages due to Hurricane Andrew to my building and adjoining parking lot at the above address.

Your adjuster estimated $238,000. The repairs are now being done and it's clear that the cost will be $291,000—$53,000 more than what your company allowed. With my $10,000 deductible, the amount of underpayment is $653,000. A full itemization and particulars are enclosed herewith.

Mr. Andrews, I want to stress that these repairs are necessary to restore my property to its prestorm condition, not to make any improvements beyond that condition.

I realize your adjuster was extraordinarily busy at the time and may have been hasty in his examination. And I'm sure that Angelou Insurance will rectify his miscalculation.

As you can imagine, this has been a terrible experience for me and my employees. It's so good to know we have placed our trust in a fine, ethical company such as Angelou.

Thank you for your time in taking care of this matter.

Truly yours,

Nicolas Dale

cc: Amalgamated Insurance Brokers

▎ A STOCKBROKER TOUTED YOU ON A BAD INVESTMENT.

SITUATION: Your stockbroker talked you into an initial public offering. He strongly suggested it would be a good moneymaker, a seldom-seen opportunity.

You are normally prudent with your hard-earned money, but you saw this as good advice from a supposed friend.

Eleven months passed, and you now have a loss of $32,400 on a $100,000 investment, which was still sliding southward when you were able to sell it.

You are distressed; it's making you physically ill; and you feel stupid about being conned. You desperately want to get your money back.

Appealing to the NASD, SEC, and Attorney General will take months of delays and mounds of paper work. It's even questionable if they would see this as important enough to launch their big guns. You have to prove duplicity or fraud. Consulting a lawyer is costly. Undoubtedly, other people have also been stung by this culprit. Could you start a class action suit? If yes, how?

STRATEGY: Send the head of the brokerage firm a registered letter, return receipt, declaring your grievance. You tell him that his company's agent gave you a glowing verbal report, making statements that were not shown in the prospectus. You note that the company, in effect, knowingly allowed you to obtain misleading information. Include all of the particulars.

The letter shows your awareness of the government authorities and industry bodies that monitor such matters, but also shows that you prefer not to involve them at this time.

Brokerage houses, and other companies that handle money and are subject to official regulations, are especially concerned about claims of misfeasance or unethical practices. They don't like to be investigated by the authorities. You have a legitimate beef that the company will probably check out thoroughly. Your loss may not be big enough in eyes to warrant a fracas, and it may want to settle this and get it out of the way.

However, the company's attorneys may consider that a payment to you could cause legal problems, such as opening up a can of worms regarding other investors in this and other offerings.

If a great deal of money is involved, or the company doesn't want to make good or has disappeared, government authorities and the courts may be the only option. You'll need a lawyer to represent you, a means of redress that is not the province of this book.

(By Registered Mail)
November 17, 1996

Mr. Bailey C. Dickinson
Chairman and CEO
Dickinson, Stanley, Matthews and Co.
Investment Counselors and Brokers

Dear Mr. Dickinson:

I am bringing to your attention a serious wrongdoing by an agent in your Detroit office, Mr. Oliver DeCamp. It has caused me a large financial loss and much personal anguish, which has affected my health.

Mr. DeCamp was very aggressive in selling me 1000 shares of the initial public offering of LEX Biotech, on January 7, 1993 for $100,000. He spoke glowingly of the company's future. He said it was a vanguard entry in a zooming market; it was doing cutting-edge research; it had new product breakthroughs in the pipeline.

I am very conservative in these matters, but I trusted Mr. DeCamp. He was eloquent in elaborating the merits of this offering. Mr. DeCamp caused me to believe I would make a profit of 20% to 30% on my investment within 12 months.

Instead, LEX, as you know, plummeted in value, causing me a loss of $32,400 when I finally sold the stock on November 8, 1993 to avoid further loss.

I realize there is risk in stock transactions, but this was a case of your agent pushing a very questionable investment with falsely optimistic information. It may well be that other people have suffered similarly severe losses as a result of this deception.

I did not contact the SEC, the Attorney General, the NASD, or the N.Y. Stock Exchange Ethics Committee. I prefer to deal directly with you, Mr. Dickinson, as the Chief Executive Officer of a well-known and reputable investment company. I demand that your company redress this egregious and unethical manipulation of my hard-earned money by putting $32,400 into my account. I will then consider it a closed matter.

If I do not hear from you by November 29, which is two weeks from the above date, I will be obliged to take further action.

Very truly yours,

Eleanor Todd Hamilton

FIGHT BACK AFTER BUYING FAULTY, UNDERPERFORMING, DEFECTIVE, OVERPRICED MERCHANDISE

RECENTLY PURCHASED OFFICE EQUIPMENT IS UNSATISFACTORY. YOU WANT TO EXCHANGE IT. PAID BY CREDIT CARD.

TWO STRATEGIES, TWO LETTERS

I: *Credit Card Charge Went Through*

II: *Credit Card Charge Did Not Go Through*

SITUATION I: An air-conditioner unit you recently bought from an appliance retailer for your conference room doesn't have enough cooling capacity. The salesperson had mistakenly told you it would be adequate. You want it removed and a more powerful unit installed. You paid by credit card.

STRATEGY I: The credit card charge went through. The seller has your money. You must invoke its good will to have it make the exchange. It's good to mention that the manager of the bank that issued your card is your ally. A retailer wants to have a good image with a credit card bank, particularly one in the area.

Send a letter by certified mail, return receipt.

STRATEGY I

(By Certified Mail)

January 13, 1996

Perfect Appliances and Electronics, Inc.

Attention: Ms. Irene Wentzel
              Vice President and Store Manager

Dear Ms. Wentzel:

I'm sure you will understand our consternation and frustration when you read this. From the glowing comments we heard about your company, I am equally sure you will set it right.

It regards an Upstart 190 room air conditioner which we purchased for our conference room on December 21, 1993. (#134702, delivered and installed December 23). This machine doesn't cool sufficiently, even though your salesperson told us it has adequate BTU capacity for our room size of 22' × 35'.

The room temperature does not go below 78 degrees on a hot day, which is certainly uncomfortable. It goes without saying that we would have ordered a more powerful unit if there had been any indication it was required.

Our credit card charge of $1,286.17 with Carol National Bank has gone through. But the manager at our branch told us it had processed many transactions from Perfect Appliances. There haven't been any problems; in fact, she told us that we shouldn't be concerned because of your fine reputation in this community. She was certain you would replace this machine with one of greater cooling capacity. We are asking this of you at this time.

Ms. Wentzel, we're sorry for any inconvenience this is causing you. But it's good to know you will rectify the situation. You will have a delighted customer who will join our bank manager and other business people in this community in vouching for your reliability.

Thanks so much. I'll talk to you soon about making the exchange.

Best regards,

SITUATION II: You were able to cancel the credit card charge with the issuing bank before the payment went through. In effect, the seller hasn't been paid.

STRATEGY II: You are virtually in control. Ask for an exchange. It's not a bad idea to bring in the name of the credit card bank manager for extra leverage.

Send a letter by certified mail, return receipt.

STRATEGY II

(By Certified Mail)

Harrison Franklin, Owner
Perfect Appliances and Electronics, Inc.

Attention: Ms. Irene Wentzel
              Vice President and Store Manager

Dear Ms. Wentzel:

I'm sure you will understand my agitation about the Upstart 190 room air conditioner we purchased from you on December 21, 1993 (#134702, delivered and installed 12/23/93).

It doesn't cool the room satisfactorily, even though your salesperson stated the BTU units were sufficient for the room size of 22' X 35'.

I have therefore asked my credit card bank to cancel your charge of $1,286.17 for this product and installation.

I would be very happy if you removed this appliance and installed another air conditioner with greater cooling capacity. And, perhaps, a different brand, which we can discuss. The manager of the bank branch that issued my card said she has many transactions with your store without any problems, so I'm confident you will make good on this.

I'm sorry for the extra work this has caused you, but it's good that it can be rectified, and you will have a happy customer who will be coming into your store for many more purchases.

Thank you so much.

Sincerely yours,

Harrison Franklin, Owner

▌ RECENTLY PURCHASED A CAR THAT HAS DEFECTS.

You didn't get satisfaction from the dealer after talking to him and even sending a letter. The next step is a certified letter to the president of the manufacturer, copy to the dealer. This will get you action.

(By Certified Mail)

February 19, 1996

Mr. Carl Longo
President and CEO
Artful Motor Co.
2001 Northeastern Rd.
Long Beach, CA 91628

Dear Mr. Longo:

It has become necessary for me to write to you about a dealer complaint that I'm sure you will agree is serious.

Please review the enclosed copy of my previous correspondence to this dealer, Sequence Motor Co., Southfield, Michigan. This indicates the issue; however, it does not address the dealer's unacceptable solution.

The repairs needed in order to have my car function satisfactorily, and to perform as you claim in your advertising, were not done, despite the dealer's claim that he restored this vehicle to peak performance. This is why I am asking you to intercede in this matter.

I am sure that as the head of a reputable manufacturer and marketer of an expensive product, you will not want this unpleasant episode to continue further.

I appreciate your time in handling this.

Sincerely,

Mrs. Ethel Bettis

cc: Mr. Harold Langer
       President, Sequence Motors

ANOTHER LETTER THAT LEFT YOU FURIOUS

Mr. Carl Longo
President and CEO
Artful Motor Co.
2001 Northeastern Rd.
Long Beach, CA 91628

Re: Your Invoice No. 34772

Dear Mr. Longo:

I have 8,000 miles on my '97 Lariat, the Laurel model. I recently visited my dealer, Sequence Motors in Southfield, Michigan for a routine oil change, but the service consultant advised me to get a 15,000 mile check since it was opportune in terms of the number of months the car had been driven.

The dealer charged me $469.82.

Enclosed is a copy of an advertisement from a neighboring Lariat dealership that I recently received. It is interesting to note that the regular 15,000 mile service price here is $369—$100 less than I paid.

The 15,000 mile service was not necessary; furthermore, Sequence Motors offers a $49.95 minor service special which would have met my requirements at the time. Therefore, I feel that I should be reimbursed by Sequence for the extra costs. A number of my associates have advised me that this is a flagrant overcharge, possibly fraudulent.

I trust that you will set this matter straight and I will receive an appropriate reimbursement which is due me, approximately $400.00, obviating the need for me to pursue this further.

Yours very truly,

Mrs. Rowena Stevens

cc: Mr. Harold Langer
       President, Sequence Motors

Less strident. You cooled down somewhat, but not entirely. A car defect was not adequately fixed. It is still causing a problem.

LETTER TO THE OWNER OF THE DEALERSHIP

Re: About my '96 Adven 85

Dear Mr. Ratigan:

I went into your shop twice for the same defect and it still hasn't been fixed. My vehicle stalls at the most inopportune times, obviously an unsafe condition. The latest incident took place on the Manchester Thruway, blocking a lane and holding up traffic.

When the engine cooled I was able to start and proceed on my way. This is not only trying, inconvenient and very vexing—but, as I said before, unsafe. Do you understand? Unsafe for me and for children who often ride in this vehicle.

I'll try your service department a third time. If this condition isn't repaired, I'll have to take steps that I'm afraid will be unpleasant for both of us.

Thank you for taking action on this.

Very truly.

Melissa Morgan

ANOTHER COOL APPROACH ... LETTER TO THE SERVICE MANAGER, COPY TO THE PRESIDENT

Dear Henry:

You deserve applause for the way you run your shop, and the excellent service you provide. And indeed, the friendly manner in which you and your staff assist customers.

With that said, my car still doesn't run right, despite having it looked over two times. I'm certain this distresses you as much as it does me. because you take so much pride in how your shop performs.

Quite likely it is not your shop that's at fault but an inherent defect in the car that can't be satisfactorily fixed.

Please call me on Wednesday and tell me what steps you will take.

Thanks for your time, and your concern about setting this right.

Cordially,

Brandon Schwartz

DECEPTIVE CLAIM, MISLEADING ADVERTISING. IT COST YOU MONEY

An appliance dealer offered three months suspension of payment without interest on any merchandise in the store. However, it required $15 a month payment during the three-month grace period, which the manager and salesman earnestly claimed was toward the principal amount and not an interest charge. When you got the bill after three months the $45 you had paid was not deducted. You feel you were duped, lied to, and are mad.

Send a letter to the financial office that sent the bill with a copy to the dealer.

Gottfried Appliance Centers
P.O. Box 1501
Minneapolis, MN

Re: Acct # 6-72-40619-4305

You have either made a mistake in your bill, or you have committed an overcharge violation, which could amount to fraud and misleading advertising.

I purchased a refrigerator on 6/19/97 from your Dallas store at a total cost of $604.72. It was done under the terms of your promotion which stated that a buyer need not make payment for three months, with no interest charge.

I was billed and paid $45 (3 monthly charges at $15 each) with the expressed provision that this was toward the principal amount and was not interest. This was explicitly confirmed by your store manager.

The only bill I received was on 10/1/97 for $624.72 (604.72 + $20.00 late fee). There is no indication of the $45 I paid against the principal amount.

The bill I received on 10/1, due date 1/22/98, is the only one for the full amount. The $20 fee is for late payment. How can there be a late fee if this was the only bill sent to me?

You are subject to a number of violations, which I will not discuss in this letter but which I think you are aware of after reading this.

I am enclosing a check for $559.72 as full payment ($604.72 less $45.00). I expect to receive a receipt for this noting that it is payment in full.

Very truly yours,

Roland Bard

cc: Gottfried Appliance Centers
        73 Hardwick Blvd.
        Dallas, TX 30412

A case of a new product that is inoperable, a fax machine. Write to the customer-service representative of the retailer chain.

Dear Mr. Hamilton:

This is in regard to an unsatisfactory product, a Bettis fax machine, purchased from you—Model #605P, priced at $699.50 plus tax.

The fax copies are far from satisfactory. While I do not expect exact duplications of the original documents, the ones I get are of such poor quality that they are difficult to read. The typewritten or printed words are somewhat smudged with broken letter characters.

For your information, I told the department manager I need highly legible copies for my business; I was assured that this machine would be more than adequate. As noted above, this is not the case. Please have this machine picked up. I will go to the store to seek another make or model that suits my need.

Thank you.

Seena Rogers

November 22, 1997

Mr. Lee Wong
Store Manager, Elec-Mart

Subject: TV Set-Finder 85, Model SQ7——
                purchased Oct. 3rd.

Dear Mr. Wong:

I'm at my wits end!

I can't get this machine to work properly. I tried every knob to get a good picture, put it in different locations, but it just seems to be a lemon.

As you know, it could happen with any machine, no matter how reliable the manufacturer is and what sort of consumer rating it got.

Considering the price I paid—$749.00 plus tax—it is, understandably, very disturbing.

Please have a repairman come to fix it to my satisfaction—or better still, have it replaced. I'll be pleased to give the manufacturer full details as to what is wrong if it cares to research this malfunction.

I want to have this straightened out by December 14.

Very truly,

Virginia Jones Donner

A FRIENDLY COMPLAINT LETTER

Find out the manager's first name, and address him that way. A warm approach with praise is usually effective, and keeps a pleasant relationship.

```
Good morning, Paul:

I have a problem, and I know you can help me. Judging from the wonder-
ful customer-friendly way you run your store, I know you are an excel-
lent business person.

The cassette player and recorder I bought from you on Feb 2—James CT,
Model XT4, price $89.95 + tax—isn't working well.

I don't want to take your time now to explain why. I'll bring it in to
the store to show you, after you've had a chance to read this letter,
and you'll see why it must be exchanged for another set. I'll call your
office to set a date/time.

I'll be looking forward to meeting you, a fast-rising executive from what
I've heard.

Warm greetings,
```

A TOO COMMON EXPERIENCE

You bought a $700 copying machine and set it up for use. The manufacturer is considered an exceptionally reliable company—among the very best. The machine was a bomb—didn't work. It had a major defect and was never used. The company claims that if there is poor performance, it will pick up the merchandise and deliver a new machine. One day service. Very commendable.

You called the customer-service number to arrange for the switch; you packed the lemon in the original shipping carton with its electric cables and instructions.

Two days later (not bad!) a replacement was delivered. The lemon was to be picked up later.

Outrage! The replacement is a refurbished model. The package did not contain cables or instructions so it could not be assembled to work.

There were numerous long- distance calls to the customer-service people, at your expense. Bottom line. . . It's the manufacturer's policy to replace new products that don't work with refurbished machines. "To all intents and purposes as good as a brand-new machine," you were told, without considering that you had paid for a brand-new machine.

The only way to get another new machine promptly is to take it to the original dealer where it was bought. No matter that the original dealer is at a distant, inconvenient location.

Send a letter to the corporate president after the product switch has been made. There are sentences and phrases in this letter which can be lifted for various other situations of a similar nature.

Mr. Benson Hopewell, President
Surefire Electron, Inc.
300 Michigan Boulevard
Chicago, IL

Dear Mr. Hopewell:

I am calling to your attention a clear customer-service defect that you are probably not aware of—one that could cause your company trouble.

I am a marketing consultant and very, very busy. But I'm taking the time to write you because I'm troubled by the unfair and cavalier way a major American company, with a heretofore impeccable reputation for quality products and customer service, could condone the outrageous policy displayed here. To save time, I'm giving the facts in outline form.

1. I purchased an office copier for $704.92—sales slip that denotes all details is enclosed.

2. The machine doesn't work. Was never used, couldn't be used.

3. Called your customer-service number. My people and I spoke with the agent who was ineffectual and we asked to be transferred to the supervisor. The supervisor provided his private number; thus all my calls to him were regular long distance at my expense.

4. We were told that Surefire's service policy is for replacements to be refurbished models. This is noted in the warranty, he said.

5. We were told to pack up the machine in the original carton and return it to the original dealer for an immediate replacement. Not good, because the dealer was two hours' distance away and it was inconvenient to get there.

6. The supervisor arranged to deliver a replacement in a day or two.

7. Replacement arrived two days later. Lo! A refurbished machine. (To your company's credit it was identified as refurbished.) In other words, I paid for a brand-new machine and got a refurbished one. Unacceptable!

8. Your customer-service supervisor assured me, "To all intents and purposes, it is as good as a new machine." A stupid statement when a customer paid for a brand new machine.

9. Further, the refurbished machine was packed without electric cables or instructions. "You should have taken these from the original machine," the supervisor said. But he didn't tell us that beforehand. It doesn't matter; I don't want the refurbished (used) machine anyway.

The bottom line: I am taking the lemon to the original dealer, which as noted before, will be about two hours travel time through dense traffic.

This egregious episode cost me money—in the form of long-distance phone calls, the time of my hourly-paid personnel, not to say my time which I make available at an hourly fee.

It is dubious if replacing a defective machine—including a never-used one—with a refurbished article would hold up legally. If, by chance, it has been upheld in some court of law, I don't think it would survive further legal challenge.

You have a problem, Mr. Hopewell, I trust you appreciate my effort to advise you of it.

Very truly,

Sinclair Lebeau

You received a fax machine by UPS, and the company charged your credit card. It was defective and you sent it back for an exchange, which was delivered. The company contends there is a price for the repair and you owe them money.

It sent you a letter on the matter, saying that if it isn't cleared up in three days, it will automatically put the charge on your credit card number. The company included a phone number to call if there are any questions. You believe you don't owe any money since the machine was defective. The company is in California, you are in New Jersey.

You called . . . voice mail asked you to wait for an available agent. Three to four minutes passed, no agent yet. You hung up in disgust.

Send a fax.

(By Fax)

From: Regis Moore

To: Persevere Technical Company

Re: Serial #KP46QR3018
        Replacement Unit #G78520031
        Defective Unit #P9801078U

I tried calling you and didn't get through after several minutes of waiting on a long-distance call that I'm paying for. (It appears your agents
are interminably busy.)

You can call me at (201) 792-2300, Ext. 31 today until 5:00 P.M. Eastern
time. On Monday after 3:00 P.M. Eastern time at (201) 794-1483. My fax
is (201) 603-7831. Otherwise give me an 800 number, or a number I can
call collect.

This matter is caused by your defective product. It has already cost me
considerable time and money in trying to negotiate the exchange procedure. Under the circumstances quoted above, I do not appreciate your
threat of automatic billing.

Kelly Mitchell

The computer you just bought isn't working right. The manufacturer is
trying to fix it, and keeps trying. Still not right.

Mr. Drew Rogers

President
Arsenal Computers

—————————————

—————————————

Dear Mr. Rogers:

If you have a bathtub overflowing you don't begin by mopping up the
floor. You turn off the tap.

My Arsenal Computer, Model 30-T, is still not functioning well after
three attemps to fix it. This has caused me grief, and needless to say,
it's costing me money.

The instinct of your customer-service staff was not to acknowledge a
product defect. Rather it tried to fix it by happenstance, tinkering,
praying that the problem would go away, hoping it would stumble on a
solution, and dealing with the defect as a freak occurrence.

It isn't fixed and I am the loser. I assume that this product line is performing well and your other customers are happy. And that I, unfortunately, happened to buy a lemon. There is no point in tinkering any longer. I'm starting to feel victimized.

I need a brand-new machine! I expect a prompt reply from you or someone in your company to confirm this very soon, please!

Respectfully,

Emily Brubaker

cc: Mr. Harry Sims, President
LON Electronics

AN OVERCHARGING SITUATION

Dear Ms. Cohen:

I bought a Harlequin video recorder at your store last week (August 22), Model #37G, after seeing your ad in which a similar model was offered as a special sale item for $179.90.

The salesperson said the sale model, sold out and not in stock at the time, would only be available at the advertised price in about a month. I therefore chose the above item which was $22 higher than the one advertised.

Another person I know bought the sale video recorder in your store at the $179.90 price three days after my purchase. How come?

This appears to be a case of bait advertising. Some people get the savings, others don't. I'm sure you are aware of the penalty for this.

I expect to be reimbursed $22.00, or replace my machine with the sale machine at the sale price.

Very truly,

Flora Jean Jackson

ANOTHER OVERCHARGE ISSUE

The owner of a plumbing repair company sent you a whopping bill. Try to get it reduced. Be nice about it, because you may need this plumber again.

Dear Mr. O'Hara:

I just got your bill. It seems to be out of line.

I know it was an emergency repair. A plumber and helper were here about six hours, and did a fine job. But $743? Isn't your charge of $148 per hour excessive?

I really appreciate your prompt response to my call, and the way your men worked, but I didn't expect the size of this bill. Could you please find your way clear to adjust it somewhat? I'm asking this because it really is more than I can afford at this time.

I would very much appreciate your consideration.

Sincerely,

Mrs. Manuel Karakas

A MORE PLEASANT APPROACH:
THE CASE OF A FAULTY FAX MACHINE
LETTER TO THE STORE MANAGER, COPY TO THE COO OF THE CHAIN

Dear Ms. Gutfreund:

How we wish that everything that should happen, does happen!

It's not always so, of course. That's the case with the Condat fax machine I purchased in your store on December 4th (sales slip enclosed). It isn't working as it should—copies are smudgy, and it usually jams when I insert 10 or more pages.

I'm certain I'm taking the proper step in writing you about this defect rather than the manufacturer. I'll call you about bringing this machine in for repair or exchange.

Thank you for giving this your attention.

Truly yours,

CRITICIZE WITHOUT BEING OVERBEARING

The report you've seen is well written, but it doesn't make a crucial point. It sorely lacks a practical solution to the problem.

Dear John:

Your report, aside from being well written, was very instructive. Thanks so much for a lucid explanation of the problem.

May I suggest that as a next step, you can show how this can develop into a solution, a practical solution we can put into action and live with. It's a tough assignment which I think can be made easier when you discuss it with some of the people involved. It goes without saying, I'm here to help.

Again, you gave some very interesting background info with a very engaging presentation—paving the way to the important next step.

Good luck!

Scott

ANOTHER LETTER:
A REPLY TO A PROPOSAL ON MARKETING VIA THE WEB

To: Larry Johnson:

Your presentation was perfect—showing a grim determination to lead our industry in marketing on the Internet. A great idea!

But it didn't discuss how to create the technology to make this possible. Let's say, so that those who read the presentation are sold. In other words—good, fine, but now what?

Get your thesis through to a successful conclusion by indicating the new
technology that is needed. You are obviously not in the position of creating the technology, but perhaps you can describe the parameters, so
that specs can be made for the software engineers to follow.

You have fathered a wonderful new avenue to market penetration.

Congratulations,

Gustina Gustafson

ANOTHER LETTER

To: Sigrid Arani

Your new publication idea is very intriguing, and well documented. But,
in my humble way of thinking, it didn't include an important aspect.
Perhaps a crucial one.

It doesn't take into account that we will need new avenues of production
and distribution.

If you get this into the equation—and it ain't easy, it requires a lot
of thinking—you will have a smash hit proposal. Good luck!

Edgar Sonenshine

A proposal on a new product idea was really bad—not practical. It
should be turned down forthwith. But try not to cause distress.

Re: Report on a new product idea

Dear Siegfried,

Your piece was quite interesting and shows good imagination. It's bold,
it's creative and smart. Unfortunately, however, it is something we are
not in a position to market.

Don't feel bad. You demonstrated what you can do. We all appreciate the
effort—and the skills you showed.

Better luck on the next one.

Johanna

ANOTHER LETTER

Greetings, Otto—

Your network on-line proposal gave us all a glimpse at future science—
which is a good thing in a way, for it points to an idea on how infor-

mation technology will advance in the next 20 or 30 years. But we're not anywhere near there yet!

A lot of inventions have to be made before we can start to think about what you described. You have a wonderful imagination, which impressed us. But keep in mind. . . revolutionary processes don't just happen from empty space, they stem from the past and present.

With admiration,

Leonard Lillen

AN ASSOCIATE WROTE A LETTER TO AN ERRANT SUPPLIER THAT WASN'T STRONG ENOUGH

To: Luisa Valdez:

Your letter to NuCycle Associates was very good. It's silly of me to say this because you are exceptionally capable in your correspondence.

I want, however, to express an opinion which you may or may not agree with. It's a question of intent.

I feel that this supplier's services have been less than "very good" of late, a few steps below its previous performance. We can't afford to receive this kind of service quality.

It should be told of our displeasure clearly, not by an obtuse reprimand. Your consideration of the supplier's feelings is laudable, but we're in a tough business, and it is too.

Let me know if you agree.

Jack Leroux

ANOTHER LETTER

To: Felicia Baker:

Your letter to the vendor who gave us a poor MIS plan was commendable in its delicacy—that is, not wanting to hurt its feelings too much. But then, I don't know the full story as to how you decided to handle this problem.

I think you showed good judgment in not putting any vituperative remarks on paper. You decided rather to vent fully when you talk in person or on e-mail which is very informal. If so, that's a class-act way to do it.

Jean Carnevale

**LETTER TO VENDOR WHO ERRED AND CAUSED YOU TO MISS A DEADLINE.
YOU DON'T WANT TO COME ON TOO STRONG.**

Dear Alphonse:

It would be untruthful if I told you I wasn't totally ticked-off at your late delivery, which caused us to miss a deadline, which caused us to lose some money, which caused us to feel the wrath of a client.

It would also be untruthful if I said that this goof turned out to be serious. We somehow got the work to our client in time for its review meeting, and the client feels good about us. As to the money, treat Jack and me to a good lunch and we'll call it square. It's not just the lunch that will be a treat, it's your company too.

Cordially,

Tom Brewer

**AN ASSOCIATE'S REPORT HAD INCORRECT NUMBERS—SLOPPY RESEARCH.
PUT HER DOWN, NOT HARD. CORRECT, MOTIVATE,
DON'T CAUSE HARD FEELINGS.**

To: Jean Towers

From: Phil Camos

The way you structured your report was exceptional and certainly innovative. It's just too bad that some of the key numbers were incorrect. It just means you have to be more careful next time in doing the research.

You have so much on your plate, at this time especially, that it's a wonder if errors don't happen, so this shouldn't be taken as a serious criticism.

What you do is much appreciated, Jean. Keep it up.

ANOTHER LETTER

To: Gus

From: Herb

Gus, don't feel badly about the error in your TUN presentation, in answer to its RFP. We sent the revised pages, and I don't think the error will affect whether we win or lose.

It was a very tough assignment and you handled it well. Next time we'll have to put some more time on the research. By all means, keep up the good work in getting out these reports. Although complex, detailed, and cut-and-dried, they still need your ingenuity to give them life.

FIRM, UNFLAGGING CRITIQUE OF A RIVAL'S WORK, BUT WITH CIVILITY, POLITENESS, CONSIDERATION. DO NOT HOLD BACK YOUR NEGATIVE OPINION.

Dear Sam:

You asked me to comment on the RET Corp. plan for the communications network you wish to set up. We are doing this with what we believe is total objectivity—no regard for the fact that Beta Computer, a division of our company, has submitted its own plan. We assume that RET has been similarly asked to give you an opinion of our plan, and we trust it will do so in the same businesslike manner.

This is the result of our review of what RET submitted. . .

- It entails a high initial cost. Is it advisable to start with a completely new infrastructure rather than build on present facilities? We think not, considering that their procedure is untried. Who knows how the market will accept it? We can enhance the equipment when demand warrants.

- It doesn't talk much about the structure for customer service which is very important and should be built into the plan. It should be thorough in all its ramifications before the sales effort starts. What about such simple and crucial things as who handles phone calls from customers? Where are the user instructions?

To sum up, Sam, RET's plan, if adopted, will entail too much risk without a pullback option. With ours you don't bet the ranch, you have an opportunity to assess the initial results and then decide how much more money you want to invest.

We're as optimistic as RET, but more businesslike, and with a wiser approach, and certainly more regard for your money.

Very truly,

Bill Singleton

OTHER LETTERS ON THIS SAME SUBJECT

Dear Ms. McNamara:

Seldom are we asked to critique the presentation of Cross Associates, one of our rivals in response to your Request for Proposal. I expect that Cross has been asked to do likewise.

I'm sure you and your people are very capable of judging the relative merits of what we submitted. But this gives you another useful perspec-

tive and you show your wisdom in requesting this kind of outside opinion—especially from a competitor!

The following pages will list the technical and cost-effective aspects
of Cross's proposal in detail. But first this is to give you a thumbnail
idea of what we concluded:

1. Cross does not suggest sufficient testing. It is depending
   almost entirely on its previous experience with other clients.
   No two companies are alike. Cultures are different, people are
   different, vital objectives are different, and so on.

2. Its costs are lower in dollar amounts—initially, that is. But,
   as you know, everybody has to make a profit. We think Cross will
   be very tight and unhappy when it sees its profits dwindle. Will
   this result in a reduction of service in subtle yet meaningful
   ways? We don't reflect on what Cross will do, but it is more
   than likely this will happen. At any rate, why chance it?

Thank you, Ms. McNamara, for allowing us to make this appraisal. With
all fairness and objectivity, we believe we have a decided edge over
Cross.

Truly yours,

Langston Smith

Try not to appear too self-serving when you make your comments—
you are elbowing your way up front in a battle to have your proposal accepted versus other submissions. Make your point with certainty, and with civil-
ity as befits the image you want to convey.

You proposed an expansion plan for the public library in your community. You want to follow up to keep reminding the Library Committee of your
plan's merits.

To the members of the Library Committee,
Arendale Township:

Re: The Levin—Wyman plan for expanding our library services.

                 It will take you three minutes to read this.
                 An important three minutes.

Our proposal can be financially painless in terms of the much
greater value to the people in the community—school children
and adults—vs. the other plans submitted. It will provide all

the additional books and reference materials you need, rather than compromising on the amount you should have.

It is completely doable, and within the budget we submitted. There are no hidden costs, no surprises. We, and others who have seen the two proposals, are convinced that ours is the most practical solution.

Further, the other plan is grandiose to the point of bad taste. It does not sufficiently take into account the nature and the culture of our town. In fact, it's a sorry reflection on our community. Despite the grandiosity, it does not provide any more books or services than the Levin-Wyman plan.

With us, there will be no deleterious effects on the environment. In addition, the engineering and architectural specifications can be started in short order.

We are prepared to back up these statements. Thank you for your time—and for your consideration.

Reginald Tisman
President

You want to strike down a competitor's proposal for a new product research project, so as to have the chance to get your proposal up front.

LETTER TO THE COO OF THE COMPANY THAT RECEIVED THE PROPOSAL

Dear Mr. Marberry:

> *"The difference between results and consequences:*
> *Results are what you expect. Consequences are what you get."*
>
> (Robert McNamara, Secretary of State,
> during the Vietnam War)

That is exactly the problem with the proposal you had received. It shows meticulous research. Iron-clad documentation. Exquisite analysis. All leading to what was supposed to be a stupendous result.

And then the proposal fell flat on its face. It pointed to a one-time final result that lacked a dimension. Longevity! What will it do over time? 5 years, 10 years or perhaps 2. What are the consequences? What will the government regulators say? Will your competition copycat the best of what was done and overrun, overpower and overwhelm you? Will consumers stick or switch?

What it amounts to is that you will be researching the product for the benefit of your competition. If it's successful competitors will pounce like hungry wolves. If it flops, well, you've done research, that's all.

We have experience with this kind of product development. We know how to build in exclusivity, protection, lasting power, the ability to thwart copy-cat competitors.

With due respect, Mr. Marberry, I'm giving you crucial advice. Don't take a short view of just looking at initial results. Take the view of long-term consequences.

We should get together and I'll give you all the reasoning behind what I'm saying here, and tell you of our experience. Please expect my call.

Best regards,

Stuart Finn
Executive Vice President

You see a report from a financial advisor that is not definitive—a lot of "approximations" of results. No definitive numbers. No categorical statements. Projected results are qualified with "about," "theoretically," "hopefully," "probably." There seems to be either sloppy research or a fear of sticking one's neck out.

Mr. Charles Malone
Check Point Financial Advisors

Subject: Your June Quarterly Analysis

Dear Chuck:

I read this report with much interest. It was intriguing, interesting, but with due respect not sufficiently informative. That is, I couldn't put my finger on a clear, stick-your-neck-out statement.

What does "should show a little growth, about 3%," or "hopefully swing to the upside," or "hovering on a plus or minus 2 to 3%" really mean?

Why are you afraid to make a specific declaration? You know, we make or lose money on differences of 1 or 2% around here. If you are not too afraid of being wrong, you will work harder, do more thorough research, in order to have the greatest chance of being right.

I would welcome your comments without caveats, hedging, timidity.

Regards,

Leo Levine
President

ANOTHER LETTER

Dear Priscilla,

This is about your Spring Report . . .

The numbers you churned out are more like penumbras. They are shadowy, not clear data, full of hedging and caveats.

It's obvious you don't want to express definitive conclusions, but we still want a conclusion—an opinion if you will—that shows you have a conviction. You write in a style so that you can never be called wrong.

It's like the weatherman saying "there is a 40% chance of rain." He is correct if it rains and correct if it doesn't.

Around here we make or lose money by following your predictions to the extent that we want to be guided by them. You are judged on the results.

Don't be afraid of being judged. Your opinions—whether through empirical data or intuitions—are very perceptive.

Stay well,

Bernie Brooks

ANOTHER LETTER

Dear Cynthia,

Our request for a progress report on the XX4 research puts you in an anomalous position.

Judging from the results to date that you told us about, you couldn't take a positive stance, which is what everyone would like to hear; and you couldn't be negative, which is what everyone doesn't want to know and will try to tear down. So you are in-between, and everyone is saying you are double-talking and not being professional.

Perhaps you could reissue this report. Start with an unequivocal point of view, such as "In my opinion at this early date" or "there are no conclusive data...yet, but indications at this preliminary stage are . . ."

It's just a thought. You are much more skillful than I when you want to express a preliminary point of view. Thanks for the important contributions you are making.

Cordially,

Jean Pia Morrow

**OTHER LETTERS OF DECIDED CRITICISM, YET SOMEWHAT EGO-SENSITIVE
AND RESTRAINED SO AS NOT TO UPSET A RELATIONSHIP**

To: Our staff who contributed marketing ideas,
        plans and proposals.

We've gotten some very good business-enhancement thinking from using our
in-house toil and sweat as opposed to outside vendors. Your presentations are very thoughtful, aggressive, and interesting.

However, when it gets down to financial truths—costs, return on investment, profit analyses—people here scamper for the exits.

Therefore, none of these would pass the hard-nosed scrutiny of the
Management Committee and the Board of Directors. You have to add the
cruel business realities to make any of these ideas fly.

Please do this. We'll try for an extension of our due date. Take the time
that's needed. Whatever we recommend has to be right from a financial
point of view.

Have a good rest-of-the day,

Peter

ANOTHER LETTER

Your new business report looks like a fiction novel about how to slay
the competitive dragons. Interesting reading—and it stops there!

We have to go beyond the penumbra to the hard-core business realities
on:

    Return on investment (ROI), the dictum that will never go away.

    How long?—When does the money hemorrhaging stop and the trans-
    fusion begin?

    Profits—now and forever—at least while we're alive.

These considerations are what makes the bean counters prevail.

You're a marvelous writer, a sharp thinker; just add what I have indicated. Ask John in accounting to help.

Good work,

Jim Tobin

CHEER UP SOMEONE WHO HAS HAD A BAD BREAK

▎YOU MUST UPLIFT MORALE AFTER A FAILURE.

SITUATION: *(Lost a Political Election)* Your friend was her party's choice for the state legislature. She was an administrator in a state regulatory board and had never run for an elective office before. You are head of a media-consulting company and worked full time on her campaign, including the fundraising effort.

It was a lot of time, a lot of money, and a bitter campaign. She lost in a close vote, 48% to 52%.

Your friend is an excellent choice for public office: brilliant, honest, idealistic and dedicated. She must keep trying. Encourage her.

You want to continue working with her with the view of preparing for her next campaign—and the next, and the next. She will have a long public career if she has good advisers and fund raisers.

STRATEGY I: Send a personal letter to her home, with copies to all the party bigwigs. Boost her morale. Encourage, even beseech her, to remain active in politics. This is just an episode in what will be a successful public-service career.

November 10, 1996

Ms. Lucille Campo

_____

_____

Dear Lu:

Winston Churchill remarked that the most important quality for success is the ability to overcome failure.

What resounding failures Churchill experienced in his public career! And what stunning successes! Many other historical figures have also had to rise from the ashes to go on to victory and fame. Success couldn't have come if they hadn't risen from cataclysmic setbacks.

You are great, Lu. You have incredible ideas that will inspire our state and our country. The party needs you.

This is a temporary lull in your road to the top. We want you to keep at it, undaunted. You are too good to take a back seat.

There will be other elections. Bigger challenges to triumph over. Keep at it, Lu, and you will win. We are behind you, more than ever. I am honored to be at your side.

With admiration and loyalty,

Chelsea

SITUATION II: *(Failed to Get a New-Business Gem)* You are the senior VP, marketing of a long-distance phone company. You formed a company team of several energetic marketing people to go after a prime piece of corporate business. An all-out effort was made with pressure-driven, crazy-long hours, but a competing company won.

STRATEGY II: Hoist up the team's morale and its pride. It didn't win, but it didn't lose either. The members truly showed themselves to be big-leaguers. They have to be recharged for the next new business, spare-no-effort push.

November 10, 1996

To: The Consummate New-Business Team
      Jerry Robinson   Bernie Schwab
      Kate Carmody   Mac Simon

From: Bill Palmer

Dear Team:

We didn't win the Hero Automobile account that we worked so hard to get, but we came out winners nevertheless.

ATD managed to snatch the brass ring this time. I want to tell you now, before you see it in the papers.

This doesn't mean it had the best presentation. We had the best. But the politics and vagaries of the battle don't always raise the hand of the best.

Everybody here is proud of the big-league presentation we put together, and how you guys did it. It was excellent, and still is. It's good enough to show off with pride to anyone. Let's clear the decks for the next big one.

With much thanks,

P.S.   We can dust this presentation off to go after another car
       account.

A friend was asked to resign from a top management post at a high-tech company. It was a high-visibility setback. Send him a fax, to his home.

To: Adrian

Congratulations!

You're rid of headaches, tribulations, dealing with the unsavory and the nonsense.

On to newer and better—and more deserving of you!

Please call on me for any assistance I can give . . . or just to talk.

Bernie

The dischargee's business theories didn't coalesce with those of the company's sales director.

Dear Alicia:

Don't fret, or even be concerned about your sudden and unexpected dis-
missal. It's unforgivable, but being bitter does no good and diminishes
you. Besides, the chemistry wasn't right; the culture didn't coincide
with your style, and you couldn't be happy there.

It was a fortuitous happening, no doubt about it! I'm sure that it is
best for you career-wise.

All the best,

Francois

To a software programmer who was a downsizing victim, as was explained to her. But really, she was simply fired.

To my dear friend, Priscilla,

Commiserations on your involuntary career change. I really mean congratulations!

It's disheartening now, but it will be good in the long run. The spot
simply didn't match your talents, your vision. It was a wrong cultural
climate for you.

In short, they didn't deserve you!

Your brains and skills will be appreciated elsewh ere. But be sure your
next move has a comfortable fit with your personality and your work
ethic. And make sure your next employer has the intelligence to admire
your relentless pursuit of technology breakthroughs.

Please be sure to call on me for advice, information, assistance or to
just talk. I'm always here to help.

Your buddy,

Lindsey

An associate where you work was fired—the victim of a browbeating supervisor that wanted him out.

```
To:     Isha Kmuno

            You made a choice, it wasn't right,
                and too late you saw the light.

            Now that the error was corrected,
                you should be happy, not dejected.

            It was predictable, what happened to you,
                now on to what's better, on to the new.

            It makes no sense that you feel sad,
                in the end you will be more than glad.

        Congratulations are appropriate for this event,
                on your next job you may rise to Vice President
                (or even President)

Your friend

Lee Raab
```

CRITICIZING PLANS, IDEAS, AND PROJECTS OF A COMPETITIVE COMPANY...OR ANOTHER PERSON IN YOUR ORGANIZATION

You are a senior executive of a computer-service company. You have the chance to critique a proposal of a competitive vendor. It was requested by a prospective client to whom you made the same pitch. This prospect is a large catalog company that sells by mail and retail stores.

A LETTER TO THE SENIOR EXECUTIVE AT THE PROSPECT WHO IS RESPONSIBLE FOR CHOOSING THE VENDOR

Dear Mr. Novak:

In comparing our presentation to the others you received, I first want to point out the differences in philosophy of the competing vendors. You need to go beyond the rhetoric, the promises, the blue-sky ambitious projections, which are not supported by facts or any businesslike rationale that rings true.

In essence, I think what you've been getting from the others is the "say anything, do anything" syndrome to get the business, the urgency to make any promise in order to get through the door and claim the prize.

That's not what you want, Mr. Novak. You want a forthright evaluation of a company's facilities, personnel abilities and philosophy, and how they will be applied to servicing your requirements and goals. You also want to know a company's ideas, thinking, creativity, and its concrete recommendations.

You don't want feel-good promises with no real foundation. It can lead you to disaster. I'm sure you want a vendor who will give you practical

316

yet innovative proposals as well as excellent service on your day-to-day requirements. This is what will help you succeed in meeting your goals.

All the best,

Philip Reuter, President

You need to lash out at an associate's proposal that diminishes your ideas. You must bring it down, no holds barred.

LETTER TO THE PEOPLE AT HEADQUARTERS AND BRANCH OFFICES WHO RECEIVED YOUR RIVAL'S PROPOSAL

Dear Laurine:

I was asked to comment about Michael Reed's proposal, so here goes. I'm afraid the chips will have to fall where they may.

I won't go into the details one by one, because it would be silly in this case. You have all the numbers, projections and so forth. It's best that I discuss the broad strokes as to method of thinking which is what you really want to know . . . . Basically, what do you want to accomplish and how are you to go about it?

To begin with, the treatise in question has big ideas and high ambitions. Fine, but that's all there is. It's a wish-list scenario with figures, trend charts, and other wrappings that are based on no empirical data, no substantiation. Essentially, they are made up figures.

I'm sorry I have to be this harsh, but my duty is to not waste time and to be forthright, because neither of us has any time to waste.

Respectfully,

Jean Marie Stoneham

cc: Li Chung
      Bob Franklin
      Liz Daniels

You are asked to comment on why you turned down a proposal from a service company.

Dear Felice:

I read your piece on clinical research proposals and I must make these comments. Don't feel offended by my statements; they are not to be taken personally in any way.

Here goes . . . Felice, you have big ideas and high ambitions for our organization. Great. Wonderful. We need more. Ideas are what ignite progress, but they are only a beginning because the world belongs to the doers. Thinkers are important, but only in an academic way. In itself, thinking creates nothing.

If you pointed with clear substantiation how your thoughts would become realities, your work-piece would be marvelous. Right now it is lacking this key element.

Truly,

Sig Arani

ANOTHER LETTER

To: Larry Humber

From: Sid Weinberg

Subject: My comments on your recommendation for new software

1. The wording was excellent. You have good skills at presenting a vision persuasively.

2. A vision is wonderful and often necessary to get something started.

3. However, it's no more than a dream. Dreams are not reality. We live in reality, Larry. We don't have the luxury of dreaming and not doing. Tell us explicitly how this can be done and you have grasped the brass ring. You will then invent something that would, I believe, make money for this company.

ANOTHER LETTER

To: Sean Brady

Re: An afterthought regarding your new-product ideas in your memo of 6/4

Sean, do you know what a profit is?

A profit is a maddeningly elusive thing that everyone wants in abundance. It means life or death to people, to companies, to institutions. It's fought over, struggled with, cried over, makes people lie awake nights.

It requires incredible skills and intelligence. Actually, it can even create deep enmities and has even caused wars.

Do you get the idea? There is nothing that tells us how we can make any profit on what you propose. I suggest you get the marketing and finance departments to give you a hand on this.

Bennett James

PUT A RIVAL IDEA TO REST AFTER YOUR CLIENT HAS LOOKED IT OVER.

TWO LETTERS:

Slash and Burn

Merciful Expiration

SITUATION: You are an account executive at a marketing-services company. Your major assignment is a medical-equipment manufacturer, which represents a big slice of your company's revenue. A firm that specializes in telemarketing presented a sales-development plan to your client that was quite ingenious. It is a marketing thrust that uses telemarketing, direct mail, and advertising, all working together. It has the stamp of the popular buzzword, *integrated marketing*, which interests your client. Its marketing director has asked you to critique it.

STRATEGY: You have to kill this proposal by an interloper who threatens your coveted client relationship. Who needs a rival in your rosy picture?

You can handle it in either of two ways. Kill it with a heavy stroke, or give it a more humane execution.

The Slash and Burn Version

March 16, 1993

Ms. Millicent Howard
Vice President, Corporate Communications
Saphire Medical Diagnostics

_____

_____

Re: Topline Report on the MacAdoo Plan

Dear Millicent:

The plan that MacAdoo Marketing Co. presented to you is moving along nicely. Off the edge of the desk and into the trash heap.

I'm glad you asked us to check this out thoroughly and give our comments. This plan sounded glamorous at first glance, but it didn't measure up under thorough investigation.

Believe me, we scrutinized it rigorously, with the aim of making it operational. But there were deficiencies that would require more expenditures than the project could recoup. We detailed all this and will send along a full report this week.

I hate to be thumbs-down on this. Our normal instincts are to build on an idea and make it work. But, in this case, there weren't enough redeeming features to offset the negatives. Briefly, MacAdoo should stick to telemarketing alone, which is what they are in business for.

We're working to develop a program that will achieve your objectives. We're poring over it from the bottom up to make sure it will work perfectly. We'll be ready to review this with you in about thirty days. I'm confident you and your top management will go for it all the way.

Regards,

Less Painful Demise

March 16, 1993

Ms. Millicent Howard
Vice President, Corporate Communications
Saphire Medical Diagnostics

_____

_____

Re: Topline Report on the MacAdoo Plan

Dear Millicent:

It was good you asked us to put a fine tooth comb to MacAdoo's proposal. It's an innovative idea, and will probably get you a lot of publicity. Our instincts might say, let's go . . . at first look, but it comes apart under careful scrutiny.

The MacAdoo shop is loaded with professional skill in telemarketing, one of the best in this industry. I wouldn't hesitate to use it for a major phone project.

But MacAdoo fell down in developing an overall marketing plan that includes advertising, direct mail, and incorporates telemarketing as one of its elements. In my opinion, it should stick to its knitting.

It was good at setting up the rationale. Its concept was good. The presentation was good. But the proposal didn't address some of the practical realities.

In other words, what MacAdoo did was almost good. But the word "almost" spells the difference between smash winner and sorry loser. It said you would get a lot of publicity, but who wants publicity for a failure?

I think we owe MacAdoo some thanks for its commendable effort. Let's keep it in mind when telemarketing expertise is needed.

A full report will be delivered to you next week.

Regards,

P.S.   We are working on a plan to do what you want and then some. We're going over it carefully to get rid of some bugs. It will be doable, profitable, and objective-oriented. In fact, it will be great. We'll be ready to show it to you in thirty days.

ANOTHER LETTER COMMENTING ON A COMPETITOR'S PROPOSAL, AS REQUESTED BY YOUR CLIENT

Dear Mr. McNulty,

I feel like an undertaker. I have the task of burying a presentation that is steeped in skillful rhetoric. It shows magnificent talent in turning illogical statements into what applies as logic, of being craftily persuasive, of building excitement on a crumbling foundation.

As they say, if you are to tell a lie, make it a big one.

I won't go further except to say that if you request it, we will be happy to write a point-by-point critique of the presentation you received that details our reasoning, and tells how we would pursue a task such as this if given the assignment.

These are harsh statements, that are meant as a warning to you. I would like the opportunity to explain them.

Warm regards,

Lemoyne Sanborn

Vice President

ANOTHER LETTER

Re: Research on product efficiency

Dear Sally Jane,

The investigation you made doesn't appear to be sufficiently thorough, which makes the conclusion subject to doubt.

It seems that the salient issues were researched selectively, mainly to confirm our theory. This is not scientific. It is quasi-science, which is really not acceptable in this case because so much depends on the outcome. I'm sorry I had to give this criticism, but how about doing it again and giving it more time? It's worth the extra effort, and you can do it so well.

All the best,

Christy McNamara

LETTERS OF APOLOGY

**APOLOGIZE FOR A RASH REMARK, OR A HURTFUL ACT,
AND TRY TO SMOOTH IT OVER WITH A TONGUE-IN-CHEEK APPROACH**

Dear Colette:

I sailed the Atlantic alone in a small boat. I'm licensed to fly a 747. I wrote a best-selling novel. I exterminated a great big horde of killer bees. I wrote an award-winning play. I won a gold medal in the Olympics decathlon.

But I can't find the words to tell you how sorry I am for the unforgivable remark that made you angry at me...most understandably.

Other than to simply say—"I'm Sorry." It was an unfortunate use of words that absolutely did not reflect what I felt, nor my very high regard for you.

Please accept this in the true sense of my feeling.

With friendship,

Melanie

ANOTHER LETTER

Dear Celeste and Rupert,

There are three reasons why I placed you and Bill at the wrong banquet table.

                    1 - Stupid!
                    2 - Stupid!
                    3 - Stupid!

In case you didn't understand the reason it happened, I will add—I was just stupid!

I allowed people who didn't know the relationships of our club members, nor their contributions, nor most everything else about them, to put the seating cards in place. And with all the harried details I had to take care of, I didn't carefully check what they did.

No excuse, just the three reasons mentioned above. Please forgive.

Sincerely,

Bob Lewis

ANOTHER WHIMSICAL APPROACH. AN UNFORTUNATE USE OF A WORD. IT WAS MISINTERPRETED

Dear Hoicho,

I now understand why you felt insulted when I included the word "manipulative" in describing you. My other comments were quite flattering, as intended, but I'm told you took issue with this particular word. Now that I think about it, I may well have felt the same way if it had been directed at me. Let me explain:

You can be sure, Hoicho, it was in a flattering sense. I meant to describe your leadership values. Very often to lead is to manipulate. To motivate is to manipulate—that is, to manipulate the efforts of others to a positive result.

The word has several dictionary meanings. Among these—skillful handling or operation...artful management or control (*Webster's New World Dictionary, Third College Edition*).

I trust this explains my true feeling. To be sure, Hoicho, I very greatly admire your personal qualities and leadership skills.

Thanks for your understanding.

Sincerely,

Seth Rogers

A LETTER WITH A TONGUE-IN-CHEEK APPROACH . . .
ABOUT AN UNINTENDED SEXUAL INNUENDO

Dear Audrey,

"You can pretend to be serious; you can't pretend to be witty" (Sacha Guitry, 1885-1957).

Unfortunately, I didn't see this wisdom before I made that unwitting remark that you objected to, for which I can't blame you.

I thought it was a harmless joke. It wasn't . . . as I found out. I tried to please you with some wit that I now see wasn't really witty. Shall I say it was half witty?

Am I forgiven?

Bob

A SIMILAR LETTER

Dear Sally Mae,

I want to apologize for the tasteless comment I made in your presence yesterday. It was by no means intended as a personal remark, but only meant to make you laugh, an inept attempt at comedy. I'm sorry you were offended—no double entendre was intended. I wasn't being two-faced.

I'll close with a statement by a very wise person, Abraham Lincoln—"If I were two-faced, would I be wearing this one?"

Hopefully still friends,

Bruce

ABOUT A REMARK THAT APPEARED TO BE AN ETHNIC SLUR

Dear Nicole,

I feel so ashamed of the remark I made about you—which in no way reflected my thoughts, opinions, sentiments, beliefs, or anything else about me. Except an unfortunate fallibility of bursting out with an unthinking and dumb choice of words when angry.

It was not me! I feel strongly enough about this shameful (and innocent) remark to express my sense of shame by writing you.

"Whatever is begun in anger ends in shame."

(Benjamin Franklin)

With shameful remorse,

Michael

MAKING LIGHT OF TELLING A JOKE WITH A RACIAL SLUR— WHILE SHOWING TRUE CONTRITION

Dear Reggie,

My dumb attempt to make you and others laugh put me in the doghouse. The worst part is that it was an unfortunate attempt to be amusing as a way of taking center stage. It did not indicate any prejudice on my part in any way.

You did a good job of berating me and diminishing me, and it has my heartfelt agreement.

I am pleading Not Guilty to racial prejudice. In fact, I revile racial prejudice. Am I simple-minded and diminished? Guilty!

I'm on probation for life and will perform civic duty.

With the hope of your forgiveness,

Ben

To: Jack Gorman

"When I make a mistake, it's a beaut!"

(Fiorello LaGuardia—
New York City Mayor in the '40s)

The mistakes I made in critiquing your essay were world-class beauts.

Jack, I was in a sorry mood when I read your piece . . . feeling low, frustrated, and with a bad case of indigestion. So I got the wrong meaning from what you said. Your words were full of wisdom, and I didn't have the wisdom to get from them what an intelligent educated person should have been able to grasp. So I unwisely panned it a bit, instead of giving it the praise it deserved.

Tell me what I can do to undo it, and I will do it!

Sincerely,

Brandon

P.S.   Pardon how this reads. I can't write as well as you, but you know what I mean.

ANOTHER APPROACH REGARDING AN
INADVERTENT SEXUAL REFERENCE

Dear Serena,

Sorry, sorry, sorry...that you took my remark about you at our town meeting the wrong way. I know you did not hear the remark, it was reported to you by overzealous troublemakers who completely misinterpreted. These gossipers were driven by jealousy or troubled minds.

I said you were pretty and dressed so tastefully—that's all. Does it mean I question your virtue, have a lack of respect, or that I'm coming on? Of course not!

I say it again, Serena. You are a pretty woman, always tastefully dressed, and I admire you for it. No leering, no hidden meaning.

I was going to put this at rest by speaking to you. But I was too embarrassed, so I'm writing. I hope we remain friends. Friends in the true sense of the word, Serena.

Thanks for your understanding,

Perry

ANOTHER WHIMSICAL APPROACH—ABOUT AN
INNOCUOUS SEXUAL REFERENCE THAT WAS TAKEN TOO SERIOUSLY

To: Betty Forrester

If I didn't go through the pain and trouble of writing this—not to say the embarrassment—I'm sure you wouldn't believe me. My sincerity is proven by putting this on paper rather than talking to you directly—at first, that is.

I'm so sorry about the way I spoke to you. It was not my nature, and I regret any negative interpretations. What I said did not convey my true intent . . .which was only an attempt to have fun. Call it a tasteless attempt at comedy.

So there! Now forgive me. I was not being disrespectful. I made the statement because I like you personally and like the way you look. And why not?—You are very likeable in both respects.

Thanks for your understanding.

John Costello

A WOMAN APOLOGIZES TO A MAN FOR MAKING
A FUSS ABOUT ADVANCES

Dear Keith,

This is the hardest letter I have ever written!

I shouldn't have taken your approaches as seriously as I did, even though they were not welcome. The same situation applies to any man here. After all, I'm out of circulation, and don't want to be in circulation. (Did I say this right?)

I'm certainly mature enough not to be insulted, outraged, or whatever, and sophisticated enough to fend off advances discreetly and with aplomb.

There, I've said it. Even more, written it. No hard feelings, as long as you know where I come from.

I have forgotten that it happened!

With friendship,

Laura

ANOTHER TONGUE-IN-CHEEK WAY TO MAKE LIGHT OF COMING
ON TO SOMEONE OF THE OPPOSITE SEX, AND BEING REBUFFED.
(PERHAPS THERE IS A CHANCE IF IT'S DONE THE RIGHT WAY)

Dear Beth,

I see now, painfully, that my approach was wrong. Doubly wrong. First, in making the come-on, and secondly, in doing it so clumsily. A case of sheer naivete, since my experience is so limited in this arena.

I insist on making amends. Please check off below what you want me to do:

    ____   Pray for forgiveness for my shameful attempt.

    ____   Take a personality course.

    ____   Allow you to flog me.

    ____   Avoid you no matter how painful this would be for me.

    ____   Try again, but with aplomb.

    ____   Continue seeing and talking to you but on good behavior.

    ____   Take a course in savoire faire.

Sincerely,

Bryan

A woman reproached a man in a shabby way, and wants to apologize and continue their former warm friendship. A fun letter would not appear to be too forward, and she would retain her dignity.

Dearest Michael:

You are undoubtedly angry with me, which, in retrospect, I certainly understand. I regret the way I spoke to you, especially since other people in the office overheard what I said.

Don't forget, you said some mean things too!

What can I do on my end to become friends again? Please check off:

    ____   Wear shorter skirts.
    ____   Change my hair color.
    ____   Pretend nothing happened and take it from there.
    ____   See a psychiatrist
    ____   Be exorbitantly humble
    ____   Send a more self-demeaning and humiliating letter.

All I ask of you is to either be contrite and humble for a week or send me a dozen roses.

With hope,

Bernadette

Your goof on a marketing report resulted in a loss of business, although the account did not go away. It was serious. You have to explain it to your management.

To: Messrs. Keith Holland, Bennett Fenner, Regina Jones

From: Cynthia Dane

I'm not going to explain the reason for the error in our ATS presentation. Excuses are not in my nature. I seek results and I don't try to explain away errors.

Nor am I going to place blame in any way on the people who worked for me on this project. The buck stops here!

All I'm saying is that I'm sorry. And it won't happen again. Period!

Jennifer Roth

OTHER LETTERS OF REMORSE ON A BAD MISTAKE,
OR AN UNFORTUNATE TURN OF EVENTS YOU SHOULD HAVE AVOIDED

To the Committee on Environmental Rehabilitation:

I'm willing to take responsibility for not getting the requested funding during my stewardship as head of the Funding Task Force.

With that said I stand humbled. We thought we worked hard, but it was not hard enough. We were too complacent since we considered this a can't-lose situation in that a clean environment has so much popular appeal.

The lesson: Don't take anything for granted, and work as if you are on the verge of losing. Nothing, especially a funding appeal, succeeds without backbreaking work, long hours, and so forth.

I will certainly live by this if you again see it clear to honor me with this important responsibility.

Sincerely,

Howard Epstein

ANOTHER LETTER

Dear Ms. Stillwell,

Re: Using several wrong questions in our public-opinion survey.

This is not an apology. An apology indicates personal responsibility for a bad mistake. This is a show of remorse for what occurred.

We didn't realize the tenor of responses the public would voice to the questions that were asked. How were we to know in advance? The fact that an unfortunate questioning technique happened before (more times than we like to think about), and will undoubtedly happen again (more times than we like to think about), does not diminish the seriousness of this error. Quite a bit of money went down the drain.

My deep regret is that I was associated with a failure. Call it a fiasco if you will. It's an inherent risk of the business we are in. Our success lies in having the bonanza drillings overshadow the dry holes.

The nature of our business is that we must keep changing our ways as experience dictates. We don't know what lies ahead and have to make corrections after it happens—good and bad.

A mistake was made, but we're not guilty.

Be well,

George Kalitis

You are culpable in a situation of morality, ethics, bad behavior. A written explanation or apology is required. You were caught in a moral transgression that reflected on your organization.

To: Mr. Roger Malone

Re: An unforgivable transgression that needs to be forgiven.

It was regrettable, it was stupid, it was immature!

I'm mature and courageous enough to say this. My behavior was a deviation from my normal lifestyle. This will never happen again. It should not be spoken of in any way. It must be forgotten. "He who is without sin cast the first stone," said Jesus when a mob wanted to stone a sinner to death.

I sinned, and I am a better person by writing you of my deep regret.

With sincerity,

Jack Cooperman

A female transgressor needs to apologize to her co-workers on a political committee for moral turpitude.

The committee chairwoman asked for a letter of regret, and wants to put the matter to rest.

Dear Melissa,

I deeply regret what went on, but I'm not ashamed even though my co-transgressor is married.

I won't go into the matter of love and sincerity and passion and such because this does not condone what happened. This is rather an act of contrition, and to advise you that I do not feel immoral. I will argue with anyone who takes a holier-than-thou attitude and will fight it tooth and nail.

Let nothing more be said—by you, by me, by anyone.

I owe a great debt of thanks to you for your understanding and compassion. Most of all for your wisdom.

Thank you so very much,

Jeannette Levitan

You flew off the handle at someone's mishap—sounded off some pretty nasty remarks. The error didn't warrant the outburst. You feel ashamed at insulting someone for what was a fairly minor misjudgment.

Send a note. You feel it would have more impact than a verbal apology.

Dear Concetta,

Sorry! Sorry! Sorry!

Putting this in writing demonstrates my utmost sincerity in seeking your pardon for going ballistic yesterday. It was far beyond the importance of the issue. What I did certainly didn't reflect on your ability, judgment, work habits, or anything about you.

Rather, it reflected on my judgment.

Next time I see you, I'll apologize verbally, but I wanted this to precede it.

With friendship (I sincerely trust)

Fahti Al-Bana

ANOTHER LETTER

Dear Richard,

May I explain why I sounded off the way I did yesterday? Something else was on my mind other than what you did. But this is not an excuse, just an apology—please accept it!

What occurred could have happened to anyone. Everyone is forgetful at times, including me, more often than I care to think about.

On a more personal note, I admire the wonderful job you are doing.

Sincerely,

Yardena

ANOTHER LETTER

Dear Donna,

How can I make up for the unpardonable way I sounded off at you yesterday? Everyone makes a mistake at times—especially me, more often than I care to say. And yours by no means deserved my ugly outburst.

I'm ashamed! And I hope my putting this down on paper demonstrates the sincerity of my apology.

Thanks for your understanding,

Lui Zhen

ANOTHER LETTER

Re: Mea Culpa

Dear Harold,

The remarks I made this morning were unwarranted, appalling, and unforgivable.

Nevertheless, please forgive me!

Some personal, unhappy events were bothering me at the time, which explains, but does not excuse, what I said. It is something I'm ashamed of.

Please accept this explanation in the true spirit in which it is intended.

Sincerely,

Steven

P.S.   Please burn this note after reading.

MAKING UP AFTER AN ARGUMENT

To: Roberta Sliwack

From: Gerri Olmert

Can you imagine the difficulty I had in writing this note? I wrote something, tore it up, wrote again—three times, and finally this. It still does not really convey how sorry I feel about the way we argued yesterday, what we said to each other.

When I woke up this morning I felt a burst of shame. We exchanged such mean, reprehensible comments as the argument got hotter.

Certainly I didn't mean what I said. You, I'm sure, didn't mean what you tossed my way. How could we both hurl such remarks at each other, insults, cusses that were patently untrue?

I'm sure, Roberta, you feel exactly as I do today. I want to be the first to express it this way. This may sound crazy, but in some way this incident further enhanced my warm feeling toward you.

Sincerely,

Gerri

ANOTHER LETTER—REGARDING A MAN-WOMAN COMEUPPANCE

Dear Hannah,

Re: Mea Culpa about yesterday

I trust you got all your dissatisfactions, discomfitures, and complaints off your chest. I sure did.

I'm so sorry about what I said, I could cry. In fact I did profusely, no kidding. Let's call it a purging, which is probably healthy once in a long while.

It further deepened my strong feeling for you. My admiration. My love.

Let's pick up again where we left off. Soon, today, now!

With all my heart,

Dennis

ANOTHER MAN-WOMAN LETTER

Subject: Let's make up and be friends (good, close, personal)

Dearest Jack—

I am seizing the opportunity to be the first to write, even though what you said (when we came pretty close to blows) was more cutting and insulting than what I said, which was less vitriolic.

Then again, why did you walk out on me?

At any rate, for some perverse reason, this incident made me feel even closer to you.

Jack, explain your appalling behavior, apologize profusely for your remarks, and then let's carry on as before. Forget your pride, as I did mine.

Truly sincere,

Judy

ASKING FOR A FAVOR

You are in the running for a prestigious volunteer assignment in your community. You need help in your campaign, such as names and addresses of certain people to contact for support, attractive literature to mail out and a strategy to employ. There is someone who can help you. You had done him a favor a few years ago, and there had been no contact since then.

Send him a letter prior to renewing the acquaintance via phone. It will help indicate how important you consider his help to be.

Dear Sam:

I guess you're surprised at my sending you this letter since we haven't been in touch for a long time—when I had given you a reference which helped you get a favorable life-insurance policy. I trust everything has been good with you since then.

Now I need your advice and expertise, Sam. Besides, I can't think of anyone, anywhere, whose advice would have as much wisdom as yours.

I'm up for the chairmanship of the Allendale Park District Rules Committee, a volunteer post that I'm very anxious to get. I find that I need some mailing literature to be sent to some of the residents here who have clout, and your expertise is much needed to compose it the right way.

I'm not asking that you write it, Sam, just edit what I give you and offer any other advice that you think is relevant.

This is a big favor, but I don't want you to take a lot of time at it because I know you are very busy. The benefit of your experience and talent is what's important.

Sam, I look forward to my being able to return this favor. I'm at your disposal any time you say.

I'll call you—and thanks so much; this means a great deal to me.

Warm regards,

Matthew

ANOTHER QUID PRO QUO LETTER

Dear Thelma,

I'm just catching up with all the things that are on my list to do—with priority when it comes to friends I really like.

How did my advice work out on the business deal you asked me about? We had quite a long discussion and I reached back to a lot of my past history—good and bad—to come up with what I think you agreed was a good solution. At any rate I'm curious to find out the result.

I must confess, however, this letter is not entirely for that reason. I'll be frank in saying that my main purpose is to ask a favor of you (although I am anxious to know about the business deal). What I'm asking doesn't involve much time on your part and it would be very important to me. You are the one person who can help me.

I'm pitching an account that would be very important in my life. It's for servicing the Palladium Company. I know you have friends who are in Palladium's upper management, and I mentioned you in my proposal as a reference. Separately I asked them to call you. If and when they do, and I think they will, I trust you will give them the right words—You know what I mean.

Thelma, I can't thank you enough. You know I will do my best for you if you ever want to call on me—regardless of whether you are able to help me in this situation.

You can expect my call to fill you in further on this deal. All the best to George and Nina.

Warm regards,

Warren

A SOMEWHAT DIFFERENT APPROACH

Dear Thelma,

Thelma, I'm going after an account that would be very important to me, especially at this time. It's the Palladium account.

I understand you know some of the top brass at Palladium and I gave your name as a reference. If and when someone calls you it would be most appreciated if you gave the "right" answers. Please understand. I'm not asking you to fabricate or exaggerate anything. I know you wouldn't do this, and there's no need to. I'm sure you think well of my work and you can candidly express good opinions.

Again, Thelma, getting the Palladium business is important in my life and I can't tell you how much I would appreciate your help.

Best regards,

Cliff

MORE SITUATIONS, MORE LETTERS

Dear Ms. O'Neill,

I need your help. It would also be so appreciated.

I know how you hate to read long letters. That's why I'm making this short, to the point, and I hope it doesn't seem abrupt.

I'm being considered for a job at Peerless Radio Syndication as an editor in the new department. Ms. O'Neill, I really want this job. I'm dying to get it—it's a great opportunity. I'll be crushed if I don't.

As a leading journalist, acclaimed throughout the country, and the world, your word obviously has great impact. A note from you to Peerless would have incalculable weight.

ANOTHER LETTER

Dear Morrie,

This is a very difficult letter for me to write. I'm asking for a favor that I desperately need. I decided to send this letter before phoning you, since a call would be too abrupt considering the magnitude of my situation. Here it is.

I've been producing your sales material for a long time, and in addition to having a pleasant client/vendor relationship, we've also been good friends. My business with you has come to about $10,000 a month for the past six months and from what I know, it will be at that rate for the next few months.

Morrie, I need $30,000 to pay off my ex-partner who is threatening to sue me, and to pay past-due print-production charges. Could I have this advance towards services I perform, which should be cleared up in three to four months? I can't get an unsecured loan like this from a bank and, believe me, I have tried. I'll pay you interest at prime rate.

I hate to take advantage of a friendship, but if you agree to this, all I can say is you'll have my deepest thanks—and my wife and kids will thank you, too.

I dislike imposing on your goodness, Morrie, but I don't know who else to turn to.

Warmest regards,

Albert

ANOTHER LETTER

Dear Ms. Sanders:

We only met a couple of times briefly, but I had a chance to show you some of my writing, including a political analysis I did in college. You said it was very good—you even added that it showed exceptional talent.

I'm being considered for a job as news editor at the Sequence Cable Network. I desperately want this job. It will launch my career. I hope I didn't presume too much by giving your name as a reference.

I also hope you do not feel I'm asking too much since we only met for a short time. But as a distinguished journalist you would have immeasurable value in recommending me for this big chance. In addition to talent, I offer determination, stick-to-it-iveness, and a burning desire to excel.

Could you please help me?

I'll call you.

Gratefully yours,

Felicia Martin

LETTERS FOR PERSONAL FAVORS, BUT NOT SERIOUS ISSUES

Dear Angela:

Please do a sweet helpful act for me! I'm asking you as a friend. This favor will take place over a period of time, which is why I'm writing instead of calling. In this way you have a reminder, every day.

I want to lose 15 pounds—desperately. I can only do this if I'm reminded daily, coaxed, and made to feel ashamed if I don't unflinchingly stick to my diet.

Angela, please call me every single morning between 8 and 10 A.M. Leave a message on my machine if you don't get me and I'll call you back. Ask me what I ate the day before, and what I'm going to have for lunch and dinner. Remind me not to eat in between. I will call you back at the end of each day to tell you what I ate that day. This will give me the motivation to stick to my diet.

Nag me, berate me, shame me if need be. This is the only way I will really diet to take off 15 pounds in six weeks.

You would be performing a humongous favor for me.

Thanks so much,

Peggy Ann

ANOTHER LETTER

(By Fax)

I need a favor, Millie:

We've been playing phone tag for three days without my being able to speak with you. So I'm faxing you because I need this favor within the next two days . . . Please!

I'm going to a formal affair, a gala event, this coming Saturday night, and I would love with all my being to borrow your beautiful red evening gown. Fred is taking me and this drop-dead gown would be a wonderful *mise en scene* for me . . . and for him.

I assume it's OK and I'll be forever in your debt.

Your really good friend,

Jennifer

ANOTHER LETTER

Dear Clifford:

Re: It's payback time.

You promised to respond to any reasonable favor I could ask of you when I recommended you for a freelance assignment, which you got. I don't have to remind you, do I? I know you'd agree to this request even if it weren't a quid pro quo payback.

In any case, now I must ask something of you. I need a letter from you as a character reference in order to get a consultant assignment from a state government special committee. I'll call you with the details.

All you have to do is write about what an honest, dependable, law abiding, patriotic citizen you have the privilege of knowing and dealing with at close hand. Me. Essentially, what a wonderful guy I am. After all it's true, isn't it?

I would really appreciate this, Cliff—it's important to me. It goes without saying, I'd do the same for you.

Your buddy,

Phil

ANOTHER LETTER

To: Larry—My friend indeed and a friend I need.

Please don't flinch when I ask this favor of you because it will not cost you anything, not a penny.

I need you to cosign a bank loan for $5,000 that I need until certain payments that are due me come through. It should be about 60 days, but I want the bank loan to hold for another six months. It will not cost you any money, there is no risk, because you have my word this loan will be paid back.

You know I would do the same for you. I've done favors for you before when you asked, but I'm not looking on this as payback time. It's just friend to friend.

Thanks so much, and warm greetings,

Clyde

ANOTHER LETTER—THIS IS ON A MAN-WOMAN LOVE THEME

Dear Elizabeth—

You were out of town and I couldn't get you on the phone, so I'm writing to make sure you receive this message.

Please do me a big favor.

Jeff and I had a big argument and I'm afraid I said some vile things. We parted and that's that. He is too proud to call me and vice versa.

Please play Cupid and intercede. I really, really must get together with Jeff and forget what happened. Jeff wants this too, I'm sure. Pride can ruin lives—don't let this happen to Jeff and me.

Elizabeth, call him and tell him how badly I feel, etc., etc. You know what to say. Please do this for me—and for Jeff. We'll both be forever in your debt.

I'm asking you with all my heart,

Maggie

FORWARDING OR ATTACHMENT LETTERS

▌ TO A BUSINESS PROPOSAL, PRESENTATION, BID, PRICE QUOTE.

Usually clipped to the front page or cover, it is the first thing to be seen by the important person who will initially review your document—with the power to toss it or act on it.

This letter must reflect the creativity and earnestness you put into your carefully written piece. It should encourage the right people to read it with a highly positive reaction.

You've got to win. This is your first try; if you strike out you're really out in this ball game.

LETTERS ATTACHED TO PROPOSALS FOR NEW BUSINESS. OFTEN IN ANSWER TO A REQUEST FOR PROPOSAL

Dear Mr. Moriarty,

Thank you so much for putting us in the running for this important assignment.

We've answered all the questions in your Request for Proposal, with full details and documentation, and we believe that it satisfactorily presents our credentials in terms of facilities and personnel.

However, this document doesn't tell the full story about our fitness to serve you. We add a vital extra value that does not lend itself to tables or graphs.

It's our corporate culture! How we serve our clients with close personal attention to all their needs. How our whole operation is structured to assure top quality on every assignment. How we take the extra step to be a vital adjunct to your production team.

You can see it, feel it, know it, by visiting our shop and watching our people work. And by talking with our clients. As a start, please call the client references who are included in this proposal.

Yes, you can best be convinced of Sigma's value to you by looking beyond the cold facts in this proposal. The facts make the case as to our ability. Your later investigation will prove our dynamism in enhancing your business.

Best regards,

Brad Thomas
President

ANOTHER ATTACHMENT LETTER
TO A NEW BUSINESS PROPOSAL

Dear Mr. Mathias,

Thanks so much for having us submit this proposal.

It is packed full of innovative ideas on increasing your business significantly—that is, in the 20% to 30% range.

It also tells of our resources, facilities and, more importantly, our people who will make it happen.

You'll also see the core purpose for hiring us. . .We show you how we will provide THE COMPETITIVE EDGE.

Yes, the COMPETITIVE EDGE that will help you outdistance your competition and raise your market share—no small achievement in this market. We look on it as our mission. We have the right stuff to do it, and we are ready and able to start doing it for you NOW!

Thanks again for this opportunity.

Best regards,

Perry Rose
Executive Vice President
& Director of Marketing

ANOTHER LETTER

Thank you so much for this opportunity to participate in your RFP.

We complied with all the items you specified, and in doing so we became more convinced than ever that we're ideally suited to serve all your needs in excellent fashion. We have the people, the technology, the philosophy, and a great deal of experience in similar industries.

We presume to say it may be an opportunity for you too. After all, you want the best.

This all adds up to giving you the very highest level of performance if we have the good fortune to service your business.

We ask that you give us a test project so that we have the opportunity to prove it!

Sincerely,

Winthrop Gibbons
Executive Vice President

You are a service vendor making aggressive new business efforts.

A LETTER TO PROSPECTS TO GO ALONG
WITH A PRINTED PIECE ABOUT YOUR COMPANY

Dear Mr. Blumenthal,

Competition has gotten very tough and trying. You know it, virtually everyone in your industry knows it.

We succeed by *not* relying on the presumed wisdom; *not* following so-called trends that have almost run their course; *not* stressing technique over substance. And *not* getting you started full blast on a strategy without having a valid measurement as to how it will work.

Yes, we go by creativity and feel, but we also have good facts and reassurance on what works best. This seems basic—many service companies say it. We *do* it. And the people we work for say we do it well.

The bottom line: our business is to make your business grow faster than that of your competition. We can prove we know how to make it happen.

Why not pick up the phone and call us?

Best regards,

Syl Overstreet
President & CEO

A new business prospect asked you to state your performance record. (You are an older established financial manager vs. some heralded newcomers.)

Dear Gene:

As you requested, I am enclosing Alpha Financial Management's performance results for the five-year period ending December 31, 1997. Our investment goal is capital appreciation regardless of whether there is a bear or a bull market. During the last five years, financial assets have had the benefit of an unprecedented bull market, and financial enhancement was easily achieved.

The investment return from stocks and bonds has been higher than sound analysis would justify, and it seems every novice is now convinced that a large gain is sure to be realized on any investment purchases. The fact is that most professionals managing money today haven't been in the business long enough to witness a stock-market decline, so the last five years aren't a true indication of investment know-how.

This favorable investment climate will not continue forever, and it is inevitable that stocks and bonds will enter a bear market one of these days. Capital preservation will then become increasingly important to you and other investors. That is the real test of our ability.

This is why we want to inform you of our longer-term investment record. A portfolio managed by us from our start in 1986 would have an average annual rate of return for the period of 17.6%, which significantly exceeds the 13.0% return for the industry's comparable benchmark. More importantly, our holdings have never suffered a negative annual return in even the most difficult investment climates. By any standard, this long-term performance history is outstanding.

Gene, I hope this answers your questions. We have over twenty years experience investing the assets of wealthy individuals, and we want you to have confidence in our qualifications to be entrusted with your portfolio.

I look ahead to working with you for many rewarding years. And I await your call if you have any questions or want further clarification.

Warm regards,

Nell Fineman

ANOTHER LETTER

Dear Dolores,

Thank you so much for considering us for the distinction of handling your business.

The Autoscript account—its size requirements, complexity and so on—happens to be in perfect sync with the way our company is structured in terms of facilities, people and experience.

We successfully service other companies whom you may consider to be competitive, but I want to assure you that we have an inordinate concern about the confidentiality of our clients' records and plans. There has never been any infraction of confidentiality. Never a leak, hint, or any other act that could compromise private information.

No client has ever had any concern about the integrity of its files. From the impeccable care we give to security, there never will be.

We look ahead to additional dialogue, and particularly to meeting you and your colleagues.

Best regards,

Tim Johnson

ANOTHER LETTER

Our warmest regards, Mr. Lee,

We feel we really know you and your company from the details you gave in your proposal specifications. The more we know, the more we're convinced we're the ideal partner to help you achieve your goals in the next year, and the years hence.

We believe you will see this in our presentation. We're eagerly looking forward to the next round of discussion.

Sincerely,

Morton Witman
Senior Vice President

Dear Chris,

Thank you for considering us for this important project. I am confident we can more than satisfy Consolidated's requirements, and that we have addressed all the issues in your Request for Proposal.

We very much appreciate this opportunity, Chris, and we eagerly anticipate continued dialogue.

Meanwhile, we stand ready to provide any further information you may need.

Best regards,

LETTERS TO CONSULTANTS WHO RECOMMEND YOU
FOR PROPOSALS TO THEIR CLIENTS

Dear Harvey:

We very much appreciate your putting our hat in the ring for the RFP business. This proposal answers all of your queries in the detail you specified.

It goes without saying, we're now head-to-head with the other companies who are vying for this business. You'll line us up and decide with your client who survives and who gets lopped off. This likely depends on—

- Reputation, dependability
- Ability to perform in accordance with the specifications
- People chemistry
- Creativity—Ability to chart new courses, new solutions
- Eagerness for the account. How important it is to the vendor
- Experience with this type of account (successful, that is)

We believe we have the edge when you add all these up and compare. But we ask that you and your client see us, talk to our people, see our non-confidential reports, talk to our clients, our suppliers, and people in the trade.

After checking us out this way, we believe you too will be convinced of the extra edge we offer.

Thanks again for giving us this opportunity to prove ourselves.

Jean Ahern
Vice President, Sales

OTHER LETTERS TO CONSULTANTS

Dear Ms. Finnegan:

We're obviously delighted you selected us for this RFP.

We have covered all the items you asked for, which is quite a comprehensive list. It certainly gives you a broad view of our resources and abilities, as well as those of the other companies you invited for this pitch.

May we suggest an added aspect to keep in mind: we have the skilled personnel on tap and ready to go to work for your client . . . NOW. We do not need to hire more personnel, which greatly cuts the tooling-up time. Considering Handy's time constraints this is an important factor.

It is against our policy to impugn our competition, but I'm not sure that the other companies can make this statement with total candor.

To this we add superior capability in carrying out all of your client's needs, and them some.

Again, many thanks for putting our name forward on this very desirable assignment.

Very truly,

Seth Gordon
Senior Vice President

Dear Adrienne:

The attached presentation in answer to your RFP answers all the items you specified in full detail. We are absolutely certain we can perform all our required duties to the full satisfaction of your client. This goes for all normal procedures and for the ad hoc requests that arise without notice and need immediate attention and extra efforts.

In all candor, however, we must advise you that we will need 30 days to clear our decks and get ready to perform at full speed. After this time, we'll be able to give your client 100% performance continuously and without qualification.

We really appreciate your having us compete for this business. Our reputation and track record show us to be a correct choice.

Warm regards,

Sy Schwebel
President

Thank you, Greg:

We're grateful for the chance you gave us to compete for this account. We believe we came through with an exemplary presentation of who we are and what we can do, and that we are perfectly suited to serve your client in excellent fashion.

We're looking forward to the next round of discussions.

All the best,

Enid Hammer
Vice President

OTHER LETTERS, DIRECTLY TO THE COMPANY

Dear Mr. Merriwether:

Despite the intensity of the work in getting this proposal completed—thoroughly and fully documented—within the time you requested, our people found great pleasure in putting it together.

We enjoyed telling about our facilities, our technology, the place where we work. But even more, we like the opportunity to tell you about our people—how their talents and experience coalesce in an atmosphere committed to excellence and to 100% client satisfaction.

Yes, our people and our corporate culture are the important extra ingredients we bring to the table.

Best regards,

Harold Candle
Senior Vice President, Marketing

Dear Mr. Perry,

We're most pleased to make this presentation to you.

Your account would be a very important piece of business for our company—and you can expect the topmost efforts of our staff, including our top management, to service your requirements.

We look forward to the opportunity of giving you whatever other information you may require . . . and, of course, to meeting with you and your colleagues.

Thank you for this chance to show our credentials. More important, to show how we will help your company grow to be an even bigger power in your industry.

Most truly,

Alfred Seymour
President

ANOTHER LETTER

Dear Ms. Hasimoto:

We greatly appreciate your considering us for this important marketing assignment.

Our aim in this document was to provide you with all the information you requested in a format that would be most helpful in evaluating Simdux.

I believe you will see that our management is dedicated to superb performance, evidenced by an enviable history of success. We will give you the most attention-grabbing and effective sales material in your industry that will surely lead to increases in your market share.

We've done this for other clients—we'll do it for you.

Best regards,

Reginald Waters
Vice President

ANOTHER LETTER

Dear Mr. Nance:

Our presentation tells how you will profit from a relationship with us. But it is only part of the story. We want to show you firsthand.

We want to demonstrate how we work, how we follow the highest standards of quality and efficiency in the industry. How we toil, and research, and discard, and test to develop powerful income—building concepts to put you ahead of your competition.

We call it aggressive marketing. You will call it smart sales building.

Let's arrange a visit—You must see it to believe it.

Best regards,

Michael Woods
Executive Vice President

ANOTHER LETTER

Dear Mr. Shine:

We're very pleased at the opportunity to put our hat in the ring for this project, which would be an extremely important addition to our business.

> Yes . . . We have complied with all your requirements in preparing this presentation.

> Yes . . . We have the facilities, the personnel, the experience, the technology to serve all your needs.

Yes . . . We are dedicated to take the extra step—a most important step—to more than comply with your requests. We want our
team that is dedicated to your business to be a vital part of
your team.

Yes . . . We can handle your business requirements in excellent fashion. But we also want to be partners in helping you
arrive at solutions. To help build your business—now and for
the years ahead.

This is the kind of relationship we will seek if we have the privilege
of servicing your business, Mr. Shine. This is the added advantage we
bring to the table that you may not fully see in the cold facts of this
presentation.

Sincerely,

Betty Sargent,
Senior Vice President

ANOTHER LETTER

Dear Mr. Douglas,

We're extremely pleased at this opportunity to tell you of our special
qualifications for this key project.

We have the people, the resources, the expertise to service the volume
and complexity of your business. This is said with careful forethought,
for in the 12 years that Spec Inc. has been in business, we have never
failed to live up to a client commitment.

It reflects Spec's dedication to excellence, and to your total satisfaction.

Very truly,

David Chiffington
President

Dear Copley:

Here is our presentation—conforming thoroughly with all your specifications and questions.

But this is only part of our story. There's a lot more to be said that
doesn't lend itself to a mere statement of facts. Such things as how we

grew to be a major player in the industry. What caused our inventiveness to flourish, and how we contribute to the success of our clients.

This would require a separate document. Better yet, why not visit us and allow us to show you?

Best regards,

Matt Harrigan,
Senior Vice President

ANOTHER LETTER

Dear Jennifer:

Here it is, our fully documented presentation for the privilege of servicing your business. Your account would be a very important addition to our client roster, accounting for almost 20% of our business. You can be sure of getting the priority attention of our entire staff to all of your needs and requirements.

You are looking for a high rate of growth over the next five years. If you grow, we will grow too. And you can be sure we will make every effort to have this happen.

Regards,

Charles Deventer
President

ANOTHER LETTER

Dear Mr. Harris:

We're extremely pleased to make this presentation to you.

In going through this, please note our plan to organize our operation to best suit your needs, within the time frame you require, and to perform the quality of service you expect and deserve.

While this is stated as our pledge, we are determined to go beyond this parameter. If we are selected to service your account, our aim will be to give you more than you expect to get. Yes, we want to exceed your expectations.

Truly yours,

Keith Freedman
Vice President

ATTACHMENTS TO PRESENTATIONS THAT WERE SUBMITTED AD HOC—
I.E. WITHOUT BEING INVITED TO PARTICIPATE

Dear Ms. O'Meara:

You didn't invite us to make a presentation—but it will pay you to see the concepts, the ideas, the executions that we are submitting. A great big wealth of creative material to look at. . . for free, no obligation. Because we know you will want to buy it later.

You will see here that we go for the innovative, the dramatic, the sit-up-and-take-notice approach. This is what pays off. This is what will give you the most effective program in the industry.

Best regards,

Ethan Quinn
Chief Creative Officer

Dear Ms. Saunders:

We are submitting this presentation because we're convinced of our exceptional capability in handling your assignment.

We believe that when you read this, you'll agree that we can likely do a better job than the other vendors who are competing for your business—as to personnel, equipment, resources and the unusually close fit of our companies in terms of a client/vendor relationship.

All of this is documented in this submission.

Most sincerely,

Fred Baldwin
Vice President

Dear Mr. Sorenson:

We are throwing our hat in the ring for this important business. This will tell you why. We fully document certain qualifications warranting serious consideration.

1. Thorough experience in your industry at the highest level.
2. An enviable track record.
3. In sync with your corporate culture.
4. Our size is just right for you. Your business will be very important to us, and you will have the continuous attention of our top management.

All this is confirmed in capsule form for quick review and we are prepared to elaborate on any aspect.

We are grateful for your attention, which involves a critical decision.
One that is of vital concern for both our companies.

Truly yours,

Noah Sedlow
President

ANOTHER LETTER

Dear Ms. Witkoff:

The marketing and sales concepts we are presenting here are not necessarily startling or excessively resplendent, nor are we engaging in
metaphoric word games. That would be catching the consumer's eye, but
not their heart and mind.

What we are showing is meant to sell and to stand the test of time. It
can be effective in many different media. It is adaptable for various
kinds of promotional campaigns.

In short, what we are showing is designed to build your business.

▮ TO A RESUME YOU ARE SENDING FOR A DESIRABLE JOB.

Keep in mind that your resume is among scores of others for the same job.
Your attachment letter must immediately spark the reader's desire to seriously review what you have sent versus the pile that arrives.

HERE'S A "TAKE NOTICE" LETTER—IT'S DARING,
BUT MAY BE APPLICABLE IN SOME CASES

Dear Mr. Horowitz:

I set production records at three companies—I was chief editor of my college newspaper—I was honored at a dinner by my church—I was on the track
and swimming teams of my college. . .

You will see this in my resume, which gives the straightforward highlights of my work record and personal attributes.

It doesn't fully relate the details of my accomplishments, my abilities, samples of my work, the laudatory comments of my peers and employers, my real worth to your company.

I'm pleased you have read this far. Now, I ask you to read the resume. And then please let's meet so I can further prove my exemplary value to Sims & Co.

Sincerely yours,

Dita Morgan

ANOTHER LETTER WITH A BOLD APPROACH

Ms. Marsha Feinbaum
Director of Human Resources
Piccadilly Associates

Dear Ms. Feinbaum,

My bio indicates that I represent a dynamic new dimension for your company. And I'm sure you will come to this conclusion when you confirm the accomplishments I have related.

> Just one example: In addition to my day-to-day functions at my previous employer, Seaport Ltd., I had the lead role in inventing a product-development system that reduced by half the time needed to get a new-product idea through the production stage and into the market.

> This innovation has become Seaport's normal operating procedure for the past two years—with much impact on its bottom line . . . and there's more that will interest you.

When we meet, I'll provide details on other bellwether accomplishments, and several references who will attest to my skills and creativity in developing new avenues of profitability. I increased productivity and income for Seaport . . . I'll certainly be able to do it for Piccadilly.

I'll call you shortly to arrange a meeting.

Very truly,

Bennett Horaldo

P.S.   I left Seaport voluntarily for personal reasons which I'll explain when we meet.

ANOTHER LETTER

To: P.O. Box 1704
        Miami Herald

This can be a wonderful opportunity for both of us.

I am one of the very few people in the country with hands-on experience in virtually all phases of the development and marketing of new investment products.

This includes creating the product concepts, writing the marketing plans and supervising the advertising and promotion. Clearly, my contributions helped raise Syntek's sales and bottom-line profits to a significantly higher plateau.

I am prepared to present factual confirmation of this and other accomplishments when we get together.

Sincerely,

Barbara Shannon

ANOTHER LETTER

Dear Ms. Hopatushu,

Gamma is one of six companies in the United States to whom this resume was sent. But you are number one in my esteem—the company I am most eager to join. It's because my experience, skills and work ethic are in close sync with your corporate vision and culture. This feeling of compatibility is further reinforced by Gamma's impeccable reputation and accomplishments.

This resume truly reveals a valuable resource for Gamma Services, Inc. I'm confident you will come to this conclusion as we go further along in our discussions.

Very truly yours,

Copley Bienstock

ANOTHER LETTER

Dear Mr. Stevens:

My bio gives you the cold facts about my experience and accomplishments. It shows how I bring excellent capability to every task I'm responsible for.

It doesn't tell you about the extra values that I will be able to bring to CPG Inc.—the extra dynamism that will bear directly on your bottom line. This is how I have been described by my supervisors—

- A people person who gets the best efforts from his staff.

- A motivater and problem solver. . . Brings people together to resolve issues, not just to get the job done.

- A leader . . . Empowers people to bring forth ideas and new concepts that deal with the incredible changes taking place in the industry.

Mr. Stevens, you no doubt agree that this is the difference between a competent manager who will do a good, creditable job, and a valuable manager who will enhance your profits.

I'll phone you about getting together.

Regards,

Jim Standos

ANOTHER RESUME LETTER IN RHYME

Dear Ms. Hyman:

I'm sending this with hopes galore
For I have great skills in store.
A track record beyond compare
And an urge to excel that seems quite rare.

There's another asset you may like to hear
I wish to be with RPF for the rest of my career.

Sincerely,

William Meyer

ANOTHER LETTER

To: P.O. Box 718
       The Wall Street Journal

Here are a few facts that relate to my resume that's enclosed:

- As a production manager at CPY Company, I set a record for monthly product output—a 13% increase over its previous highest performance.

- Despite rising expenses, my cost per product unit was reduced by 7%.
- My group outpaced competition for quality, based on industry standards.
- Despite rising costs and fierce competition, my employer cited me for "setting production records which helped enhance our business."

I left CPY because a downsizing caused its headquarters office to be integrated with another facility in Baltimore, and I am unable to transfer there for family reasons. Thus, I'm now available for the position you described, which I'm eager to discuss with you.

I believe this could be a wonderful opportunity for both of us.

Sincerely yours,

Oleg Lachkovsky

ANOTHER LETTER

To: PL 418
       Los Angeles Times

This may be the best response to your ad.

You are no doubt being flooded with resumes, but it will benefit both of us if you put this one on top. There are a number of crucial qualifications and several impressive disclosures of performance that I have listed. I'm sure this will be confirmed when you check my references.

I believe the next step is a personal meeting, and I wait eagerly to hear from you.

Very truly,

Irwin Vetrov

ANOTHER LETTER IN RHYME—REQUESTING A MANAGEMENT-TRAINEE POSITION. TO BE SENT TO A SCORE OF COMPANIES

Dear Ms. Hertz:

> I'm sending this with boldness
>   for I am very sure,
>
> That my training and my background
>   to your company has allure.

> It's to your benefit to see me,
>   to discover how I rate.
>
> As a management trainee
>   I'm an ideal candidate.
>
> My resume gives cold facts
>   but certainly that's not all,
>
> There's much more that will please you.
>   I eagerly await your call.

Most sincerely,

Ludwig Rachlin

GETTING BACK INTO THE JOB MARKET AFTER A HIATUS

Dear Mr. Pettigrew,

My resume documents how I will be an extraordinary addition to your company, I'm confident you'll be convinced when you interview me.

I've been out of the workplace for the past five years due to family responsibilities. But I'm as skilled and resourceful as before—and likely more so—in enhancing profit—making opportunities.

I kept in close touch with the industry during my hiatus, studying all the trends, changes, new techniques. In fact, I researched your company before sending this in order to gain a broader perspective of its structure and vision.

I'll give you a call about arranging a meeting.

Very truly,

Rosemary Higgins

ANOTHER LETTER—SIMILAR SITUATION

Dear Mr. Lemuel,

I'm back, ready and eager to work after a five-year hiatus following the birth of my child.

My most recent employment was at Beam Industries where I spent five years as top assistant to the Senior Vice President in charge of MIS, handling the myriad details of in-house information and computer services. This included expansive responsibilites, including trafficking the work of seven managers and technicians.

The company's management was extremely pleased with the way I handled these responsibilites without any lost motion. However, the company has been reorganized since my departure and is now fully staffed in all departments.

The attached resume briefly outlines my career experience and relevant personal data. It goes without saying, my attributes are adaptable to various departmental areas in addition to MIS.

I'll call you to arrange an interview.

Very truly yours,

Hannah Raab

You have great confidence in an up-and-coming talented young artist and you want to help her exhibit.

LETTER TO THE JUDGING COMMITTEE
OF A PRESTIGIOUS ART SHOW

Dr. Henry Rotondi, Chairman;
Members of the Judging Committee

I know you want to bring into prominence little known but tremendously talented artists. With this in mind, I want to introduce Hortense Silvers, who is starting her rise to acclaim on the current art scene among dealers and collectors. This youthful American artist, born in 1968, now resides in San Francisco.

Ms Silvers' bold, vivid, even startling elucidations of the feelings, ambitions, anguishes of modern human endeavor, are captured in huge, brilliant expressionism.

Although her art pieces are clearly individualistic, a number of art enthusiasts have related Ms. Silvers' works to those of Georgia O'Keefe in her early years, and some have likened them to Haring's modern sur-realistic conceptualism.

Hortense Silvers studied at The Art Students League in New York City and her pieces were shown at several New York exhibits that emphasize strong, contemporary messages by rising young artists.

Thank you for this opportunity to present the talents of Ms. Silvers' work for this auspicious showing.

Bruno Castellano

INDEX